Conversations with Madeleine L'Engle

Literary Conversations Series
Monika Gehlawat
General Editor

Conversations with Madeleine L'Engle

Edited by Jackie C. Horne

University Press of Mississippi / Jackson

The University Press of Mississippi is the scholarly publishing agency of
the Mississippi Institutions of Higher Learning: Alcorn State University,
Delta State University, Jackson State University, Mississippi State University,
Mississippi University for Women, Mississippi Valley State University,
University of Mississippi, and University of Southern Mississippi.

www.upress.state.ms.us

The University Press of Mississippi is a member of
the Association of University Presses.

The Estate of Madeleine L'Engle has not approved or endorsed the publication of this anthology, *Conversations with Madeleine L'Engle*.

First printing 2019
∞

Library of Congress Cataloging-in-Publication Data

Names: Horne, Jackie C., 1965– editor. | L'Engle, Madeleine, interviewee
Title: Conversations with Madeleine L'Engle : / edited by Jackie C. Horne.
Description: Jackson : University Press of Mississippi,
[2018] | Series: Literary conversations series |
Identifiers: LCCN 2018014108 (print) | LCCN 2018018626 (ebook) | ISBN
9781496819857 (epub single) | ISBN 9781496819864 (epub instititional) | ISBN
9781496819871 (pdf single) | ISBN 9781496819888 (pdf institutional) | ISBN
9781496819833 (cloth : alk. paper) | ISBN 9781496819840 (pbk. : alk. paper)
Subjects: LCSH: L'Engle, Madeleine—Interviews. | L'Engle, Madeleine—Criticism
and interpretation. | Authors, American—20th century—Interviews.
Classification: LCC PS3523.E55 (ebook) | LCC PS3523.
E55 Z46 2018 (print) | DDC 813/.54 [B]—dc23
LC record available at https://lccn.loc.gov/2018014108

British Library Cataloging-in-Publication Data available

Novels, Plays, and Nonfiction by Madeleine L'Engle

18 Washington Square South: A Comedy in One Act (1944) (Walter H. Baker)

The Small Rain (1945) (Vanguard)

Ilsa (1946) (Vanguard)

And Both Were Young (1949) (Lothrop, Lee & Shepard)

Camilla Dickinson (1951) (Simon & Schuster)

A Winter's Love (1957) (Lippincott)

Meet the Austins (Austin Family Chronicles #1) (1960) (Vanguard)

A Wrinkle in Time (Time Quintet #1) (1962) (Farrar, Straus and Giroux)

The Moon by Night (Austin Family Chronicles #2) (1963) (Farrar, Straus and Giroux)

The Twenty-Four Days Before Christmas (Austin Family Chronicles #3) (1964) (Ariel)

The Arm of the Starfish (O'Keefe Family #1) (1965) (Farrar, Straus and Giroux)

Camilla (revised edition of *Camilla Dickinson*) (1965) (Crowell)

The Love Letters (1966) (Farrar, Straus and Giroux)

The Journey with Jonah (1967) (Farrar, Straus and Giroux)

The Young Unicorns (Austin Family Chronicles #4) (1968) (Farrar, Straus and Giroux)

Prelude (adaptation of *The Small Rain*) (1968) (Vanguard)

Dance in the Desert (1969) (Farrar, Straus and Giroux)

Lines Scribbled on an Envelope, and Other Poems (1969) (Farrar, Straus and Giroux)

The Other Side of the Sun (1971) (Farrar, Straus and Giroux)

A Circle of Quiet (Crosswick Journals #1) (1971) (Farrar, Straus and Giroux)

The Wind in the Door (Time Quintet #2) (1973) (Farrar, Straus and Giroux)

Everyday Prayers (1974) (Morehouse-Barlow)

Prayers for Sunday (1974) (Morehouse-Barlow)

The Risk of Birth: A Gift Book of Poems (1974) (Harold Shaw Publishers)

The Summer of the Great-Grandmother (Crosswick Journals #2) (1974) (Farrar, Straus and Giroux)

Dragons in the Waters (O'Keefe Family #2) (1976) (Farrar, Straus and Giroux)

The Irrational Season (Crosswick Journals #3) (1977) (Seabury Press)

A Swiftly Tilting Planet (Time Quintet #3) (1978) (Farrar, Straus and Giroux)

The Weather of the Heart: Selected Poems (1978) (Shaw)

Ladder of Angels: Scenes from the Bible Illustrated by Children of the World (1979) (Seabury Press)

A Ring of Endless Light (Austin Family Chronicles #5) (1980) (Farrar, Straus and Giroux)

The Anti-Muffins (Austin Family Chronicles #6) (1980) (Pilgrim Press)

Walking on Water: Reflections on Faith and Art (1980) (Shaw)

A Severed Wasp (1982) (Farrar, Straus and Giroux)

The Sphinx at Dawn: Two Stories (1982) (Seabury Press)

And It Was Good: Reflections on Beginnings (Genesis Trilogy #1) (1983) (Shaw)

A House Like a Lotus (O'Keefe Family #3) (1984) (Farrar, Straus and Giroux)

Trailing Clouds of Glory: Spiritual Values in Children's Literature (1985) (Westminster Press)

Many Waters (Time Quintet #4) (1986) (Farrar, Straus and Giroux)

A Stone for a Pillow: Journeys with Jacob (Genesis Trilogy #2) (1986) (Shaw)

A Cry Like a Bell (1987) (Shaw)

Two-Part Invention (Crosswick Journals #4) (1988) (Farrar, Straus and Giroux)

An Acceptable Time (Time Quintet #5) (1989) (Farrar, Straus and Giroux)

Sold Into Egypt: Joseph's Journey into Human Being (Genesis Trilogy #3) (1989) (Shaw)

The Glorious Impossible (1990) (Simon & Schuster)

Certain Women (1992) (Farrar, Straus and Giroux)

The Rock That Is Higher: Story as Truth (1993) (Shaw)

Anytime Prayers (1994) (Shaw)

Troubling a Star (Austin Family Chronicles #7) (1994) (Farrar, Straus and Giroux)

Glimpses of Grace: Daily Thoughts and Reflections (edited by Carole F. Chase) (1996) (Harper)

Penguins and Golden Calves: Icons and Idols in Antarctica and Other Unexpected Places
    (1996) (Shaw)

A Live Coal in the Sea (1996) (Farrar, Straus and Giroux)

Wintersong (with Luci Shaw) (1996) (Shaw)

Bright Evening Star: Mystery of the Incarnation (1997) (Shaw)

Friends for the Journey (with Luci Shaw) (1997) (Vine Books/Servant Publications)

Mothers and Daughters (with Maria Rooney) (1997) (Northstone Publishing)

Miracle on 10th Street and Other Christmas Writings (Austin Family Chronicles #8) (1998) (Shaw)

A Full House: An Austin Family Christmas (Austin Family Chronicles #9) (1999) (Shaw)

A Prayerbook for Spiritual Friends (with Luci Shaw) (1999) (Augsburg Fortress Publishing)

Mothers and Sons (with Maria Rooney) (2000) (Shaw)

Madeleine L'Engle Herself: Reflections on a Writing Life (compiled by Carole Chase) (2001) (Shaw)

The Other Dog (2001) (Chronicle Books)

The Ordering of Love: The New and Collected Poems of Madeleine L'Engle (2005) (Shaw)

The Joys of Love (2008) (Farrar, Straus and Giroux)

Contents

Introduction   ix

Chronology   xxv

Madeleine L'Engle   3
  Roy Newquist / 1967

An Interview with Madeleine L'Engle   18
  Ruth Rausen / 1975

Madeleine L'Engle   26
  Linda Chisholm / 1976

Allegorical Fantasy: Mortal Dealings with Cosmic Questions   69
  Cheryl Forbes / 1978

Madeleine L'Engle: An Interview   79
  Ted Baehr / 1980

"Listen to Your Work": An Interview with Madeleine L'Engle   91
  Connie Soth / 1980

Madeleine L'Engle and Studs Terkel in Conversation   103
  Studs Terkel / 1980

Interview with Author Madeleine L'Engle   130
  Katie Pauley / 1983

An Interview with Madeleine L'Engle   136
  James S. Jacobs and Jay Fox / 1987

Luci Shaw—Madeleine L'Engle Interview   150
   Fay Lapka / 1991

The Story as Teller: An Interview with Madeleine L'Engle   160
   Gary Schmidt / 1991

A Mind in Motion   170
   Betsy Hearne / 1998

Madeleine L'Engle   181
   Leonard S. Marcus / 2006

Index   189

Introduction

"In my experience, conventional wisdom about children's and young adult publishing may cover ninety-nine percent of the titles being published. But there's that one percent—the wild cards, the jokers, the books that challenge everything we know about books—the books that change everything we know about books . . . We desperately need the creators who will give our children books that they do not even know they want—until, that is, they read them."
—**Anita Silvey,** *editor of* Horn Book

In 1962, when Farrar, Straus and Giroux (FSG) released the children's book *A Wrinkle in Time*, few at the publishing firm gave the odd, unconventional novel, a hitherto unheard of generic mishmash of science fiction, fantasy, and family tale, much chance of commercial success. In later years, its author, Madeleine L'Engle, often delighted in recounting the story of FSG's attempts to lower the expectations of the new-to-their-list writer. "Dear, now we do not expect this book to sell well. We're doing it as a sort of self-indulgence. We don't want you to be unhappy when it doesn't sell," she mimicked during a 1980 radio interview with Studs Terkel. The editors and salespeople at FSG may have been intrigued by L'Engle's story, but they didn't think too many other readers would share their enthusiasm. With its time- and space-traveling protagonists, its forays into hard science, its joyful interplay of both the fantastic and the religious, *A Wrinkle in Time* was just too different, too odd, too *difficult* to appeal to a broad popular audience, especially an audience of children.

But *A Wrinkle in Time* did appeal to a group of children's librarians who were serving on the selection committee for the 1963 Newbery Medal, an award given each year by the American Library Association to the "author of the most distinguished contribution to literature for children." After this group awarded its coveted medal to *A Wrinkle in Time*, L'Engle's novel became a "must-have" for every library in the country. There, it was discovered and claimed by generations of readers eager to rise to the challenge of the questions—ethical, philosophical, scientific, and psychological—that it dared to pose.

But *A Wrinkle in Time* was not the only book Madeleine L'Engle wrote. And she did not only write books for children. The author's books, as well as her life, were often marked by contradictions, including the contradictions inherent in writing for multiple audiences. A few telling examples: Contemporary advances in scientific knowledge, about which L'Engle had a voracious curiosity, never led her to question her deeply held Christian faith, as they had so many other intellectuals and writers of the twentieth century. Though she spent a large portion of her life teaching writing workshops, she continually claimed that "it is the story itself that is the narrator," not the writer (Schmidt). Despite insisting that the personal journals she assiduously kept were never meant to be published, she drew on them extensively in creating her four popular memoirs now known as the *Crosswicks Journals*. At the same time, L'Engle's family members regard those memoirs as "pure fiction" and consider her novels to be far more autobiographical (Zarin). While L'Engle often argued that to be creative one needed to be open, to be vulnerable, she kept many of the more painful aspects of her personal life hidden, both from her public and sometimes even from herself. For Madeleine L'Engle, facts were one thing, but truth was something else entirely.

Pinning down such a contradictory writer could be a challenge for an interviewer. L'Engle, born in 1918, first began to be interviewed when she was in her forties, after *A Wrinkle in Time* won the Newbery. Though she had been a shy outsider as a child growing up in the intellectual, social register world of New York City, by middle adulthood she had crafted a persona which she was happy and eager to share with the world. A consummate storyteller not only on the page, but in person (she spent several years working professionally in the theater after graduating from Smith College), L'Engle took great pleasure in recounting the anecdotes she held as exemplars of her own personal truths: how so many publishers rejected *A Wrinkle in Time* because it was ahead of its time; how she never wrote for children or adults, only for herself; how children could understand the sophisticated science in her books more easily than adults could, to list only a few. These and other favorite anecdotes appear in different guises in many of the interviews in this collection.

L'Engle could also redirect an interviewer by ignoring unwelcome questions or by switching the focus to stories with which she was most comfortable. Many friends, family members, and acquaintances have remarked on her generosity, her kindness, and her warmth, but she could also prove quite the grand dame, growing impatient with the few interviewers knowledgeable enough, or canny enough, to push her beyond her set pieces. Betsy Hearne, who interviewed L'Engle for *School Library Journal*, uses the words "stonewalled" and "sidestepped" to describe L'Engle's responses to her challenging questions and concludes, "There are people in the business I can argue and debate with, but I had realized by then [late in the interview] that I could not argue with Madeleine. As we talked, I felt I was being managed. . . . I think she managed her audience as well as her characters" (Marcus, *Listening* 353, 354, 355).

Many of the details of her management of her own public image came to light via Cynthia Zarin's *New Yorker* profile of 2004. Zarin uncovered, or was told by L'Engle's family members, about half-truths and self-deceptions L'Engle told not only herself, but others, about certain painful details in her life. How, then, should a reader approach the earlier interviews in this collection, knowing that a selective self-fashioning is being constructed through them? The opening lines of the first piece of this volume, an interview with Roy Newquist for his book *Conversations*, can be read as both warning and guide: "My husband claims that I've used my early life in so many books that I no longer know fact from fiction, so I'll have to admit that I may have things somewhat confused. Yet what I'll say is more or less true" (230). Weaving through the documentable facts in these interviews are partial lies, misdirections, and out-and-out wish-fulfillment fantasies. But when read against her fictions, these "truths" can help us see L'Engle more deeply—see what she wanted for herself and for her children, what she believed about good and evil, what she thought was the right way and the wrong way to be a family—than if she had been able to articulate such "truths" more directly. We can read her continual assertion that the negative things in her life often turned into positives for her as a writer as a way to contain her own disappointment, her own grief, at the difficulties she experienced both as a child and as an adult. By recognizing what she has left out of her story, as well as what she has added or embellished, we can begin to see not only the gap between the intellectual, well-bred white culture in which L'Engle was raised and that of our own ("It seemed to be a trend in this day and age for the young to feel they had to announce defiantly whatever was wrong, instead of, as she had been taught, keeping it decently private" says one of L'Engle's many fictional avatars, Katherine Forrester of *A Severed Wasp* [285]). We can also see what for L'Engle was simply too painful to be explored, except through the displacement of fiction—absent and distant parents, marital infidelity, alcoholism, and the continual desire, yet inability, to connect with those to whom we are closest.

The interviews also chart changes in L'Engle's religious beliefs and in the way she talks about her religious beliefs to others. In Linda Chisholm's 1976 interview, L'Engle speaks of her agnosticism while living in Goshen, Connecticut, during the 1950s, when she and her husband became involved in the town's Congregational church community despite her own religious doubts. "I'm still an agnostic," she tells Chisholm, not because she doesn't believe, but rather because her religion is not about provable fact: "Mencken says the deepest, most strong and mystical religion is larded with agnosticism because you take with great faith something you do not know" (11). In later interviews in the 1970s and early 1980s, L'Engle would claim she was an "unhappy agnostic" during her Goshen days. But during this same period, L'Engle began to write essays on religion at the urging of her new friend Luci Shaw, wife of Harold Shaw and cofounder of Harold Shaw Publishers. Her second book with Shaw, *Walking on Water*, a meditation on the relationship between Christianity and art, became a bestseller in the Christian market. In the following years, L'Engle began lecturing and preaching at religious colleges and religious retreats, not just about writing, but about theology, especially the role of art and imagination in Christianity. Significantly, after *Walking on Water* became a bestseller, the word "agnostic" did not again appear when interviewers asked about the development of her religious beliefs.

These interviews also give hints of her thoughts on the increasing calls for censorship of her novels. Both her nonfiction with Harold Shaw and her public speeches on religion and art drew new, not always welcome, attention to L'Engle's fiction. Some early literary critics had taken her children's books to task for being too overtly religious; during the 1980s and '90s, evangelical Christians began to protest precisely the opposite, that the "neo-Orthodox and New Age world-view" of *A Wrinkle in Time* and L'Engle's other children's novels undermined Christianity. "It is well documented that Madeline [sic] L'Engle teaches universalism in her books and denigrates organized Christianity and promotes an occultist world view" warned Craig Branch in the *Watchman Expositor* in 2003, urging readers to "Contact Watchman Fellowship if you would like a detailed analysis of Madeline [*sic*] L'Engle" (Branch). The American Library Association's list of "100 most frequently challenged books" for the period 1990–1999 lists L'Engle's *A Wrinkle in Time* at number 23 (although by the following decade, after L'Engle's health led to a sharp decrease in her public appearances, it had dropped to 90) ("100 Most Challenged"). The interviews in this collection move between bemusement, annoyance, and anger to pride in her new role as champion of the artist and critic of biblical literalism to fundamentalist religious believers.

The interviews also document L'Engle's increasing influence on the larger American Christian community. During the 1980s and early '90s, her growing body of religious writings, as well as her outspoken championing of the importance of imagination to religious belief in her speeches and talks to religious groups, led thousands of Christians to take L'Engle as a role model. As Dick Staub of *The Kindlings*, "a movement devoted to rekindling the creative, intellectual, and spiritual legacy of Christians in culture," noted upon her death, L'Engle's "willingness to write what she saw, say what she thought, and do so succinctly, provocatively, and imaginatively made her a hero for those for whom faith seemed a set of manacles instead of a source of encouragement and inspiration" (Staub, *Missing*).

L'Engle clearly enjoyed her role as theological and personal advisor; as she told one interviewer, "I'm old enough now to appear as a wise old woman, and that's a plus" (Webb 57). And people clearly felt drawn to her, to her wisdom, her theatricality, her kindness. Questions from attendees of the Sarasota Quaker Monthly Meeting, which appear in a transcription of an interview conducted by Steven and Martha Swerdfeger, give a sense of what her fans were looking for from her as Madeleine the sage:

"I am wondering about your opinion about whether or not the way we interpret that verse [Genesis I:28] is related to the terrible way we've treated the earth, and your opinion about how we can recover a sane relationship with this planet we live on." (7)

"Could you comment on the hard things in the Bible and how we so effectively ignore them?" (8)

"Could you comment about good and evil?" (9)

"How can we learn to live into the questions of faith? How can we learn, not only to accept, but to love the questions, and how can we be content to move and dwell within the mysteries, the mystery of faith questions?" (9)

"In your opinion, why do we seem to be so much more threatened by those of our own faith family who differ from us than we are by those of other religious groups who have much greater difference? And how can we help change that fact?" (10)

Being regarded as a sage could be deeply satisfying, especially to a woman who had spent much of her childhood alone, but being thought a hero could prove also trying. As Luci Shaw recalls,

> Madeleine had fans who would show up wherever she was scheduled to speak, and I think this was a bit of a struggle for her. Everybody wanted a piece of Madeleine. Everybody wanted to be counted as a close friend. . . . She said that some people viewed her more as some kind of hero rather than as a real person. And it is true that when you are famous, you are on a pedestal that removes you from the real life that you live. It becomes hard for the other person to understand that you can be tired or cranky or quixotic, all of which Madeleine often was (Marcus, *Listening* 289).

L'Engle herself echoes this frustration in another passage from *A Severed Wasp*: "Katherine waved her away and walked off. The child was adoring her and she did not like to be adored. Appreciated, yes. But adoration turns one into an idol, and when the one who idolizes discovers flesh and blood instead of marble perfection, there is apt to be trouble, if not disaster" (84). L'Engle's *Penguins and Golden Calves: Idols and Icons in Antarctica and Other Unexpected Places* reflects on the dangers of turning one's icons, "open windows to God," into idols, things that are worshipped for themselves rather than as pointers to God.

L'Engle's donning the robe of sage also led to tensions within her family, as later revealed by Zarin's *New Yorker* article. Understanding the frustrations some of her children and grandchildren felt over her public role, L'Engle once again articulated in fiction what she could not say in interviews: "I suppose the world is beating at your door, as usual, people pouring out their woes? There's something about you that makes people want to bare their hearts to you. Sometimes we used to get jealous, afraid you'd love some wounded sparrow more than us" (*Severed* 233). But L'Engle, like *A Severed Wasp*'s protagonist Katherine Forrester, kept such tensions private, allowing no hint of any family dissension to leak out to the public. As Katherine, a famous pianist, notes, "Who could blame her for more than skimming the surface with the journalists? If there were the normal family tensions, there was no need for them to be revealed" (*Severed* 105).

But those who read L'Engle's quartet of memoirs, published between 1972 and 1988, felt they knew Madeleine, sometimes better than her own family did. Many fans came to treat her as an idol, rather than an icon, wishing they, too, could live the charmed life she portrayed in the *Crosswicks*

Journals, a life with a devoted husband, loving children, and a wide circle of artistic and intellectual friends. The gap between icon and reality frustrated L'Engle's family, and shortly after the turn of the century, they determined to right the record.

The result was Cynthia Zarin's controversial 2004 *New Yorker* profile, "The Storyteller: Fact, Fiction, and the Books of Madeleine L'Engle." Zarin had envisioned her profile would be a "kind of appreciation" but gradually discovered over four years of interviewing and investigating that many of the details of the public persona L'Engle had crafted and honed were more wish fulfillment than fact (Marcus, *Listening* 361). The piece, then, developed into not quite an exposé but certainly into a debunking of the personal myth-making of the famed author.

The article proved upsetting, especially to friends and fans who had put L'Engle on a pedestal. As Luci Shaw notes, "The fact that some of the family members aired the family dirty linen in front of the public was horrifying to us. Not that it was all false, but we just didn't see how it was helpful. . . . But there was a lot of buzz among her friends about that article. It felt cheapening, demeaning, a betrayal" (Marcus, *Listening* 293). But did L'Engle find it so? An attentive reader of her fiction might wonder. As a character in *A Severed Wasp* remarks to Katherine, "Most of us distort our childhoods one way or another, rearrange that past to make it more bearable" (194). Through her character, L'Engle seems to suggest that such self-fashioning is not unusual but should rather be expected, especially from public figures.

Zarin herself doesn't regard her profile to be a betrayal; rather, she believes "that Madeleine was extremely conscious of what I was doing—that the jig was up—and that she had decided to participate in it" (Marcus, *Listening* 363). Instead of painting a portrait of a hypocrite, Zarin believes she helped debunk the harmful hagiography that had grown up about the writer, even if that hagiography had stemmed largely from L'Engle's own idealized storytelling. "It's the responsibility of readers and admirers to understand that hagiography is a dangerous business because there's no way that anybody can live up to it," Zarin asserts (Marcus, *Listening* 361). As Cara Parks notes in her review of Marcus's composite biography of L'Engle: "The contradictions of L'Engle's life offer the best insights into the complicated acrobatics we perform in the modern world in order to satisfy the competing claims of love, family, success, and ambition. Here, explained by her friends and loved ones, L'Engle's shortcomings don't come across as condemnations but as humanizing counterpoints to her iconic status."

Perhaps we can understand L'Engle's desire to reveal herself at last by reading the Zarin profile against the thoughts of melancholy Henry Porcher, the
narrator of L'Engle's second novel, *Ilsa*:

> All my life the people I have loved . . . have accepted me as a friend, have
> confided in me—but, somehow, there has been no actual contact made. It has
> been almost as though they could talk to me because I didn't exist. I think
> that's because there has been no give and take. I have been a pitcher into
> which the people I love have poured themselves. I have accepted everything
> and been allowed to give nothing. When they discover that I have passions of
> my own it seems to jar them. (139–40)

◆ ◆ ◆

Leonard Marcus, author of *Listening for Madeleine*, an "impressionistic
biography" of L'Engle, suggests that his subject "carefully departmentalized
her vast and densely populated universe. People important to her in one
sphere of her life typically did not meet those important to her in the others" (22). Because of this departmentalization, the interviews in this collection were taken from a wide variety of sources: journals for scholars or
practitioners of children's literature; popular Christian magazines; and radio
shows for both general (Studs Terkel) and specific (Episcopal Radio) audiences. Some interviewers are most interested in her work as a children's
book author and innovator. Others focus more on her religious writings and
beliefs. Still others wish to understand L'Engle as an embodiment of the
"new woman" of second-wave feminism, a woman who could juggle marriage, motherhood, and a career and keep all in the air without everything
crashing to the ground.

The first piece in this volume, taken from Roy Newquist's book
Conversations, a collection of interviews with forty-three "prominent figures in contemporary literature," was published in 1967, four years after *A
Wrinkle in Time* was awarded the Newbery Medal. Newquist himself does
not appear in the interview; instead, the account is related entirely from
L'Engle's point of view. L'Engle recounts many of the major events in her
life, from her lonely childhood to her early adulthood working in the theater to her life as a young mother living in a rural Connecticut town and
her family's subsequent move back to the city a decade later so that her
husband, actor Hugh Franklin, could once again return to the stage. Her
descriptions of her frustrations trying to balance work and domestic life,

her insistence that "I am first and foremost a writer" (234), and the decid-edly un-child-centered household she and her husband created come across as strikingly progressive for America of the 1950s. She also articulates many of her pet themes, themes that will be reiterated in various forms in sub-sequent interviews throughout her life: her frustrations with being labeled a "children's book writer"; her valuing of the "true" over the "factual"; her thoughts about the purposes of writing; and her belief that a responsible writer needs to write every day, just like a violinist needs to practice every day "to make his instrument as good as it can possibly be so that it can be kept constantly fit for playing" (240).

The next piece in this collection, which was originally published in the academic journal *Children's Literature in Education* in 1975, reproduces a conversation between L'Engle and Ruth Rausen, a teacher and coordina-tor of young adult services at the New York Public Library. Rausen, who addresses her subject as "Miss L'Engle," focuses on L'Engle as a writer of children's books and solicits her thoughts about the current state of writing for young people. They also discuss L'Engle's writing workshops for children in the city, motivated, L'Engle reports, by "pressure put on writers to have protagonists from minority groups," which L'Engle felt "was not my right or my privilege to do . . . because this is not my own background" (202). Instead, she felt "the only thing I could do was to try to give some of these kids the equipment of vocabulary and learning to tell a story that would make them able to write out of their own experience" (202). There's more than a hint of the white savior in her comments, but there is also a recogni-tion that what today we would call #ownvoices stories are vitally important, especially for children.

One year later, Linda Chisholm conducted a long interview with L'Engle as part of an assignment for her oral history course at Columbia University. This interview, as well as an additional interview conducted two months later, subsequently became a part of the Oral History Project at Columbia. On the paper transcript in the archives at Wheaton College, the typewritten tag "Mrs. Franklin" has been crossed out, replaced with simply "L'Engle," presumably at L'Engle's request (Chisholm notes that L'Engle reviewed the transcript and "made only minor corrections and emendations"). Chisholm asks L'Engle to give her an "educational biography," a summary of the major "formative influences" on her life "both as a writer and as a person" (2); her answer touches upon many of the same incidents as in her Newquist inter-view, but in more detail. Chisholm is also the first interviewer to ask L'Engle about religion. L'Engle labels her religious belief while living in Goshen,

Connecticut, during the 1950s, when she and her husband were drawn into the town's Congregational church community, as agnostic. "I would like to come to church, but he [the minister] would have to accept the fact that I simply had to live *as though* I believed in God, but I could not say that I did" (10–11). Despite L'Engle's doubts, the minister asked her to teach Sunday school; he and other local ministers suggested L'Engle try to find her faith by reading the works of German theologians. L'Engle's religious belief was awakened not by reading those texts, but rather by her discovery of Einstein and Planck and quantum theory.

Chisholm's second interview also touches upon L'Engle's views on gender and sexism, highlighting both the author's engagement with, and rejection of, many key concepts of second-wave feminism. L'Engle claims, "I identified just as easily with men as with women," and takes women's lib to task for "sexual pigeonholing," what she sees as wanting no differentiation between the sexes. In her vision of enlightened gender relations, "we enjoy both our masculine and feminine attributes. . . . If we limit ourselves only to masculine attributes or only to feminine attributes, we're horribly limited." She also worries that gendered "intellect and intuition are at war instead of at love" (38). She dislikes what she sees as the more extreme branches of the women's liberation movement's denial of sexuality and boldly proclaims her enjoyment of her own body and her own sexual life. A reactionary response? Or that of a third-wave feminist in the making?

L'Engle's frequent speaking engagements at Wheaton College began to draw the attention of Christian publications in the late 1970s and early 1980s. The next three interviews in this collection are taken from religious magazines and journals of three different Christian denominations, but all focus on L'Engle's path to Christianity, her spiritual beliefs, and the importance of story and metaphor in teaching religious doctrine. Cheryl Forbes, writing for the evangelical *Christianity Today* in 1979, asks if L'Engle is a universalist, a belief that worried conservative evangelical groups. "No. I am a particular incarnationalist," she argues; "I can understand God only through one specific particular, the incarnation of Jesus of Nazareth . . . which gives me my understanding of the Creator and of the beauty of life" (18). In Ted Baehr's 1980 interview for the Episcopal Radio program *Searching*, L'Engle takes pleasure in being a harbinger, bringing the message to doubtful evangelicals that art "can, in fact, be Christian instead of sinful. That's a very fine discovery." She also speaks to another theme that will become increasingly important to her as her profile as a religious speaker grows: the idea that the search for answers is more important than the answers themselves. Congregationalist librarian (and clear fangirl) Connie Soth also met with L'Engle in 1980; her interview, "Listen to Your Work," portrays a more playful side to the author, whom Soth interviewed in the parking lot of the University of Hartford before a conference. Soth, writing for *Arkenstone*, a "journal created to provide an area for artistic expression and discussion within an historical biblical perspective" (*Arkenstone* table of contents), asks L'Engle to speak about her work in the theater, as well as her writing and how she experienced each as a Christian.

After reading three religion-focused pieces, it is fascinating to jump to the next interview, "Madeleine L'Engle and Studs Terkel in Conversation," and witness L'Engle shift tone to speak to a more general audience while still returning to many of the same themes as in the earlier pieces. Recorded in 1980, during one of L'Engle's several appearances on *The Studs Terkel Program*, much of the pair's conversation focuses on L'Engle's recently published young adult novel *A Ring of Endless Light*, exploring her purposes and goals in writing a book so focused on death and dying for a young audience. While L'Engle does not speak of religion, her discussion of her dolphin research does show how, for her, fantasy and reality are not split into distinct, uncrossable categories, but rather that reality is imbued with the numinous:

> **L'Engle:** I was leaning over the public petting pen one day. Most of the kids come, they pat the dolphin on the head, and they go away. I was just staying there, thinking to the dolphins, "Tell me where you want me to scratch you." And one dolphin came over and said, "Scratch my chest."
>
> **Terkel:** You knew he said that?
>
> **L'Engle:** Yes, and I scratched his chest. This went on: I'd try to stop, and he'd come back and say, "Hah, come on; scratch my chest." And some of the kids said, "Hey, that dolphin really likes that lady!" You do establish an incredible rapport, a real relationship.
>
> **Terkel:** So there is that communication without words.
>
> **L'Engle:** Yes.

Terkel is also fascinated by L'Engle's belief that children can more easily understand some of the more sophisticated scientific concepts in her books than adults can and clearly appreciates the challenge her books present to his own previously patronizing attitude towards children and their reading, an attitude that his admiration demands his listeners also question in themselves.

Katie Pauley returns our attention to Madeleine L'Engle as a role model for the Christian working wife, mother, and now grandmother, examining "her lasting marriage and her timeless books." Writing for *Family Life Today*, a magazine committed to "Building strong marriages, equipping the Christian home," Pauley asks L'Engle about her marriage and for her advice to other young people looking forward to marrying. L'Engle also speaks about why she does not write for Christians, despite her belief that through all her writing she is spreading the good news of Christian scripture, as well as the responsibility she feels not as a Christian writer, a label she eschewed throughout her life, but as a "writer who is a Christian," "There have been people who've turned to Christ because of my work. That's a very terrifying, humbling thing" (15).

James S. Fox and Jay Jacobs engage with both of L'Engle's two writerly identities in their interview for the Brigham Young University journal *Literature and Belief*. L'Engle argues for the need to accept both paradox and contradiction in her faith and in her own writing. Though she continues to eschew labels, particularly that of Christian author, she does admit to being a "theological searcher," constantly striving to find God through her writing. By 1987, L'Engle had grown more frustrated with her evangelical critics, questioning their focus on fear rather than on the hope and courage that faith inspires in her. She finds a similar rejection of hope in contemporary literature, a situation that concerns her deeply. "I don't like to read books about antiheroes. I don't want to be left depressed and cynical at the end of a book. I want to be opened, enlarged, given hope and courage" (7). L'Engle's focus on hope rather than cynicism may be one reason why she found such a welcoming home in children's literature, a genre which rests largely on providing hope to young readers.

Fay Lapka's joint interview with L'Engle and her friend and editor, evangelical publisher Luci Shaw, conducted while the two took part in the 1991 C. S. Lewis Summer Institute on the Christian and the Imagination, highlights the influence the two women have had on both each other's writing and religious beliefs over the course of their twenty-year friendship. They talk about the theological fights they would have during the editing process and how they most often ended up on the same side, rather than with one winning out over the other. Lapka is particularly interested in how writers can differentiate between "trustworthy, safe" work and work that is coming from the sinful parts of our human nature. L'Engle's answer shows her characteristic self-deprecating humor:

> **ML:** Does it have in it for me any of the three temptations that Satan offered Jesus? If it does, I won't go on.

FL: You don't mean that all your characters need to be saints . . .

ML: No, I mean, am I writing while thinking, "What's in it for me? Is Madeleine going to look good? Will this sell on the marketplace?" (3)

In the sixteen years between Ruth Rausen's 1975 conversation with L'Engle and Gary Schmidt's 1991 interview for the *ALAN Review* (the journal of the Assembly on Literature for Adolescents of the National Council of Teachers of English), the academic study of children's literature had become far more professionalized, a shift reflected in the different kinds of questions posed by each interviewer. Schmidt is most interested in the literary aspects of L'Engle's work—he questions her about issues of genre, narrative voice, and authorial intention. The exchanges have at times almost a combative air; L'Engle takes particular exception to questions that suggest she as author is manipulating or controlling the story, an approach to writing in marked contrast to her belief that she is the conduit, or servant of, the story, not its creator. She also brings up religious issues several times herself, highlighting how much more important her own faith, and her own religious writing and audience, have become to her by her eighth decade.

In 1998, Betsy Hearne interviewed L'Engle for *School Library Journal*, another children's literature–focused magazine. L'Engle had just won the Margaret A. Edwards Award for lifetime achievement in young adult literature, given annually by ALA's Young Adult Library Services Association, but Hearne's aim in the interview was not only to pay homage to the revered author, but also to try and understand why the moral complexity of L'Engle's thinking and writing often seemed to contradict her tendency, at least in her writing for children and young adults, to "cast her characters into either all-good or all-evil roles" (Marcus, *Listening* 354). Hearne's challenging questions were often met with resistance from the seventy-nine-year-old author, and Hearne had the impression that L'Engle's "energies were waning and that she felt that her time was short. It was harder for her now than in the past to concentrate and to do all the things she was used to doing" (Marcus, *Listening* 354). Hearne understood that it was more important to get L'Engle's "thoughts and words out to the reader" than "push her into areas that I might have wanted to go if we had been having a personal conversation" (355). L'Engle may have had less energy than in the past, but she could still use that energy to maintain her strong, opinionated public persona.

Over the course of several years of meetings with L'Engle, and with the author's friends and family members, Cynthia Zarin was able to accomplish what Hearne, in one short telephone interview, could not. She discovered the far more complex, far more flawed person behind the polished author persona L'Engle had presented to the world for so many decades. Many friends and fans felt that Zarin's 2004 profile for the *New Yorker* (not reprinted in this collection, but accessible via the *New Yorker* website) took advantage of L'Engle's growing cognitive difficulties, but Zarin disagrees, "I think that Madeleine was a lot sharper than she let on at that time. She was extremely sharp when she wanted to be present" (Marcus, *Listening* 361). If one insists on regarding L'Engle as idol, one is likely to find the Zarin profile upsetting. But for those familiar with the complexities of L'Engle's fiction, especially her adult fiction, the woman and the family presented in Zarin's piece will not seem at all unfamiliar.

In 2002, children's literature scholar Leonard Marcus conducted one of the last formal interviews L'Engle gave. L'Engle had recently suffered a stroke, and her granddaughter warned Marcus that she had "'good days and bad days' and that the interview might well have to be cut short or canceled" (Marcus, *Listening* 22). When Marcus arrived in Connecticut, it seemed as if it might be one of L'Engle's bad days; the author struck Marcus as disengaged when he attempted to talk with her. He remained at Crosswicks, reading the paper while he waited, disappointed, for his scheduled bus back to New York. But then, about an hour after she had left for a nap, L'Engle returned, a far more animated and engaged presence. While several of her stories struck Marcus as familiar, "much of what she said, [he] thought, was new" (24). The most poignant moment came when L'Engle, talking about a fan letter from a cancer sufferer, told Marcus, "My books are not bad books to die with. . . . When I read a book, if it makes me feel more alive, then it's a good book to die with" (24).

Perhaps dissatisfied with his own interview or with the knowledge that Zarin's *New Yorker* profile would have the "final word" on L'Engle after the author's death in 2007, Leonard Marcus interviewed over fifty of L'Engle's friends, family members, literary and religious acquaintances, and others whose lives had been touched by the esteemed author. Rather than writing a formal biography, Marcus allowed each of the interviewees several pages to speak their often contradictory truths about L'Engle. As Cara Parks's brief review of *Listening for Madeleine: A Portrait of Madeleine L'Engle in Many Voices* notes, Marcus's bricolage biography strives to paint a portrait not just of "contradiction," but "of a woman who was balancing—sometimes ineptly—the roles of mother, wife, and celebrated author." I would encourage readers to seek out Marcus's book as a worthy companion to L'Engle's own words about herself and her writing.

Readers do not have to tesser, only to turn the page, to find themselves back in 1967 America, bearing witness to the skillful construction of a public persona undertaken by an intelligent, intellectual, and increasingly spiritual writer in mid- and late-twentieth-century America.

Acknowledgments

Many thanks to my University Press of Mississippi editor Katie Keene, whose enthusiasm for children's literature and for Madeleine L'Engle, in particular, inspired me to take on this project. I am grateful to all of the rights holders who welcomed this project and graciously provided permission for their essays and interviews to be reprinted. Special thanks to Keith Call of the Wheaton College Library, an enthusiastic scholar and fan of L'Engle, who kindly scanned many interviews from the L'Engle papers archived at the college that I would have had difficulty tracking down on my own; and to Maddie Smith, who read the first draft of the introduction for this project and gave me invaluable feedback on ways to improve it. Finally, I wish to thank the Children's Literature Association, which has supported and encouraged my writing throughout my not-quite-conventional scholarly career.

The Estate of Madeleine L'Engle has not approved or endorsed the publication of this anthology, *Conversations with Madeleine L'Engle*.

JCH

Works Cited

American Library Association. "100 Most Frequently Challenged Books by Decade." *Banned and Challenged Books*. http://www.ala.org/advocacy/bbooks/frequently challengedbooks/top100.

Branch, Craig. "New Age Infiltrates American Life." *Believer's Web*. 2 May 2003, www. believersweb.org/view.cfm?ID=706. Reprinted from the *Watchman Expositor*.

Carroll, Margaret. "A Full Life: Madeleine L'Engle Continues to Add Titles to Her Bibliography." *Chicago Tribune*, 30 September 1990, articles.chicagotribune.com/1990–09 –30/features/9003210523_1_revisions-smith-college-cherry-orchard.

L'Engle, Madeleine. *Ilsa*. Vanguard, 1947.

———. *A Severed Wasp*. Farrar, Straus and Giroux, 1982.

Marcus, Leonard S. *Listening for Madeleine: A Portrait of Madeleine L'Engle in Many Voices*. Farrar, Straus and Giroux, 2012.

Parks, Cara. "Ironing Out the Wrinkles—The Complexities of Madeleine L'Engle." *New Republic*, 27 November 2012, newrepublic.com/article/110453/wrinkle-in-time -complexities-madeline-lengle-leonard-marcus.

Schmidt, Gary. "The Story as Teller: An Interview with Madeleine L'Engle." *ALAN Review*, vol. 18, no. 2, Winter 1991, pp.10–14.

Silvey, Anita. "The Problem with Trends." *Horn Book*, vol. 70, no. 5, September/October 1995, pp. 515–17.

Staub, Dick. "Missing Madeleine L'Engle." *Dick Staub* blog. CRS Communications, 2007, dickstaub.com/staublog/missing-madeleine-l-engle/.

Swerdfeger, Steven and Martha. "Transcript of Two Telephone Interviews with Madeleine L'Engle." Madeleine L'Engle Papers 1918–2006. Wheaton College Special Collections.

Terkel, Studs. "Madeleine L'Engle and Studs Terkel in Conversation." *The Studs Terkel Program* WFMT, 28 May, 1980. The Studs Terkel Radio Archive.

Webb, Heather. "A Conversation with Madeleine L'Engle." *Mars Hill Review* 4 (Winter/Spring 1996): 51–65.

Zarin, Cynthia. "The Storyteller: Fact, Fiction, and the Books of Madeleine L'Engle." *The New Yorker*, 12 April 2004. www.newyorker.com/magazine/2004/04/12/ the-storyteller-cynthia-zarin.

Chronology

1918   Born in New York City on November 29 to Charles Wadsworth Camp and Madeleine Hall Barnett Camp.

1926–30 Attends Brearly, a private New York girls school catering to the city's socially prestigious families; unhappy there, she is transferred to a series of city day schools.

1930   The Camps move to the French Alps and send Madeleine to Chatelard, a boarding school in Switzerland.

1933   The Camps return to America, settling in Jacksonville, Florida; Madeleine is sent to Ashley Hall, in Charleston, South Carolina, to complete her schooling.

1936   Father Charles Wadsworth Camp dies.

1937   Enrolls in Smith College.

1941   Graduates from Smith College with honors in English; moves to New York City and takes a job working in the theater.

1945   *The Small Rain*, first novel for adults, published.

1946   Marries actor Hugh Franklin.

1947   Josephine Franklin born.

1949   Publishes *And Both Were Young*, her first book for teens.

1950   Moves to Goshen, Connecticut, with her husband and daughter; the family takes over the town's General Store.

1952   Bion Franklin born.

1956   Adopts Maria, the child of friends of the Franklins who had recently died.

1959   Ten-week cross-country camping trip with Hugh and the children; during the trip, the words "Mrs. Whatsit, Mrs. Who, and Mrs. Which" pop into L'Engle's mind.

1960   The Franklins move back to New York City, settling on the Upper West Side; Hugh Franklin returns to acting.

1960   Begins six years of teaching at St. Hilda's and St. Hugh's School.

1960   Publishes *Meet the Austins*, her first book for children.

1961	Edward Mason West, canon sacrist of the Cathedral Church of St. John the Divine, becomes "her spiritual adviser, confidant, trusted reader, and the model for Canon Tallis" (Zarin).
1962	Publishes *A Wrinkle in Time*.
1963	Wins Newbery Medal for *A Wrinkle in Time*.
1966	Begins a three-decade tenure as volunteer, then later librarian and writer in residence, at the Cathedral Church of St. John the Divine.
1970	Hugh Franklin begins a thirteen-year-run as Dr. Charles Tyler on the daytime soap opera *All My Children*; Madeleine begins a long career as a speaker on the literary, college, and Christian lecture circuits.
1972	Publishes her first memoir, *A Circle of Quiet*; together with *The Summer of the Great-Grandmother*, *The Irrational Season*, and *Two-Part Invention*, the memoirs come to be known as *The Crosswick Journals*.
1972	Meets Luci Shaw at Wheaton College Writers' Conference.
1978	Publishes *A Swiftly Tilting Planet*; publishes *The Weather of the Heart*, her first book with religious publisher Harold Shaw.
1977	Granddaughter Lena Jones is hit by a truck but survives.
1978	Awarded University of Southern Mississippi Medallion for lifetime contribution to children's literature.
1979	Awarded National Religious Book Award for *The Weather of the Heart*.
1980	Publishes *Walking on Water: Reflections on Faith and Art*.
1980	Awarded an American Book Award for *A Swiftly Tilting Planet*; awarded National Religious Book Award for *A Ladder of Angels*.
1981	Awarded a Newbery Honor Medal for *A Ring of Endless Light*.
1984	Awarded the Regina Medal of the Catholic Library Association for distinguished contributions to children's literature.
1985–86	Serves as President of the Authors Guild.
1986	Hugh Franklin dies.
1986	Receives ALAN Award for outstanding contribution to adolescent literature from the National Council of Teachers of English.
1990	Edward Mason West dies.
1990	Wins the University of Minnesota's Kerlan Award in children's literature.
1991	Severely injured in a car accident.
1995	Writer-in-residence for *Victoria* magazine.

1997   Publishes *Mothers and Daughters* with her photographer daughter Maria Rooney.

1998   Awarded the American Library Association's Margaret A. Edwards Award for lifetime achievement in writing for the teen ages.

1999   Son Bion Franklin dies at forty-seven from complications from alcoholism.

2001   Suffers a stroke that curtails travels and writing.

2007   Dies at eighty-eight.

2008   *The Joys of Love*, originally written in the 1940s, published posthumously.

Conversations with
Madeleine L'Engle

Madeleine L'Engle

Roy Newquist / 1967

From *Conversations...*, 1967, pp. 230–43.

"We're afraid to say what we really want to say. We're afraid to communicate because by doing so we become vulnerable... take off your armor, do violence to jargon and platitudes and make yourself vulnerable. Talk and write about the things that matter, even if people think you're silly. This is the only thing that will give language back its dignity and joy."

L'Engle: My husband claims that I've used my early life in so many books that I no longer know fact from fiction, so I'll have to admit that I may have things somewhat confused. Yet what I'll say is more or less true.

I was born shortly after the First World War. My father was a foreign correspondent and a writer of all sorts. He was gassed during the war, so I never knew him as the volatile, fascinating, attractive person he must have been. I saw him dying for eighteen years; the gas just went on eating. My mother had studied to be a pianist until she married, and for a while, when we lived in New York, my father was drama and music critic for the *Herald-Evening Sun*. The house was full of peculiar people.

I always wanted to write, but I wasn't encouraged at home because my father was a writer. (I certainly would not encourage my children to write. None of them show any tendency to do so, thank God.) My early teachers didn't encourage me to write either.

I was well into adolescence when I started really doing something about writing. This was when I attended a perfectly ghastly school. I was quite lame, and at this school they placed a tremendous emphasis on prowess in the gym. It was also faintly social. A really repulsive New York–type school. I remember coming home and saying, "All right, so I'm the unpopular one," and I began a life purely of the imagination. I wrote to keep *myself* company, to make myself happy. The homeroom teacher went along with the kids in labeling me the lame and unpopular one, and she also decided I wasn't very bright. Her name was Miss Pepper or Miss Salt, I forget which, and she was dreadful. I probably didn't change her opinion by the way I didn't study. The last year I was there they had a poetry contest in the spring that was to be judged by the head of the English department. The submissions went right to her without screening; otherwise, I wouldn't have had an entry. I won it, and there was great sound and fury because my homeroom teacher said, "Madeleine isn't bright. She couldn't have written that poem; she must have copied it." So my mother had to go to school with the mass of poems, novels, and stories I'd written, and they finally had to allow that I probably had written the winning poem.

Also at school (and this I put into *Camilla)* I had to go to the bathroom, and the teacher wouldn't let me go, so I wet my pants. My mother went to the principal about it, but the teacher denied what she'd done and was believed. I learned about adult perfidy from her.

I was twelve when it became apparent that my father couldn't stand living in the city anymore. He adored London, he adored Paris, and he adored New York, but the fumes were just too much for his lungs. It was cheaper for us to go to live in Europe than for him to be ill in America, so we moved to France. My parents stayed in the French Alps, and I was sent to a boarding school in England. After the completely solitary life I'd led in New York, I was suddenly in a dormitory with twelve other girls. The only American, the foreigner. It was absolutely splendidly horrible. I still get books out of it, but I honestly learned all sorts of valuable things. I learned to concentrate anywhere; consequently, I wrote my first book when I was on tour with a play, wrote it in railway stations, on trains, in dressing rooms. I remember saying once, "No, no, I can't talk quite yet; I'm in the middle of a seduction scene. Wait."

While at this school, I also resolved, after deciding I would not die of anguish, that I would show them. This is not really good motivation, but quite a lot can come from it. When I graduated I was president of student government and everything else you can be president of.

I wrote my first novel when I was twelve. I still think it quite splendid. All about triplets: one was great at sports, one a great intellect, and one marvelous socially. So they pretended to be one person and were very successful as one great person. Then one of them fell in love, and he had to confess to the girl that he was only one-third of himself. The last line as she left him was, "He said nothing. What was there to say?" I suppose that twelve is the classic age to write the first novel.

I went on writing reams of poetry and reams of short stories and did nothing about them; I think this was wise. I simply wrote them to pile up experiences. I went to Smith and was graduated with honors. I'm probably the only Smith graduate who lost Phi Beta Kappa for misbehavior.

After I got out of college I decided it was time that I get published. All the magazines that paid turned me down with not-surprising regularity. I began, however, to get things into little magazines. I didn't know then that publishers read little magazines and contact writers they think might show promise. So I did get letters from several publishers. Bernard Perry, now the head of Indiana University Press, was then with Vanguard, and he wrote and asked if I had a novel. I told them I was in the middle of one. They said, "Show it to us when you finish it." I did. It was very rough. (I must always do a great deal of rewriting, but I don't mind doing it.) They offered what seemed to be a fabulous sum of money—a hundred dollars—and I spent the entire summer sitting alone in an apartment in the village rewriting *The Small Rain*, which they bought with some trepidation; it surprised them by doing very well. (It was good, in other ways, to sit that summer out; I was recuperating from my first wild love affair.)

Vanguard then published my second novel exactly as I wrote it. It was a damned good first draft, but it had no business being published.

Then, at Bernard's suggestion, I wrote my first so-called children's book. In *The Small Rain* I wrote about the dark side of the English boarding school; in the children's book I touched the slightly brighter side of it. It's still doing very well.

Then came the phase when nobody would publish me. The decade of the 1930s was absolutely ghastly. I had married Hugh by then, and he had decided to leave the theater because it wasn't fair for children to have a father whose profession was so precarious. He left, and we decided that if I got pregnant within a month we'd settle in the country. So I got pregnant, and then what do you do? He thought that thirty-five was a young enough age to start a new career. Well, it's not—not when you have only a degree from Northwestern in speech. Fortunately, we had bought a house the first spring we were married, an absolutely marvelous old white farmhouse in the northwestern corner of Connecticut, for $6,300. So we went there to put roots down. There was a town nearby, and he went to see about getting jobs in various factories. He didn't have an engineering degree, so they couldn't use him in a white-collar job. He said he would just as soon work on a machine, so they gave him tests, and he came out rated "Genius." They said he'd disrupt the men, so he was just plain unemployable.

I took the baby to visit mother in South Carolina; I hadn't been there long when Hugh called me and said, "I bought the Goshen general store." This was a completely dead general store in the center of town, and he had mortgaged us to the hilt to buy it. He had no experience in this sort of thing. He comes from a family of lawyers, and being an actor is strange enough but a general store operator! Yet we ran that store for many years. He built it from a completely dead store to a flourishing business; it reached the point where the only thing to do would be to buy more stores. One night, when we were sitting in front of the fire having a drink, I said, "Hugh, are you still happy with the store?" and he said, "No." I said, "Sell it."

We lived there nine years. The children were little, the house was drafty, and there were days in winter when we couldn't get the kitchen above forty-five degrees. I was struggling with diapers. I was in the store for three hours every day so Hugh could come home for lunch and have the kids nap. I wrote at night after the kids fell asleep. Frequently, I fell asleep over the typewriter. I learned a tremendous amount during that decade. I wouldn't give it up for anything, but I hope never to live through anything like it again. . . .

The only thing I was selling during this decade was stuff from the store, and I was fairly successful in talking people into buying things they didn't want. I have a splendid imagination.

I do remember, with fondness, the carnival people. They had a real old-fashioned country fair in Goshen, and during the winter they rented the fair buildings to carnival men. They're basic dirty-clean marvelous people, and most of the town stood off from them a bit. But I wasn't afraid of them. I always came to the store at noon, and one day the carnival men were there. And one of them said to Hugh, "Where's the boss?" Hugh said, "What do you mean?" and he said, "Ah, come on now you know who the boss is!" And Hugh said, "I'm the boss." At that point I walked in, and Hugh raised his finger and said, "Madeleine! Down on your knees!" Naturally I dropped to my knees as any good wife would and the carnival men thought this was the loveliest thing they'd ever seen, and they treated me like a queen after that.

During this decade I was looking forward to my fortieth birthday. Instead of dreading it I was dying to have it because it seemed to me that things would have to change; somebody would have to buy something I'd written. I had a book out at Simon and Schuster, and I knew that three editors were very strong for it, one hated it, and a fifth had to be heard from. They'd had it for three months, and I was hopeful. But on that longed-for day Hugh called me from the store and said, "I'm sorry; I know it's your birthday, but the answer is no." That almost finished me.

During that decade it seemed I had two alternatives. Once in a while I would come very close to doing a Gauguin, just leaving diapers and washing machines that froze, the whole household bit. The other—and because I do have a strong conscience it popped up more often—"It's not fair to Hugh and the children. I'm not selling. I'm not pulling my weight financially. I don't sweep in the corners. I can't bake pies. I should stop writing and be a proper housewife and mother."

So Hugh's call seemed that the message had gotten through, and this was it. I should stop. Each time a book got rejected, I had to go off somewhere and bawl, and it was hard on the family because the mother sets the tone of the house. If I wasn't gay, nobody was gay. So I went to the typewriter and covered it with a great gesture of renunciation, vowing that I would learn to bake a cherry pie. I bawled at the top of my lungs as though I was four, not forty (thank God the kids were at school), when all of a sudden I realized what my subconscious was doing. My subconscious was very busy writing a book on failure, so I went to the typewriter, took off the cover, and said, "Okay, this is it. If nobody ever publishes anything I write again, it is nevertheless what I am." When Hugh asked me to marry him it was, "Yes, I too want a family and would be as good a wife and mother as I could, but I am first and foremost a writer." And I'm forever grateful that I made my sweeping decision in a moment of absolute failure, when I really believed I'd never be published again. But during that fortieth year things did change. I began to sell what I wrote, and things have gone considerably better ever since.

Meet the Austins was taken that year by Vanguard. It was turned down by most publishers because it begins with a death, and we mustn't let children know about death. It is also a book about things that happened in our family, and I wrote it purely as a love letter to my husband. But I don't believe that children should be cushioned from the darker things. A clergyman friend and his wife once attended a seminar conducted by a very famous child psychologist. It was a question-and-answer affair, and she asked him, "Why is it that everything in the household falls apart around dinnertime?" He said, "The obvious reason is that it's the time of day when children are tired; they want their dinner. You're tired too; you've been struggling with diapers and formula and all the household routine. Your husband comes home at the end of his day, and he's tired too. But the real reason—and you'll probably contradict me—is that we're all afraid of the dark."

They all did contradict him, and he said, "The very violence of your reaction proves the truth of my words." This hit home because I think we all are afraid of the dark. Part of the reason for this is because in the child-centered life of the average American home children aren't allowed to know that there is such a thing as the dark or that it's perfectly all right to be afraid of the dark. It's *fine* to be afraid of the dark. You're afraid of existing evil, and you look for the light instead. If we try to cushion our children, we are really pushing them into the dark, denying them a chance to find a light to see by.

We have never had a child-centered household. We adore the children, but Hugh is first. In every family there has to be an apex, and I'm dead against the matriarchal setup which usually goes with a child-centered household. When we came back to New York the kids were seven, ten, and twelve, and Hugh went back to the theater. We ran into a problem because I was trying to get up with the kids and get them off to school, then stay up with Hugh when he came home from the theater at night. I think he has a right to expect a wife ready to sit and eat with him and talk to him. It just didn't work; I ended up in the hospital.

So we called a family conference, and I said to the kids, "You don't need me in the morning as much as Daddy needs me at night. You're old enough to get yourselves off to school, and when you get home from school, from then until you go to bed at night, I'm wholeheartedly yours. But you're on your own in the morning. Get up and make your own sandwiches, get yourselves decently dressed and off." I don't think they suffered abominably from it.

We do have a good family relationship. The kids think I'm a nice kind of moron. They like my books, and they like my cooking. But they do think I'm a nut. I was so determined not to get in the girls' hair when they got into their early teens that when it was time to get clothes I'd say, "All right, we have just this much that you can spend; here you are. Go buy what you want." Finally they came to me and said, "Look, Mother, we know the other girls all gripe because their mothers go out and choose all their clothes, but won't you come with us just once?" and I said, "No. You all have very good taste, and if I go you'll just waste my time and yours." I held off until this spring when our eighteen-year-old finished her second year at Smith, had exams, and planned a June 8 wedding. I told her to get her clothes in Northampton so things wouldn't be so rushed, and she said, "No. I'm not going to get one single thing without you this time." So we shopped when she got back.

Back to books. After *Meet the Austins* I wrote *A Wrinkle in Time*, which got rejected by everybody. It was turned down for about the twentieth time just before Christmas, when I was sitting on the bed wrapping Christmas presents, and I thought, "Madeleine, you've really grown up; you're being terribly brave about all this." I didn't realize until later that I had sent a necktie to a three-year-old girl, some perfume to a bachelor friend. So I called Theron, my agent, and said, "Theron, it's not fair to you or my family because this is such a peculiar book that nobody will buy it. Just send it back. I love it, but forget it."

So he sent it back.

My mother was up for Christmas. After Christmas I had a small party for her, and one of my friends said, "You must meet John Farrar." I said, "Yeah," because I was down on publishers at that point, but she insisted on setting up an appointment. I took the book when I went to keep it. What did I have to lose?

John Farrar had read my first book, *The Small Rain*, and liked it and asked if I had anything else. I said, "Yes, here's a book nobody likes." He asked if he could read it, and two weeks later I signed the contract. They said, "Now, don't be disappointed if it doesn't do well; we're publishing it because we love it." And it did very well indeed. It is still doing very well, and with it things certainly changed.

Farrar, Straus and Giroux have been wonderful for me—perfectly willing to let me write a different book every time. I don't have to do the same thing in a different color, which was my problem before, which must be a problem for most writers. I've done five books for Farrar, Straus and Giroux. Each has been completely different from the others, and they don't mind. They're wonderful.

Now, I feel a bit strongly about this categorizing of "children's books." All of the so-called children's books I care about passionately are not children's books. I don't write children's books. I think anybody who writes for children is being intolerable to children. I don't think they read children's books except as they read comic books, and this is a stage they outgrow, we hope. The real children's books are those they go on reading all their lives, books that come to terms with man's place in the universe. They are written because the writer is trying to work something out, and the only way the finite can say anything about the infinite is through paradox, through telling a story. I don't think it's any coincidence that, with the exception of the Sermon on the Mount, Christ taught entirely by telling stories. Anything lasting that has been said about man's relationship to creation has always been in the form of what is now called "fantastic fiction." It is the only possible way we have of doing it. And children, who haven't been taught that they must be terrified of this, love it.

Perhaps I'm being unfair to many parents and teachers because I'm gen-eralizing, but as children are taught by parents and teachers they are apt to lose their concept of imagination. In schools today they're taught only the material things. They're taken on field trips. They're taught only the provable because people are afraid that anything which isn't provable isn't true. Thus what children are being denied are vital areas of real truth. Is Shakespeare's *The Tempest* true? Is Dante's *Inferno* true? What is truth? It's more than provable fact. And in imaginative fiction writers are usually groping, in one form or another, trying to come to terms with proof.

I think that even the funniest of books in this field usually come out of tremendous personal anguish. *Alice in Wonderland* is the classic example. Lewis Carroll was an Anglican clergyman and a mathematician, but what he really wanted to say he said in *Alice*. His excuse was to write it for a little girl, but he obviously wrote it for himself. George MacDonald, a Congregational pastor, wrote hundreds of books of sermons that nobody reads, but his fairy tales are read over and over again by children and adults. The same is true of C. S. Lewis. He wrote theology and fiction simultaneously, both dealing with the same theological problem. The most challenging thing in writing stories is to absolutely avoid showing the bones of the problem you're dealing with. If you show them, you're not being a storyteller. You write beyond what you actually are at that time, beyond what you are capable of knowing in the field.

I find that when I'm writing poetry or fantasy I'll make progress in my subconscious thinking. My subconscious works far ahead of my conscious, freeing it.

This kind of book is always written on many levels. Children will respond to some of them; they will always respond to the story. In fact, it must be, first and foremost, a good story. If you are a storyteller, not a theologian or philologist or whatever, you are successful at the most important level. Then, beneath that story, come the subterranean currents, the things you are really writing about. Without these currents there would be no writing, no music, no painting, no art of any form. This is our attempt to make order out of chaos, to see all of the seeming confusion of the world and put it into a pattern so that life becomes not only bearable, but joyous. You can't have joy in carelessness or lack of discipline or disorder; there is only confusion, which leads to sickness.

Writing is a way of our being healthy, I suppose. And there's always a paradox, always contradictions of pain and happiness, of opposites. I find that when I'm teaching I will frequently contradict myself, and I will have to say, "The contradictions stand because of these things that are true."

To bring things up to date: *The Love Letters* has a strange history. I have to call it a totally adult book, and this kills me because here I am, making this division again. In one way or another I've been working on it for almost six years, but it started as a play based purely on the tiny bit that is known of the seventeenth-century nun, Maryana Alcoforado, who was seduced by a French soldier of fortune. When he abandoned her she wrote him five wild love letters, and he allowed them to be pirated and published. They became what we might call the first best seller.

We know, from the letters, that she was not thrown out of the convent. She was demoted to sister portress, which was far more drastic a thing in those days than it would be today because in the convents the choir sisters were the nobility, and the sister portress was a lay nun who could have been a peasant.

The only other thing we know about her is from her death notice, which discloses that she was made abbess of the convent after thirty years of penance.

There are more or less two things you can do with this story. You can write a nasty, scandalous, blasphemous shocker. I knew I didn't want to do this, but I also knew I was going to have to come to terms with love (in both upper and lower case) and with sin, repentance, and regeneration. I had to do a great deal of theological thinking about this which I hadn't anticipated.

The play I wrote was read by several people, and finally George Shaffer, who does the Compass productions, read it and got quite excited. But I told him that there were problems with the third act I couldn't resolve. He agreed and thought it would make a much better movie than it would a play and would I like to try a film treatment? I'm usually willing to tackle almost anything anyone suggests. I knew this would be difficult because it meant a completely new medium, thinking in completely new terms, but I went into high gear and had a marvelous time until my body gave up and put me in the hospital. (My body does this to me.) The film treatment worked, probably because I was in a semicomatose state, and George liked it. Then, because it is a ticklish subject, I took it to Father Harold Gardner, the Jesuit who was editor of *America* and was at that time on leave of absence from Catholic University. He liked it and said that he would be interested in advising if it were made into a movie.

So then I wrote a scenario, but before I wrote the scenario I went to Portugal because I realized I had to see the actual places where the story occurred. Hugh was in a soap opera at the time, and they wrote him out of it for ten days, and we left for Portugal the day after Christmas. We couldn't land at Lisbon because of fog, so we went on to Madrid. It was cold in Portugal, terribly cold, and we weren't prepared for it. We had some language problems. They thought Hugh was English, and I was his French concubine. But we loved it. I saw the convent where Maryana had lived, and the curator was delighted because I was the only author who had ever dealt with Maryana who'd come to see the convent. We also found how little was known about her and how some people don't even think she existed.

I came away untrammeled by fact. I could never write a historical novel; I'm uncomfortable if my imagination isn't free to do what it wants. If you write a historical novel you're stuck with what happened, with what people actually did. The exciting thing in writing a book is to have your characters do what you didn't expect of them. Anyway, I finished the scenario, and everybody promptly got worried about it as the subject for a movie.

Simultaneously, everyone involved thought it would be a great idea if I wrote it as a novel, and if Farrar, Straus and Giroux did it, this would help us past any real or implied censure. (FSG simply would not publish a blasphemous book.) I wanted to do it as a novel anyway, but I had trouble switching mediums and turned out one treatment after another instead of a novel, until it finally (I don't know how) came out in the form it's in. Theron Raines, my agent, read it and said, "Thank God you didn't tell me what you were going to do because I would have told you not to do it; it couldn't be done." But it's done, and people at FSG call it "ambitious." But to me— well, what I've done is to write from two places in time. I start with a young American woman whose marriage has broken up. She flees to Portugal and discovers Maryana's love letters. I move back and forth in time between Charlotte, the American, having to learn what love means, what marriage is, and Maryana having to learn what love means, what faithfulness is. In some places it isn't even clear whether it's Maryana or Charlotte I'm talking about, which is deliberate. So I suppose it is ambitious, but if I'd thought of it that way I'd have scared myself off.

But it's done. Rewritten, cut, edited, cut again, and enhanced by a good editor, a good copy editor, all sorts of nice people.

I don't think my objectives as a writer have anything to do with the size of my talent, be that talent small, medium-size, or whatever. Being a writer is the premise upon which I have always based my life. It's what I am, so I suppose it is not only a profession. I care very much about being professional, but it is also a vocation.

I feel that no matter what I do, whether it's a little tiny book or something in which I am (knowingly or not) being ambitious, I have a responsibility to the reader. Now there is a tendency in some writing, some by tremendous writers at that, to use the reader as a psychiatric couch and the book as a self-indulgence. This is what you should do in your first draft. An awful lot of first drafts are getting published, but you should take the book beyond the self-indulgence of the first draft and write it for your readers.

I'll use acting as an example. If an actor cries onstage, the audience may be impressed by it, but the audience will not cry. If a comedian laughs at his own jokes, the audience won't laugh. All of this "onstage indulgence" must be weeded out in rehearsal. In rehearsing a tragic part the actor will probably bawl his head off, but this is necessary. But when he performs for an audience he has to pattern his performance to wring emotion from the audience, not put on a mere display. When all you give your audience, either onstage or from a book, is a slice of life, what's the point of going to the theater or reading a book? They might as well sit in the middle of Broadway and watch people.

A piece of art, no matter what it is, is discipline. It's got pattern; it fakes chaos. It says something about our place in the world, even if it's a very tiny thing. You don't have to be very ambitious to interpret the meanings of life. Or you can be ambitious beyond your capacity, which is an extremely good thing—I think you expand your capacity only by trying to do things that are more than you can do.

In last Sunday's *Times* there was a fascinating article by a historian who said that things were accomplished only by people who acted "as if." England, during the blitz, acted "as if" it could overcome Germany. You "as if" the impossibles; then you do them. I think this is the premise upon which all real writers write. We write as if we could write a better book than we can. It may not be the book we want to write, but it's probably better than the book would be if we were willing to stay within the limitations of our talent.

Then there's an English poet who said that poetry is like ice cream. Tremendous heat is needed in the generating of it, but in the actual writing there has to be ice, for otherwise the ice cream will melt. This is true. The more emotional a scene is, the cooler I am when I write it. This is not intentional; perhaps it's another part of the subconscious working as a guide. You can call it your subconscious or unconscious or (I'm still thinking in theological terms) grace or whatever.

I think also that a writer has a tremendous responsibility to his work, to make his instrument as good as it can possibly be so that it can be kept constantly fit for playing. I know writers who write only when inspiration comes. How would Isaac Stern play if he played the violin only when he felt like it? He would be lousy. Perhaps every concert he gives isn't as great as every other concert, but if he didn't practice and work constantly he wouldn't have an instrument for the great work when the time came to perform it. The same is true for art of every type. It may be that what we do in practice, what we throw away, is almost as important as what we keep. I know that for each page I keep I've probably thrown away a hundred.

As I said before, I resent the book as a self-indulgence. I don't think this is fair to the writer's talent or to the reader's time. I'm always a number of years behind reading current books because I usually wait to see if they're still around in five years. I'm not going to live long enough to read everything, so I've got to do a certain amount of sifting. I find, after my plunge into theology while writing *The Love Letters,* that I'm reading more philosophy. Oddly enough, I also read a lot of physics; I get very excited by physics. I was terrible in that area at school, but in reading physics, I get more of a sense of theology than I do in reading many theologians. One of the books that to me was most filled with God was *Limitations of Science* by Sullivan, which never once mentioned the word "God." And I read science fiction in the bathtub; I love it, but it doesn't matter if it falls in.

In fact, I discovered science fiction when I was eight years old. I read Oscar Wilde's fairy tales along with H. G. Wells. *Happy Prince* and *The War of the Worlds* go beautifully together.

I do regret that I sound pompous when I talk about myself as a writer, but maybe it can't be helped. I have to regard being a writer as the most important thing in the world; otherwise, there is no point to my life. I also have to constantly balance "being a writer" with being a wife and a mother. It's a matter of putting two different things first, simultaneously. This obviously makes for some frustrations, tensions, and conflicts, but that's fine—out of them comes creativity in what I write and in family relationships. I get terribly excited about things and passionately enjoy things. I enjoy life tremendously. Last spring I was going on about one of my great enthusiasms to my eldest daughter when she threw her arms around me and said, "Oh, Mother, you are such a child." I must have looked appalled, so she very quickly said, "But we love you this way. We wouldn't want you to be any different."

I'm afraid the children think I am rather immodest both in conversation and behavior. We will talk about absolutely anything. If I'm taking a bath and I suddenly have an idea, I'll plop right out and sit down at the typewriter, and they'll say, "Mother, really!"

This summer our young son, fourteen, was about to go away to boarding school for the first time. He said, "I want to have an embarrassing conversation with you, Mother," and I said, "Fine, what about?" He said, "What do fourteen-year-olds usually have on their minds?" I said, "Sex." And he said, "Yup," so we went through the whole thing. He said, "All the other boys are going to know all the words, and I want to know all the words, too." So we just went through all the words.

No wonder the kids think I'm sweet but nuts.

I know I'm regarded as a happy person, and I think I am. But I think that being happy (again we come to contradictions) involves pain and anguish as well as laughter and good feeling. Only the contented moron can have joy without pain, night without day. Light means nothing unless there is dark. A candle is useless if there's no night.

I'm not very bright; I'm not an intellectual. I got through college with honors on the gift of gab because I could write things that appealed to professors. But as far as having an intellectual mind, I don't. I have an instinctual mind. Without my husband's patience and tolerance, heaven only knows where I'd be. Not only that, but he is an absolutely magnificent editor, and when he reads something of mine and criticizes it I know that he's right and that I'm going to have a tremendous amount of rewriting to do. I get absolutely furious and behave abominably. I scream at him, I defend what I've done, I shriek, and I yell. I don't know why he puts up with it. Then I go back and do what he says.

With *The Arm of the Starfish* he was out of town with a play, but my agent read it, was excited by it, and thought it the best thing I'd done. Hugh read it and said, "No, no. It's good, but you left strings untied here; you left strings untied there. The plot isn't tight enough. The book isn't nearly good enough." I got really furious with him because I knew this meant rewriting the whole book.

I did. I rewrote the whole thing, and the last third was completely changed. The strings he pointed out meant that I had to change the whole resolution, and it was a much better book because of him.

The next thing he does which is absolutely invaluable, and saves both Theron and my publishers a great deal of time, is the way he goes over a manuscript with me word for word, cutting. "You don't need this word," or even "You don't need this comma." I scream, "You want me to cut the whole thing; you don't want anything left!" But it ends up tighter and tidier because of his vigilance. I always put in too much overcerebration, and he takes it right out. And he's right. It doesn't belong in a novel; it belongs in an essay. The world has lost a good editor in having him a great actor.

Finally, in this matter of advising the young writer, hoping for him, I suppose I have to assume that he shares my aims: to be published, to be read, and to communicate. The only school for this is reading other writers—the great writers, over and over. Some writers say, no, that you become derivative, but in the great writers you find the right things done the way they must be done, and certain things that are never done. And you can learn from these.

I think you must also write constantly, whether you feel like it or not. I have kept copious, unpublishable journals since I was eight; they are my self-indulgence, my safety valve. When I'm miserable I let it all out in there, not in published first drafts. Into the journals go everything I see, any ideas I have, and pictures and anecdotes of the children (which have been invaluable material for the Austin books). I copied down, for example, Chekhov's letters to his wife, great reams of his advice on acting, because it applied to what I felt was true about writing.

In college I majored in English, but most of my friends majored in theater. I spent most of my time in the theater making them put on my plays. This was terribly good experience, so when I came to New York to make my fortune I went into the theater for two reasons: to get over my horrible shyness and to gain experience as a writer, to see what happened to words night after night on the stage. I have a flair as an actress, but I'm much too tall to have ever been serious about it. My flair was for the comic, but I was perfectly happy to get understudy jobs. I did learn most of the things about words I hoped to learn, and I did get over being shy. Also, working in the Goshen general store helped me in overcoming my shyness. I had to pay attention to the person on the other side of the counter. I can't advise every young writer to go into the theater, but it could be a great help.

I think the journal is important, both to absorb self-indulgence and furnish source material. Experimentation with all forms of writing is important.

At dinner once my new son-in-law talked about some theologians who claim that God is not dead, as some theologists are claiming, but that language is dead and that if we are to revive language so that it will have any meaning then violence must be done to it. I got very upset. I felt very threatened by this because if language is dead so is my profession. Then I began to realize that doing violence to language didn't mean at all what I thought he'd meant at first. It didn't mean doing anything different with the words or reversing the order of words or of doing anything strange with words. What it meant was not being afraid to use words directly to communicate with each other. This applies very much to writing, just as it does to our personal relationships. In today's world what we've done is to cushion language so that we don't communicate with each other; we retreat into jargon. We talk about things being relevant and meaningful in order to avoid relevance and meaning. We're afraid to say what we really want to say. We're afraid to communicate because by doing so we become vulnerable. I'm being vulnerable right now because I'm being very open. Yet I realize more and more that you cannot be creative in any way—in personal relationships or in work—unless you completely take off your armor, do violence to jargon and platitudes, and make yourself vulnerable. Talk about the things that matter, and write about the things that matter, even if people think you're silly.

This is the only thing that will give language back its dignity and joy.

An Interview with Madeleine L'Engle

Ruth Rausen / 1975

From *Children's Literature in Education*, Winter 1975, pp. 198–205. Reprinted with permission of Springer.

Ruth Rausen: Miss L'Engle, can you remember when the idea first occurred to you that you might be a writer?

Madeleine L'Engle: I think the idea occurred to me so early that it wasn't at all a conscious idea. My mother kept my stories, which I wrote when I was five and which were all about a little G-R-U-L because I hadn't learned to spell yet. I've always written. I don't ever remember when writing stories wasn't a complete part of my life, just as necessary as breathing and sleeping.

RR: And all the writers that I've ever met were great readers. Were you a great reader as a child?

L'Engle: Oh, an enormously great reader because I was an only child here in New York City, with my mother: she was almost forty when I was born, I think. She had wanted a baby for nearly twenty years, and she hadn't been able to carry a child through beyond three months until she got me—stubborn then, stubborn now. So I was terribly overprotected; I wasn't allowed to go out alone. There wasn't a library near, so I simply had to read what my parents had, what I had been given, and when I had read everything four or five times I just started to write my own stories.

RR: Do you remember which kinds of books appealed to you most? Information? Did you like fantasy, or were you looking for books of philosophy, ideas? Can you remember which gave you the most satisfaction as a young child?

L'Engle: What's always given me the most satisfaction is a story which is a story on the top level and underneath has something mythic to say about life, about the human condition. I loved Oscar Wilde's fairy tales. I loved George MacDonald's fantasies. I loved L. M. Montgomery, particularly her books about *Emily of New Moon*, much more than *Anne of Green Gables*, because Emily wanted to be a writer. Also in *Emily of New Moon* there is a touch of what is now called the "occult" in that Emily had extraordinary dreams, and I believe in that world, which is around our conscious minds and which I think art of all kinds comes from.

RR: We often talk about the influence of books when we're doing our criticism and our book selection in libraries, and I wonder how you feel about this question. Do you think books are a major influence? Were they with you?
L'Engle: I think that in all the books that I read, and particularly the books that I reread, there's a way of looking at life which involves a sense of responsibility, that the human being is a responsible human being, that honor does mean something, and I think that there are times when I've had choices to make where I have been guided to make a more difficult choice because that's what the heroes in the books that I loved most did. They didn't just take the easiest ways out. They did what they thought was right, knowing that they really weren't strong enough to do it, but they had to do it anyhow. So it's a sense of knowing your own fallibility, your own human weakness and brokenness, and that despite all of this, great things can happen. I think that's underneath one of the terribly popular books of the last ten to fifteen years, the *Lord of the Rings*, when Frodo does more than Frodo can do, and that's behind all of the great fairy tales. Not long after *A Wrinkle in Time* came out—and as you know that was rejected by publisher after publisher for nearly two years—a librarian in Baltimore was asked which book had meant most to her children during the period that we almost went to war over Cuba, and she said, "*A Wrinkle in Time*, without question, because it gave them courage." So if I was able to give other people courage, it was because of the books that gave me courage and which still influence me. I still reread my favorite children's books. Some of them were my mother's books. Some of them came out during my childhood. They're my children's favorites, and now my grandchildren are five and six. I'm beginning to read to them.

RR: When you became a parent, did you try to direct your own children's reading?
L'Engle: I wouldn't read them anything I wasn't interested in. I'd read them any book once, and if I didn't like it, if I was bored by it, I wouldn't read it twice. I'd say, "Read it yourself. I'm bored."

RR: The world has changed quite a bit from the time you were a child. Television has come along, and that has brought children a much bigger world, we know. It's a world that parents can't control for them. It's so easy for them to watch television and have all these influences coming to them that their parents are not part of now.

L'Engle: I think the basic change in the world was before television. I was born right after the armistice that ended the First World War, and l think that that war was *the* major change. I see in people who are five or ten years older than I am a different way of looking at the world. I grew up in a world where, although there wasn't television, there was still instant communication. There was radio. There was the telephone. If there was an explosion in Leningrad, we would know about it. And I think it's the instant knowledge of too much. Now, when you know all the horrors that are going on in the world, I think the worst thing that happens is that you begin to lose compassion because you simply can't cope with that much. I remember hearing on the radio, "Only seventy-five killed this week." "Only seventy-five"—you can't say, "Only seventy-five." I think the worst thing that television does is to teach passivity. The kids sit there, and they absorb passively. They don't have to do any creating of their own, whereas when you read a book, the reader is creating the book just as much as the writer. It's an act of collaboration.

RR: Well, fortunately, there are still many young people around who love books. They love words, and we know that you love words. We're delighted in the library that we have many requests for *A Wrinkle in Time* and *The Arm of the Starfish*.

L'Engle: I know that kids love the books and love words because I get so many letters. At least once a week there will be a letter saying, "I love words. I love your new words." I have written another book in the same area as *A Wrinkle in Time* called *The Wind in the Door*. It's more adventures of Meg and Calvin and Charles Wallace, although it can stand on its own, and right now I'm writing a book which will be a sort of third along with *The Arm of the Starfish* and *The Young Unicorns*. It has some characters from both those books meeting each other, and it has a brand new character as chief protagonist. But a lot of old friends meet because I get terribly involved with my characters and I want to find out what goes on, so this is that kind of international intrigue science fiction. We're all passionately concerned about what's happening to the earth, and Dr. O'Keefe has been asked to go see a lake in Venezuela that's dying. The abuse by greed of our earth's resources is very much in my thinking now, and what I'm thinking about is bound to be reflected in my writing.

RR: Do young people in their letters ask you about your books and what *A Wrinkle in Time* means?

L'Engle: Oh, yes. I suppose I average five to ten letters a day, which is a lot of letters, and I will treasure every single one of them. If you've gone through as long a period of absolute failure as I did, ten years where I couldn't see anything I wrote, then each of those letters is just such a marvelous affirmation to me that I was right to keep on struggling and not to give up and learn to bake cherry pie properly (which I never have learned to do). I answer every letter I get.

RR: I remember quite some years ago a young boy asking me about *A Wrinkle in Time* and asking me whether I thought Calvin was the religious teacher. I said, "I wouldn't be at all surprised, but you really ought to write Miss L'Engle a letter and ask her whether this came from Calvin."

L'Engle: Well, I just thought that Calvin, who is so Protestant, and O'Keefe—such an Irish name!—made a marvelous conflict and that Calvin himself is a slightly paradoxical person. He's born in a family where nobody reads a book, and here is Calvin with this passion to learn and to know and to understand. So I just did it as a sort of pleasurable paradox.

RR: How do you view the current books being written specifically for young teenagers? They have taken as their theme very serious adult problems: drug addiction, unwed parenthood, and homosexuality.

L'Engle: When they're written to teach a lesson, I don't like them, even if they only teach in the last five pages. But when they're written because this is what the author is passionately concerned with and has to get it out onto paper, that's fine. I don't t think there's any such thing as a taboo subject. I think it's the attitude behind the subject which makes the book acceptable or not acceptable. Where a writer has been—is—himself concerned with drugs, where he's been involved in them or has been with someone who's been involved with them, and is writing out of his own urgent need, then that book can be a real book. But when it's because it's fashionable, it's selling, and it's what's going right now, then the book is usually phony. Kids can spot that in a second.

RR: "Relevancy" has become the big word.

L'Engle: "Relevant" and "meaningful" and . . .

RR: It is probably inevitable that we get a book such as Robert Cormier's *The Chocolate War*. Have you read that? That's a book intended for children.

L'Engle: No. I've heard a great deal about it; I very much want to read it. One thing about writing books is it takes an enormous amount of time to write, and then when I'm writing a book I usually have to do a lot of scientific research for whatever the science underneath the book is. But in *The Young Unicorns* when I was writing about the simulation of the pleasure center of the brain, that hadn't become a thing. We now have L-ads. That's really kind of scary because in almost every book I write about something that hasn't happened yet. My agent said, "I wish you'd stop being so prophetic."

RR: You've worked a great deal with young people in many ways, and you've had writing workshops for them.
L'Engle: I do every year.

RR: Are these young people from the inner city?
L'Engle: I try to have a totally mixed group. I don't like all inner city or all outer city. The group I have now I would say is basically a third black, a third Oriental, and a third white, and the whites are partly Christian, Jew, or atheist. So it's a beautifully mixed group, and the nicest thing about this kind of a group is to watch a trust slowly building up in the kids.

RR: Did you make any general observations on what they were seeking and what they were writing?
L'Engle: Mostly they want somebody to say, "Yes, you *are.* You exist, you matter, and what you do with your life matters." The distressing thing is that it takes me a little longer each year to get the trust going among the kids and to get the trust going to me. So this is why trust always comes into it because we tend to put people on pedestals, and that always leads to disaster. We suddenly find out that this person we've had on a pedestal has feet of clay. I want them to accept the feet of clay right from the start. I got involved with trying to teach this kind of mixed group because ten or fifteen years ago there was pressure put on writers to have protagonists from minority groups, from the inner city, and I felt that it was not my right or my privilege to do this because this is not in my own background. I don't come from an affluent background. I was on the fringe of inner city. But I wasn't in it, so I felt the only thing l could do was to try to give some of these kids the equipment of vocabulary and learning to tell a story that would make them able to write out of their own experience because a story which is not based on experience never is really real. My two most talented students were both black.

RR: Do you see that the situation has changed since you started the writing workshops? I know a few years ago the young people didn't trust anyone and were very hostile to adults. They refused even to think about a future because they couldn't deal with the present, and they were sure that there would be no hope for them in the future. Do you see those attitudes changing?

L'Engle: I find there's a more marked discrepancy—that those who are negative are more negative than they used to be and that those who are positive are more positive. There are always a few kids who really give me extraordinary hope for the future, but there are some who are so negative that I sometimes come close to despairing. But usually a chink will open, and there'll be at least a small ray of "Yes, one day it may be possible to hope," and that's enough. It's not very much, but it helps.

RR: Do you think that sometimes in the young people who are totally negative that it's just a pose with them—that they feel it's a necessary part of their role playing?

L'Engle: I think it basically comes from playing it safe, really, more than attention-getting because everything we see on television, particularly the commercials, is leading us into a world that is just about as secure and dull as the womb. The scientists now talk about the refusal of the baby to be born. The baby does not want to be born, to get out of his nice cozy amniotic fluid, and suddenly to have to breathe and eat and function. In a lot of kids there is, I think, a rejection of being born. But our lives are a constant series of being born and reborn and reborn and reborn from one stage to another, and we do tend to reject birth because Jung said there is no coming to life without pain. We're taught that pain is bad and pleasure is good. I think pain *is* bad, but on the other hand I have learned that almost everything good that has happened to me has followed a pained birth experience and that simply is a statistical fact which I can't evade.

RR: We're aware of the low reading scores here in the New York area, and they're explained by the educators as the result of poor attendance in school, lack of motivation. A basic nonunderstanding of the English language seems to be a large part of it too. And it's all so sad to us who know the joy and excitement that reading a good book can bring. In your writing, especially in *A Wrinkle in Time*, we feel your enjoyment of the richness of language, texture, and sound and meaning of words, all of it. Do you see any merit in controlled vocabulary books?

L'Engle: I get a vision of a large hairy man with horns sitting and twitching his tail happily as he gets these books out. I think they're immoral; they're horrible. If you keep a child within the vocabulary, how is he going to learn new words? Kids love great big, unwieldy, cumbersome, exciting words. I think one of the reasons that *Wrinkle* was rejected so often was—who's ever heard of a "tesseract"? Well, it's a real concept. It's an honest-to-goodness scientific word, which you'll find in the footnotes of large dictionaries. I think it's terrible to limit vocabulary.

RR: I think they did discover that there were a great many young people who could not read. They simply could not take on a book that had too many unfamiliar words. And it was a noble experiment.

L'Engle: I think it was a total lack of trust in the fact that a good writer will always use the simplest word possible. Mark Twain said he never used "metropolis" because he could use "city," and that when a writer uses a complicated word it's because it's the only word that he can possibly use. I had to use "tesseract"; there wasn't any other word because I needed the actual, accurate scientific word. I remember Beatrix Potter uses "soporific"; lettuce has a "soporific" effect. She wouldn't be allowed to do that today. They'd say, "You can say it makes them sleepy." She'd say, "No, that's not what I mean; I mean 'soporific.'"

RR: Do you like libraries?

L'Engle: I adore libraries.

RR: Do you have any advice for librarians? Because we feel that we're losing out and I wonder . . . I'm sure you're not the kind of person who likes to give advice, someone who thinks you have the answers or anything like that, but what can we do, do you think?

L'Engle: I don't have the answers, and what I'm going to say may sound slightly pompous, but I believe it. That is, I think, that love *is* just as contagious as hate. Emerson said, "What you are speaks so loudly over your head that I cannot hear what you say." So if you really come in every morning loving books, and loving to share them with people, then that's catching. Did you know that I'm a librarian?

RR: Yes, at the Cathedral of St. John the Divine.

L'Engle: Right. I walk into that lovely beautiful room every day, and my heart just sings. When I went into that library it was absolutely empty. I went there to write because I knew nobody used it, and I hadn't been there very long when the young librarian was called to be on jury duty. He got in an awful flap, and I said, "Oh, relax. Just go tell them I'll keep it open for you as long as I can use the electric typewriter." So I kept it open for two weeks and used the electric typewriter and was terribly happy, and when he got back they kept calling him over to other offices because there wasn't really enough to do there to justify a salary. Then he left. I said, "Why don't you just leave me here? I'll write my books here, and you don't have to pay me." So we have sort of a nice reciprocal trade treaty. Well, the thing is that I love the library so much that other people have discovered it too. We now have a part-time paid librarian, so I can get my writing done!

RR: Do young people talk to you about what they've read?
L'Engle: Yes. It's a good setting. It's a beautiful room with high ceilings and paneled walls and great bay windows which look across the Cathedral close to the Cathedral building itself. And there I am at a lovely desk which sort of puts me (no matter who I am) in the position of being somebody who's there and can be talked to. The first thing I did was to keep the teapot going so that people could have a cup of tea. I think that every adolescent needs somebody to whom they're not biologically bound, as they are to their parents, to talk to, to throw ideas off, to see what makes you happy—and a lot of grownups aren't happy—and when they see somebody like you, obviously doing something you are qualified to do and doing it well, and see somebody like me also doing what I love to do and want to do, that gives them a sense of, "Okay, maybe I can grow up, and it's not disastrous after all. Maybe I am born to grow up."

Madeleine L'Engle

Linda Chisholm / 1976

This memoir is the result of a series of tape-recorded interviews conducted for the Oral History Research Office by Linda Chisholm with Madeleine L'Engle in April and June of 1976. The first of these interviews were conducted in conjunction with the Oral History course of 1976. Ms. L'Engle has read the transcript and has made only minor corrections and emendations.

Madeleine L'Engle is the author of books of fantasy and science fiction for children, novels for adults, and books of reflection and meditation. She is the wife of Hugh Franklin, actor, mother, grandmother, librarian of the Cathedral of St. John the Divine, and lay theologian of the Episcopal Church. Her Newbery Medal winner, *A Wrinkle in Time*, has, in the fourteen years since its publication, become a children's classic.

In the following interview Madeleine L'Engle tells of the formative influences on her life as a writer, her parents and early schooling, her years at Smith College, her marriage to Hugh Franklin, and her experiences and philosophy of mothering. She describes the events between her first novels and *A Wrinkle in Time*, when her children were young, a decade of rejection slips, when she experienced the support of a Christian community in a small Connecticut town. She tells how *Wrinkle* was born of her interest in science, a trip West, and her search for religious truth. She speaks of her understanding of God and His manifestation in the events of her life, especially in the time of her mother's dying. She describes Canon Edward Nason West, sub-dean of the Cathedral of St. John the Divine, as her friend, colleague and confessor, and the source of one of her most beloved characters, Canon Tallis. She talks about the lack of sexism in her upbringing and its effect upon her books, of her job as collaborator and servant of the books she writes, of the sources of her rich vocabulary, of the heroes of her childhood, and finally of her plans for future books.

Interview 1: Cathedral Library, St. John the Divine, New York, New York, April 15, 1976

Q: The first thing I need to do, Madeleine, is ask for your permission to use this in the Oral History Collection at Columbia University and to quote parts of the tape for my class.

L'Engle: Of course I give you my permission, and I understand that this does not put the tape into the public domain and that I will retain copyright.

Q: That's right. We'll want to talk about your books, Madeleine, but before we do that, I'd like you to give me what I would call an educational biography. Now, by that, I want to hasten to say I don't mean a listing of your schools. I mean to ask you to identify a few of what you would call themes, important formative influences on your life, and what brought you to the place you are today, both as a writer and as a person.

L'Engle: I think it was very important that I was born in New York City and born an only child of parents who had tried for twenty years to produce a full-term baby. I was stubborn then, and I'm stubborn now. I lasted the full nine months, but this also meant that I was horribly overprotected because my mother lost another baby after me. I was going to be *it*. So, out of this rather negative thing of overprotection came my first positive experiences in writing because if you're an only child and you're not allowed out to libraries, when you've finished the books that you have, how do you get more books? You write them.

So I wrote my first story when I was five. It was about a little g-r-u-l because I couldn't spell. I wrote my first novel when I was ten because my father got a new typewriter and I got his old one. And what do you do if you're given a typewriter? Obviously, you write a novel.

Another seemingly negative thing which was very positive for me as a writer was that I was in fourth, fifth, and sixth grades in a school here in New York City, where there was a lot of emphasis put on athletics, and any team I was on automatically lost. If they chose up teams, the poor team who got me at the end groaned loudly, and my home room teacher very quickly took up the assessment of the kids and decided I was dumb. I learned quickly there was no point in doing any homework for her because she was going to hold it up for ridicule. I was not going to please her, so I stopped doing homework. And what did I do instead? I wrote. I established then a pattern of discipline in writing, which I never would have done had I been happy in school.

Then another terribly important thing happened. My father had been gassed in the First World War, and mustard gas just goes on eating up a man's lungs very slowly, and when I was twelve it became apparent he could not live in any city anymore. Cities were not polluted the way they are now, but even so, a city was too much for his lungs. My parents went to the Alps to try to find a place where Father could breathe, and what do you do with a twelve-year-old girl? They put me in an English boarding school. This was an incredible experience, having to sink or swim. I went down three or four times before I learned to swim. But the important [thing] that that school taught me was to concentrate in any kind of noise. We never had a moment of privacy, so I learned to put a force field of concentration around myself and to simply eliminate all outside sound. I can still do that as long as I'm not responsible for the noise. I wrote my first novel while I was on tour with a play, in trains, in dressing rooms that I shared with other people, in hotel rooms I shared with other people.

Q: I suspect not every child learned that at an English boarding school.
L'Engle: Well, I might not have learned it if I already hadn't established the pattern of writing, of needing the world of story, from which I sorted out what was happening. It wasn't an escape. It was a way of coming to terms with things. And I love to write on airplanes and in airports, which I do when I'm traveling to lecture. The only time that I can't do this, I discovered, was when I had children. I could not block out the sounds for which I was responsible, but if I'm not having to take care of the noise, it doesn't bother me a bit.

Then we came back to this country, and I went to another boarding school in Charleston, South Carolina, which is where many of my forebears on my mother's side come from. I responded enormously to the beauty. The school was in one of the old beautiful houses in Charleston, and I was very happy there. I was allowed to be a writer. I was allowed to be what in the other schools had been considered eccentric. I then went to Smith, and I was at Smith when the English Department was at its height.

Q: Who were some of your teachers?
L'Engle: I had Mary Ellen Chase, with whom I immediately had a battle. I was taking her—

Q: Would you like to—?

L'Engle: Yes. I was taking her survey of the novel course. It was a very popular course, and she did try to weed out those who were just taking it because they wanted to take Mary Ellen Chase and those who were really interested. The first mid-semester quiz was a hundred questions, and I remember only one of them, which was "What color dress did Jane Eyre have on when she met Mr. Rochester?" I looked at these idiotic questions, and I didn't know the answer to more than two of them. I was furious. So I grabbed about ten of those sheets and turned them over, and in my naive rage I wrote, "Dear Miss Chase, I don't know the answer to these questions. I think this is a silly quiz. But I have read the books, and I'll tell you what I think of them." Which I proceeded to do and Miss Chase, being a marvelous woman and a marvelous teacher, just simply wrote back, "Take no more quizzes," and made me do a lot of extra work, which was marvelous.

I also had Esther Cloudman Dunn for Shakespeare and for seventeenth-century literature, and she was so on fire with her work that you couldn't help catching it. I think the most important, single thing that she taught me was, in discussing Shakespeare's plays and the rudeness of the Elizabethan audience—particularly the boys in the pit—that if they didn't like what was going on onstage they threw rotten eggs and rotten fruit, and she said you note that every single one of the plays starts with an attention-getter. *Hamlet* starts with a ghost, *Macbeth* with three witches, *The Tempest* with a tempest, and *Twelfth Night* with a shipwreck. And only after Shakespeare gets the attention of the audience can he go on into the deepness of the soliloquies. Well, that's just as true for any kind of fiction as it is for the theater.

Another thing I just loved: There were two of Shakespeare's plays, which she had not read because she said, "I can't bear to have read all of Shakespeare."

Q: Some people feel that way about your books, Madeleine. They hold back.

L'Engle: Then my next hunk of education was when college was over. I had been in female institutions for ten years, and I was terribly, terribly shy. I knew I wanted to write, but you don't earn your living as a writer immediately. So I decided I would earn my living in the theater. Now, that's not quite as naive as it sounds. I had no illusions about myself as a great actress, but—I'm much too tall—I'm an adequate actress, and because I didn't care what jobs I got, I did get work. I was usually an understudy, assistant stage manager, and things like that, and I did this for two reasons: one, because I knew it would help me get over my shyness, particularly with the opposite sex. I was terrified often, but I knew I could work with them. If I met a man in a social situation, I completely froze, but when I was working with somebody, I was free to be me. The other was that I thought it was a good school for a writer. And it was. I learned—I suppose the most important thing that I learned was not every word which drops from a writer's pen is a precious pearl. I saw playwrights go back and sit up in a hotel room all night, cut one scene entirely, and write something else. I learned the necessity for revision. The play I learned most from, though, was—I was for a year on Broadway and a year on the road in Chekhov's *The Cherry Orchard*, and that was just a fantastic experience for a writer.

Q: It's a wonderful play.

L'Engle: It was a new play every night. Then, another odd negative was turned into a positive. When it was being cast for the road, there was an actor I was madly in love with, who was, I knew, up for the role of Petya Trofimov, Chekhov's mouthpiece, the young student. I was sure he was going to get it, and he didn't. At the first rehearsal I was introduced to a tall, black-haired, blue-eyed young man named Hugh Franklin, and I was not pleased. Then, at about the third rehearsal, we went out for a bite to eat at three o'clock in the afternoon, and he took me home at three o'clock in the morning. And I was pleased. We've been married thirty years this past January.

Q: Do you want to talk more about Hugh? Or would you—?

L'Engle: All right. Yes, marriage is certainly an educational procedure, and we did a lot of things that for our day were rather avant garde, without realizing it. When I was pregnant with our first baby, I had noticed the theater wives who were getting up at six a.m. with their babies and being exhausted when their husbands came home from the theater at night. I thought, "This is nonsense." I also wanted to nurse my baby, which at that time was not being done. And I had to fight. I mean, my doctor said, "Nobody nurses babies nowadays. It's really not very scientific." I said, "I don't care. I'm nursing my baby. I think it's natural." And she was a very robust, healthy specimen, so they told me in the hospital that they would cut the two a.m. feeding. I said, "No, my husband is an actor. We are up at two a.m. We will cut the six a.m. feeding." That was not hospital procedure. But this time I had all the cards in my hand in fighting the Institution, and I said, "It's my milk. You bring the baby in at six a.m., and I'm turning my breast to the wall." And I won.

You see, this worked very well indeed. I would put her to bed when Hugh went to the theater and have my evening writing. Then, he'd come home and I got the baby up, and we had our evening together. He had the fun of his child, and she had the fun of her father. An infant very much responds to touch, so we'd put her to bed when we went to bed, about two or three, and then get her up about noon. We'd take her to the pediatrician for her various shots, and he would call in the other mothers and say, "Now, I want you to look at this baby. Now, isn't she beautiful? Now, I'm going to tell you the schedule she's on."

Of course this is fine until school rears its ugly head, and things have to change. We also, with our last child, before natural childbirth had become a thing, decided that this was what we wanted to do. We had him in the country by a general practitioner, and one of our friends who was a nurse who had just stopped nursing to stay home with her baby simply said she was going to the hospital to special me. I had Hugh with me, and there he was to see his son's head come out. And it was just—again I learned an awful lot about love, and that it made us much more strong as a couple in that we shared all the time.

When I married Hugh I'd had one book already published and another in galleys, so I didn't have to fight to say, "I am Madeleine. I am not just an appendage." The night he asked me to marry him, again in my naiveté, I said, "You know, writing takes time, and I like to cook, but you'll have to do the dishes." Now, the division hasn't been rigid all down the line, but we have always shared. Then, when the kids came along, they had to share, too, in the household chores, in order for me to have time to work.

Q: You do say, however, in—I believe it's *Circle of Quiet* or possibly *Summer of the Great Grandmother* that you've had troubled times and if it weren't for the promises once made—
L'Engle: Oh, yes. If you choose to be a wife and a mother and a writer, you're choosing a life that has a lot of conflict in it. There's just no getting around it. It's full of conflict. And when Hugh left the theater forever, during the nine years of forever—thank God it was only nine years—not only were we having a hard time feeding ourselves, we were running a general store which was a . . . I guess today that's called downgrading. Well, we didn't consider it that, but I was working three hours a day in the store. I was trying to run a house that's over two hundred years old—and it's drafty—and I don't know how those first people survived. There were times when I thought of being like Gauguin, just simply walking out on them all. I didn't think about

it very long, not more than five minutes, but I did think about it. But I had chosen this myself. Nobody forced me to marry. Nobody forced me to have children. I wanted them. Even when I was at my most exhausted and my most frustrated, I really wouldn't have taken it back, but the thing that compounded it all was that nothing I wrote during that decade sold. I got nothing but rejection slips, rejection slips, rejection slips. And this is not easy.

Q: Is this where your family was a great emotional support? Or did you often feel very alone?
L'Engle: I felt very alone. My children were not old enough to be supportive, except that they supported Mother, you know. I think one of the most marvelous things that my oldest child ever did—she must have been, oh, maybe six or seven—one night she said, "Oh, Mother, you're so exciting." Now, there I was down and depressed, and that picked me back up. They were—well, they are absolutely marvelous kids. They're now marvelous grownups.

But there were times when I felt that there was not one single person in the world who believed in me as a writer. My husband was working; he was too tired, he was too tired to read me. I felt terribly isolated, terribly alone, and—

Q: Is this the point at which the Church began to have special meaning for you, Madeleine, or—?
L'Engle: No. God, yes. Church, no.

Q: All right.
L'Engle: I have often been closest to God when I am most angry with Him, but you cannot be angry at somebody who isn't there. I remind myself, when I'm like this, of our youngest, who, when he had done something which he knew was not up to his standard, even age two, would begin to beat *me*, and what I would do at that moment was (because I saw the same kind of rage in me and I knew what *I* needed) I'd simply grab him and hold him very, very tight. Then the dragon would vanish and the loving child would return.

Another thing about the time in the country: the little village that we live in, nobody's very poor, nobody's very rich, nobody's deprived, nobody's on welfare, but at that time, there was no kindergarten. You went right into first grade, and the first grade teacher told me that half of the kids going into first grade had never ever seen a book. Ever.

Q: Never seen a book?

L'Engle: Never seen a book. Now, this gives you an idea of what people might think of somebody who writes books. My conversation on diapers and cooking lasts just so far. There was nobody to talk to. I did talk with the Congregational ministers because they were the only people who wanted to discuss ideas, and they too were starved for conversation.

Q: I sympathize with them, having lived in a small town.

L'Engle: Yes. I was very much an agnostic and went back to church as an agnostic, saying to the young Congregational minister that yes, I would like to come to church, but he would have to accept the fact that I simply had to live *as though* I believed in God, but I could not say that I did. He immediately had me teaching high school Sunday school. I'm still an agnostic, but it's a totally different kind of thing. I was hung up on the usual American thing of wanting provable fact. Well, nothing that's worth anything can be seen in terms of provable fact. God can neither be proved nor disproved. But Mencken says the deepest, most strong and mystical religion is larded with agnosticism because you take with great faith something you do not know. You do not know in terms of provable fact. You may know in other terms.

Q: Does this explain what really seems to me to be a quantum leap from *Meet the Austins* to *A Wrinkle in Time*?

L'Engle: I suppose, yes. My Crosstalk journey.

Q: The time when you were first of all hurting because of the loneliness of being a writer without . . .

L'Engle: Yet, at that same time, I really did experience, I think very much in the sense of the very first century as a Christian community—there were about, oh, six or eight couples of us, all with small children, all with our lives centered in the church, all from different denominational backgrounds. It really was an ecumenical church before I'd ever heard of the word. And we really did care for each other. If one of the mothers was sick, the rest of us would go in and clean house, take the kids, bring in food. The father of one couple—the youngest child was an infant—got cancer of the lymph nodes, and while he was dying, these kids were already used to being in four or five other houses so that it was not the trauma that it would have been for them if they were suddenly taken out of their own house and put in other houses.

Q: This was a new experience for you, wasn't it?
L'Engle: Totally.

Q: Having been an only child and traveled a great deal?
L'Engle: I'd never been in a community before, and we did nourish each other. We *could* be known by how we loved one another although we didn't realize it. I don't think it can ever be realized. I think it has to be something so spontaneous you don't know it while it's going on. And I think it was that community which carried me through a lot of bad times. It was directing the choir. I directed the choir not because I'm qualified, but because everybody else was less qualified. The only music I knew was Anglican, so we sang the church year, although nobody else knew it. I even had them singing in Latin. I didn't know that Congregationalists don't process and recess. We processed and recessed. And it was—I learned an incredible amount. Directing the choir was an enormous teaching/educational experience for me. As I say in *Circle of Quiet*, the most important thing I learned was that I had to put every person in that choir ahead of music, no matter what the voice was like.

Q: And then you go on to say . . .
L'Engle: Ultimately, the music became better. We were known as the best choir in northwest Connecticut. Totally volunteer. And these people supported me and loved me and didn't have to understand me, which, Heaven knows, they didn't. Nor I, them.

Q: Did you then begin to read more and more of the theological writings and—
L'Engle: Oh, yes.

Q:—and the Bible and so on. You are known as quite a scholar now.
L'Engle: Well, Smith gave me—Smith gave me a very, very good education. As far as my theological reading at that point was concerned, my Congregational minister friends wanted to convert me, and I was eager to be converted because I didn't like being an agnostic. They gave me a lot of German theologians to read, and I kept reading them and thinking, "Well, if I have to believe all this bunk, I'm not—Christianity's not for me." And my true theological reading turned out to be my discovery of higher mathematics. Lower mathematics lost me years ago, but I found higher mathematics a lot easier than lower mathematics. Higher mathematics deals with ideas, where, for instance, you have an equation that does not have one answer. You have choices of answers.

Q: How did you get involved in this?

L'Engle: I read some Einstein. From there, I simply went on, and I read James Jeans and Eddington and Planck and the quantum theory and books on these people. A book called *The Limitations of Science* by A. E. W. Sullivan, which never mentions God, was for me an enormously theological book. These people talked about a universe in which I felt I could believe in God, whereas the theologians had turned me off. Totally.

Then, "forever" ended, and we took the kids out of school in May, bought a tent and five sleeping bags, and to bridge the transition between living in a little tiny rural New England village and the island of Manhattan, we took a ten-week camping trip from the Atlantic to the Pacific southerly and back again to the Atlantic northerly. I had a lot of these books with us, and after the kids were asleep, Hugh and I would sit out and talk by the embers of the campfire over which I had cooked dinner. This was before camping was big business. In any case, we were ahead of the camping season, and we were quite often the only people in a campsite. And there were all the stars with nothing to dim them. All of those stars are suns, and many of those suns had planets. Surely it's megalomaniacal of us to think of ourselves as being the only planet with sentient life, the only planet which is the focus of God's attention. So, this too was for me a religious experience.

We were driving along one day, and the words "Mrs. Whatsit," "Mrs. Who," and "Mrs. Which" simply popped into my mind. I don't know where they came from. They arrived. I turned around in the car, and I said, "Hey, kids, I've just thought of three great names: Mrs. Whatsit, Mrs. Who, and Mrs. Which. I'll have to write a book about them." Now, this book then, was working in my subconscious mind all during this trip. When we got back and I started to write it—Hugh went right off in a play—I started to write; it very much for me was a theological affirmation. I thought it was a very heretical book. It was heretical if you put it against the point of view of some of those German theologians I was reading. It turns out, of course, to be an intensely orthodox book, but I had to find it out for myself. I'm a storyteller, and therefore, my job, first and foremost, is to tell a good story. My internal searchings are underneath the story line. If I don't tell a good story, I shouldn't be writing fiction. I think it is a good story.

Q: It certainly is.

L'Engle: But it also does grapple with concepts, which were intensely important to me. Now, some of these concepts, I think, were aired in my high school Sunday school class, which was a marvelous, marvelous group.

I used no text of any kind. No books. We simply talked about what was happening in our lives and in the world and tried to set it in the context of the world where a loving Creator was concerned. If He was concerned, then what was our concern? So, in other words, I helped to convert myself.

Q: So your interest in mathematics and your growing interest in the church, even if it was at times a rebellion against—
L'Engle: It's always a rebellion against the establishment.

Q: And your trip all came together in *A Wrinkle in Time*. It wasn't a choice of using science fiction to write a work of ascetical theology?
L'Engle: Oh, no, no, no, no.

Q: And what the age level at which it's directed—
L'Engle: It's not directed to any age level. It was directed to me. I always write for me. That's not selfish; it's the only way to share. Now, the one thing that is very, very important for a writer of fiction is memory. You may not forget what it was like to be six or twelve or fourteen or twenty-seven or whatever. I was talking about this to a psychiatrist friend, just because it fascinates me, and I know I have a much better memory than a lot of people do because it's simply essential to my vocation. And he said that most of his patients are afraid to remember because they're afraid to find out who they are.

Q: It's very painful sometimes.
L'Engle: Yes, and I don't know why I have not been afraid of it. I suppose it's simply because when I remember and then I can set it down, either in my journal or in story, then I can see it objectively. One thing, of course, that turned me off the church, and always has, is this idiotic thing that God is impassible and cannot suffer. Now, thank God we're getting over that. If God doesn't suffer, he's not God. If he doesn't care—also this horrendous idea that part of the joy of the blessed in Heaven is watching the tortures of the damned in hell! That's still around. There are people who still believe that. Not necessarily that they're going to rejoice in it, but that there are people who are going to be damned forever and ever and ever.

I go along with Origen, who was declared a heretic for the belief, and Gregory of Nysa, who was made a saint, for believing that God's loving kindness towards his creation is going to outlast all of our willfulness, our rebellion, and resentment, and that ultimately, all of Creation is going to return to Him in joy, including Satan.

Q: Are you going to say some of this tomorrow in your sermon?

L'Engle: Yes, as a matter of fact, I am. So I do fight the establishment always, but I feel that I have to—I must not separate myself from it. I've learned that intuitively during our Congregational Church days. Just as I wear a wedding ring as a public witness to a private commitment, so I also have to stay with the church because the church has always been a mess. I think of my favorite theologians—Gregory of Nysa and St. Chrysostom and Basil the Great and all of them—in those early days, they fought with each other, much worse than we do. But they were incredibly human people, just as we are, and it's a great comfort to me when I get terribly angry with the church to realize that this is the way the church has always been. The church too is part of a fallen, but redeemed, world.

Q: As one of my dear friends, Roman Catholic friends, says, "The church must be right. It survives all these bad popes and others."

L'Engle: Yes. Somehow or another, the one thing that holds the church together, which is God's love, manages to be stronger than all of Satan's attempts to destroy it. Where else is he going to work hardest except within the church? Which is basically a tool for his redemption. We're very bad about Satan nowadays. We don't believe in him. I do. I mean, if I believe in the incarnation—

Q: What do you think we've substituted for him?

L'Engle: For Satan? I don't think we even see the success with which he's striding over the earth right now, rejoicing in all that he's doing. In many of the new liturgies, we seem to be congratulating ourselves for what great people we are. In the Confession, the—which is, you don't have to say the General Confession if you don't want to, which I find extraordinary, in the Green Book and the Zebra Book and also in certain services and new Dinosaur Book [Episcopalian nicknames for the Books of Trial Liturgies]—

Q: That's a phrase I haven't heard yet.

L'Engle:—it seems to me the only suitable response to the Confession in the Second Service is for the choir to burst out singing "For We Are Jolly Good Fellows." If we really look, we see an incredible mess that we're responsible for—starvation, earthquake, and man's incredible inhumanity to man. I've learned in my own life I cannot rejoice. I cannot get peace until I have really got off of my heart all the things I need to say, "Forgive me," for. And certainly, in family life, when—at dinner time, which has always been and still is the focus of our day, if somebody had done something wrong, if this had been confessed and got out, then we would have a meal full of laughter and joy. If one of us, either a child or parent, still had something bothering us, the meal was ruined for the entire family. So it's confession first and rejoicing next. Then through the confession and the rejoicing, you get given the strength to try to do something about what is wrong.

Now, something that is becoming increasingly important to me is that we far too often get hung up on large causes, and this frees us from seeing the people who make up the causes. We are also hung up on the success syndrome, that we have to feed all of the poor or we are a failure.

Now, Jesus did not feed all the poor or heal all of the sick. Just a few, really. When I see somebody getting passionately interested in, say, the cause of the leper and shoving the leper in his path aside as he gets on with the cause, I remember that Jesus couldn't have cared less about the cause of the leper or for the rights of the leper, but when He saw one in His path, He stopped. So, what I think we ought to be doing is simply seeing what is put in our path day by day to do, to help feed somebody, or something as simple as seeing the same people in the morning when I walk over here and smiling.

Q: Some people would say that's a very private and narrow view, Madeleine.
L'Engle: I know. But it seems to me it's not because as my grandmother was fond of saying, "It is little drops of water, little grains of sand that make the mighty ocean and the pleasant land."

Q: You don't think that allows us then to ignore people we don't see, such as the Africans?
L'Engle: Oh, no. I think that is what helps me to see the African. If I don't feed the stranger who comes to my door, I'm not going to send money to Africa. By seeing somebody who is hungry, seeing an incarnation of the hungry person, then I'm going to understand the hunger in Africa and South America as I wouldn't understand if I didn't see one hungry person. Hunger, therefore, can no longer be a generality for me. It's a particularity and, therefore, I'm very careful about our diet. We're trying to eat a diet suitable for a hungry planet, but if I didn't see this made particular in one person, I could just send a check and forget it.

Q: Do you think it's that confrontation by the particular and the fear of that confrontation that causes us to move into suburbs, where everyone is alike, put older people in homes, to shunt aside these problems?
L'Engle: Yes, I do. We went through the suburban question when we were moving back from the country—Hugh was going back to the theater.

Walter and Jean Kerr are very old friends of ours. As a matter of fact, Hugh introduced them to each other. They were very eager to have us move to Larchmont, and after a while, Hugh said to me, "You're not enthusiastic about this, are you?" And I said, "No," and he said, "Why?" because it seemed ideal. I said, "Well, Jean can go into the theater with Walter every night. I can't come sit in your dressing room. Walter and Jean have a live-in maid. We don't have anybody. You would have one life in the city. I would have another life in the suburbs with the kids. I wouldn't have a husband. They wouldn't have a father." And we moved to the upper West Side of New York City, where Hugh could come home matinee days for dinner, where the children did have a father. It was a real decision to take our children from our protected village and put them in the upper West Side of New York City. When they walked to school, they walked past winos and junkies. So, they saw the particularity of suffering, but also wine and dope could have no glamor for them. They saw what too much booze and too much drugs did to people. I think the upper West Side was a very realistic world to bring these kids into. All parents—when we do the right things, it's inadvertently. With the greatest love in the world, we do things that are wrong. I think the one thing we did that was right was to keep the family together, not separate.

Q: Of course, you made that decision about your mother, too, having her with you.
L'Engle: Yes, we did. And that summer of my mother's nintieth year, it was the family, it was the kids particularly, who ministered to me. That summer would not have been possible without my children and their friends, who were all determined that grandmother die at home. While it was one of the most incredibly painful summers I've ever undergone, it was also a marvelous summer. Now, it cost us undoubtedly less than a nursing home would have done, in money, but it cost us a lot more, in pain, but it was—again, we were a community, and we were doing what I think we are supposed to do, sharing death and pain as well as affluence.

Q: And what a moment for your son.
L'Engle: That moment made a man of him.

Q: Of course, it did.
L'Engle: And he is a marvelous young man. Not only my children, but my two sons-in-law were instrumental in ministering to me that summer. I was the only child, and they all realized what seeing this happen to my mother

was doing to me. The loving concern of somebody just coming upstairs with a cup of hot cocoa with a marshmallow at night would be enough to redeem a terrible day.

Now, that was a religious experience for these kids, again, who were every denomination—Polish Roman Catholic, New England Congregational, Episcopalian, atheist, agnostic, Jew—but they were unified in the one real visible symbol of religion, which is self-sacrificing love, which you are not conscious of self-sacrifice. I think the second you begin to think, "I am self-sacrificing," you're not. This was a purely intuitive, affirmative, unself-conscious love of giving of yourself for what you know is needed. Again, I learned just an incredible amount as a human being, as a writer, and as a Christian. For me the moment the church was most incredibly the church was when Canon West came up to do the requiem mass in the living room for all of these people who had helped take care of this old woman dying so badly. And when each of these kids held out their hands for the bread and wine, that was the Body made absolutely tangible for me.

Q: Canon West has been a dear friend, hasn't he?
L'Engle: Canon West has been more than a dear friend. He has been responsible for teaching me a great deal of theology. He's been my confessor for over fifteen years. I was in emotional trouble within myself, and I did not think I needed a psychiatrist. I thought I needed a priest, and I think I was absolutely right. I have a hunch that if you keep an absolutely honest journal and you have a good spiritual director, you're never going to need a psychiatrist. He has just been a marvelous family friend for the entire family. He's our younger son's godfather. He's our younger grandchild's godfather. We work together a good bit now. Together we conducted a retreat for over fifty Yale students at Holy Cross Monastery. And we've been doing some of the Cathedral Lenten programs. He will not let me know ahead of time what I'm supposed to do. He says, "Go away. Don't think. You're better off when you don't think." What he did at the Lenten program was that he has been reading some very, very deep Russian mysticism, and then I am to respond with a parenesis, and the parenesis is an example drawn from nature, a parable, a story. In other words, I am to enflesh the theology with a particular example. When we are doing a retreat together, he simply takes the ball and throws it to me, and I have to catch it and throw it back. So I have to be on my toes, and I cannot get in the way then because I have to listen so intensely.

Q: Can you remember an example to give me from the—

L'Engle: Oh, sure, because—well, in the Yale retreat, we were moving towards talking about the Jesus prayer, what we got into talking about the difference between healing and caring. And I brought up somebody who used to work here, who got a peculiarly painful form of cancer. A woman who was warm and loving, had no faith in herself at all. We knew she couldn't tolerate the kind of pain that she was going to have to suffer. She had no faith in her own prayers. She had absolute faith in the prayers of, say, half a dozen of us. I don't think that any of us prayed that she be cured, but we did pray that she be healed and that she not have more pain than she could manage.

Now, we were told that the doctors said that she never should have left the hospital. She left the hospital, came back here, and took aspirin for what she thought was her arthritis. When she went back, she was only in the hospital for about a week before she died. The pain never got beyond the reach of help. She simply slipped out easily, and the doctor simply said this was impossible. It was a miracle. She was healed.

But you find that in praying for healing everybody who prays is healed. This is something that's very important for prayer groups. They quite often make the mistake of thinking that if the person is not cured, then that person is not willing to accept it, and they miss the difference between healing and curing. You can die and still be healed. Or you can accept the physical disability and still be healed. God's answer is not always the one we want.

Another thing which is profoundly important to me is that very often a "No" from God is the essential prelude to a "Yes" far greater than what we were asking for. And, of course, the prototypical example of this is Jesus asking in the garden that he be spared. God said, "No," but the cross was essential for the "Yes" of the Resurrection. So over and over again, what seems to be an absolute "No" from God has been essential for something—a "Yes" I couldn't have dreamed of. I've been very grateful to Him, later on, for having said "No" to me about certain things although I have bellowed about it at the time. I've never been afraid to bellow at God.

One of the responses to *The Summer of the Great-Grandmother* that has been quite frequent in marvelous letters which come from it is, "I didn't know I was allowed to be angry." Also, "I didn't know I was allowed to have doubts." Of course, we have doubts. Of course, we're angry. I don't know where we get this idea of some kind of sterile perfectionism. That's not what Christianity is about.

Q: I think you say that in *Wrinkle* and in the other books, too, to children, which is important.

L'Engle: Yes. The fascinating thing about *Wrinkle* and *A Wind in the Door* is that these are books which are very, very difficult for many adults. Many adults said they find them too frightening to handle.

Q: Is that why they were rejected?

L'Engle: That's one of the reasons. Also, the total underestimation of the capacity of the child. Even when my present publisher took it, nobody expected it to be read below high school.

Q: Well, my own children have had it read aloud to them, the youngest being seven at the time. She seemed to understand it.

L'Engle: Yes. Well, my kids were seven, ten, and twelve when I was writing it, and I was reading it aloud to them while I was writing it. And the seven-year-old—

Q: Did they make suggestions?

L'Engle: I knew that when they said, "Oh, Mother, write some more," that the day's work was good. And if they didn't, I had better go over it. As they have grown older, they have become much more conscious in their criticism, and they're very good editors. My husband is a marvelous editor—a ruthless editor, but marvelous.

Q: Does Canon West read your manuscripts?

L'Engle: Oh, yes, he's also ruthless. He usually has me in tears. Well, they both have me in tears.

Q: Tell me—let's go back to him for just a moment. He does appear as Canon Tallis—

L'Engle: Oh, yes. Very definitely.

Q: Certainly, as a fictional character in some books, but you chose not to identify him as Canon West in *Summer of the Great-Grandmother*.

L'Engle: He chose not to be identified.

Q: He chose?

L'Engle: Now, only twice have I known consciously where characters have come from, and in both cases I had no idea of having this character appear. They simply walked into my books and would not stay out. One is Canon

West, and the other is Rob Austin, who is our youngest child. And that's that. When you are writing from a character that you know, it's very difficult because you're limited by your knowledge of that person. When I put Tallis in a situation, it has to be a situation in which I think Canon West might act in the same way. So in my new book—the publication date is today, by the way—

Q: Oh, is it? Congratulations.
L'Engle: Thanks! *Dragons in the Waters*, Canon Tallis is dumped by a helicopter—

Q: *Dragons in the*—?
L'Engle: *Dragons*.

Q: *Dragons?*
L'Engle: *In the Waters*. He's dumped into a Venezuelan jungle.

Q: I see. Is that the reason for the rose? (Earlier in the interview a friend had come in quietly and left a red rose on her desk).
L'Engle: He's dumped into a Venezuelan jungle from a helicopter and has to kill a wild boar, as well as solve a murder. I had a lot of fun with this book. I invented a tribe of Indians and a culture and religion and got so involved in my Indians that my young hero does not come back to this country. Now, if I had not seen individual people being starved, I could not have taken this intense interest in a larger number of people who are starving in South America.

So, it really—rather than being any kind of a private thing, it is the best way for me to understand a more public commitment.

Q: Canon West's choice was for what reason not to be identified?
L'Engle: Humility, I think. He comes off rather well.

Q: Yes. He does. For good reason.
L'Engle: An awful lot of people know who he is.

Q: Let me ask you this. To go back to *Wrinkle* and, really, others, was the choice a conscious one to make Meg and her mother strong women? This is a book that really predates the feminist movement of our own time, doesn't it?
L'Engle: Well, I was very lucky, growing up in a household where sexism never occurred to anybody. My mother had been trained to be a concert pianist. She hated playing publicly, so it was nothing for her to give it up

as a public career when she married. But she came from a family where women simply assumed they were going to be equally educated with the men. She and my father had a reciprocal relationship. Daniel Day Williams talks about love which is possession as being bad and real love as being participation. My parents had a very participatory love, so I had an example of it. Then, when we came back to New York and into the theater, again there's no sexism there. The women I understand, all my friends, my closest friends, are people who have had vocations. My eldest and closest friend is a physician. So—Meg is me, of course, with all of the faults and flaws and gawkiness and clumsiness and unattractiveness and getting into trouble with the—whatever institution. In her case, school.

But I have a theory which is that every work of art, whether it's a great work of genius or something very small, has its own identity, and it comes to somebody and it says, "Hey! Here I am. Enflesh me. Write me. Or paint me. Or compose me." Proof of this to me comes from *Wrinkle*, and that is—my husband is on a television soap opera, *All My Children*, where he plays Dr. Charles Tyler. His television wife was on the *TODAY* show with Ed Mitchell. You remember Ed Mitchell as one of the second astronauts who actually walked on the moon?

Q: Yes.
L'Engle: Did I tell you this before?

Q: No. I've heard it, but I'd like hear you repeat it.
L'Engle: Ed Mitchell works now for one of the governmental alphabetical agencies, and his job is to get scientific concepts of space over to laymen. He finds this very difficult to do, and he said, "There's this book that really does it far better than I could. It's supposed to be a children's book. It really isn't. It's called *A Wrinkle in Time*." Now, what this tells me is that my book knows more about physics than I know, and I find that intensely exciting. It's got to know more about physics than I know. I can teach myself just so much in a crash course while I'm writing a book, but the book knows more than I know.

Q: But you did actually read quite a bit of physics while—
L'Engle: Yes, but I never took a course of physics in my life. So the book knows more than I know, and so does *The Wind in the Door* know more about cellular biology than I know. This is marvelous. I just found this terribly exciting. I feel that in a day when servanthood is very unpopular that

my job is to be the servant of my books. When art is at its greatest, the artist becomes the collaborator as well as the servant, and that's a marvelous conception to me. Can we turn this off for second? [pause]

Q: Madeleine, a few years ago I succumbed to the compact edition of the OED, and I must tell you, you're running ahead of any other authors in sending me to it.
L'Engle: Oh, dear.

Q: It's lots of fun, but I'm fascinated by your vocabulary in your books, where the words come from. In some cases, they're words of your own fabrication?
L'Engle: Yes. Occasionally. Tesseract is a real word.

Q: Is it really?
L'Engle: I read about a half-page small scientific article, simply about the tesseract being something you cannot diagram properly. You can diagram the square and square squared but you can't do the square squared squared. And I got fascinated   it's usually a footnote in a large dictionary. Kything—

Q: Yes, that's another word for—
L'Engle: that word—I knew I needed a word, which there wasn't in our vocabulary, and I have an ancient Scottish dictionary of my grandfather's. I began going through that, and I found the word "kythe," which is really totally opening up yourself and giving. So that's where I got that word from. I think it's a marvelous word. I love it.

Q: Yes, it is a marvelous word.
L'Engle: Some of the other words are simply theological words that I pick up either from Canon West or from Alan Jones, who is also my other theological teacher. Then Peter, my other son-in-law, the theoretical chemist—now, theoretical chemistry has nothing to do with test tubes and retorts and Bunsen burners, it's all up there with his numbers and his Greek letters. He looks like Einstein and he thinks like Einstein and he expects me to understand his theories. I get just enough glimpses so that he keeps on. So I learn an awful lot from my sons-in-law who—both of them are my dear friends, which is just marvelous. And our son's girlfriend is a medical student, so when all of us get together around the dinner table, the conversation is just very exciting.

Q: Do you have a little journal that you pull out when they begin to use these words and cite these theories?
L'Engle: No, I just go after them and say, "Now, what was that word?"

Q: Could I ask you about some of your favorite fictional historical heroines, as a child or subsequently?
L'Engle: Emily Brontë has always been a very great favorite of mine. Her sisters. There was a series of books about a little girl called *Emily of New Moon* by L. M. Montgomery, who also wrote *Anne of Green Gables*, but it was Emily that I identified with because Emily was growing into being a writer.

There are so many people, I just don't even know where to begin. I will have to think more on that one. Shakespeare. Dostoyevsky.

Q: You mentioned Dorothy Sayers earlier. Would you like to say something about how you feel about her work, her life?
L'Engle: Well, I love her work. I wish she didn't underestimate her Peter Wimsey books as much as she does. We work from a totally different attitude, in that she was writing her Peter Wimsey books to get enough money so that she could forget them and write about theology. I don't see any difference between the two. I think her theology in the Wimsey books is super. I guess I feel that I want to communicate what I feel, and I can communicate best through fiction. I wrote my two nonfiction books really pretty inadvertently. They certainly were not part of my plan as a writer. Nor is the one I'm on now because I think that in fiction we again move out and beyond that world of provable fact, where you get closer to reality. Also in fiction you get the conscious mind and the unconscious mind in collaboration.

Theophon the Recluse talks about praying with the mind in the heart, and it's true of prayer. It's also true of writing. In writing, I use my intellect as far as it will take me. It never takes me far enough. I have to get out beyond the other side of it. And then, when I sort of go into overdrive or whatever you want to call it, then I can—then my subconscious mind is working together with my conscious mind. I'm convinced that the subconscious mind knows a great deal more than the conscious mind, and we're afraid of it. We call that—well, the right hemisphere of the brain controls the left side of the body, the intuitive part of a person, and the left hemisphere of the brain controls the right side of the body, the intellectual part. We see things upside down, and our brain turns them right side up for us. Sometimes the work of the artist is to see things upside down. Then we call left sinister and right dexterous. The French call left *gauche* and right *droite*, right on. We're afraid of this part of us that we don't know. I guess it's like my friend Barry saying that his patients are afraid of the memories, afraid of themselves. What I repressed, I guess then, can hurt me; and through writing, things which might otherwise stay underwater get released.

Also, I have a hunch that in our subconscious mind we are not bound and limited by individuality, that we do know more when we are in touch with ourselves. We can tap more strands than we can when we are simply alone with our intellect. I realize now from hindsight that the reason the villain in *A Wrinkle in Time* is the naked brain—I didn't know this when I was writing it—but it's that the brain when it is not informed by the heart is vicious. It's evil. I know that only from hindsight. Again, my book knew more than I knew. My books are way ahead of me in thinking, always. I sort of stumble along after them and catch up, if I can. Sometimes, years later.

Q: You've been somewhat critical of psychoanalysis in your books.
L'Engle: It's not fair of me because I don't know anything about it. I think I'm critical of the abuse of it. I do think that it is still very much of an infant science, almost as surgery was when the barbers did it and you went to a barber if you had gangrene in your leg but not if you had a splinter. I've known too many people rushing to psychiatrists and therapists, and I've seen them becoming more and more self-centered and not being helped. Now, getting to know one or two psychiatrists as personal friends has helped me, but I've also known some real weirdos.

I don't mean to be critical. If I ever got writer's block, I go running for help fast.

Q: Finally, would you say something about the work you're working on now? Are you willing to do that or is that—?
L'Engle: I'm working on two books now, but the one I'm emphasizing at the moment—Reid Isaac from Seabury came to me and asked me if I would like to write a book for Seabury. I said, "No." Just "No." Then an idea for a book came to me of writing about my own personal liturgical year, which would include the twenty-sixth of January. This is my wedding anniversary. I wrote a few pages, and he was very excited about it and wanted it for this year's Lenten book. I said, "You can't judge a book on eight pages, and, besides, I couldn't possibly get it done. But I'll write some more." I wrote about ninety pages, and he was really very enthusiastic. I said, "But you know I am under contract to Farrar, Straus and Giroux, but I don't think they're going to want this kind of book." Then I showed it to Bob Giroux, and he wants it.

So what's probably going to happen is that Seabury will pick it up as a book club for the next year's Lenten thing. That is, if when I'm done with it, everybody still likes it. I suppose it would just follow along after the *Summer of the Great-Grandmother*, but the structure is the cycle of the year.

Q: And its meditations on these events, both in the year, are personal for you and also the calendar?
L'Engle: Yes, the calendar but I illustrated always with personal illustrations, again, with my theory that until I'm particular I cannot go any further.

This is the only way I can understand the incarnation. So that it makes any sense to me is that just as in writing, the hero is particular, not a faceless generality. I have to understand God in a particular way through a particular person, so I come to my understanding of incarnation through literature, as usual. And the other book is a novel.

Q: Do you want to talk about it?
L'Engle: Yes, I'll talk about it very briefly—a novel set in an English cathedral town. It's a cathedral novel, and I think I'm going to do it under—

Q: Lincoln by any chance?
L'Engle: That's the only cathedral town I know well enough, yes. Only it's called Westerham. I'm really very seriously contemplating doing it under a pseudonym, not because it's a cathedral book but because I've had letters from about six states saying, "Oh, I finally found *Summer of the Great-Grandmother* in the children's section." That's what's really done it. I'm so slotted as a children's writer that it never occurred to anybody that I would write for an adult, whereas about half of my books are for adults.

Q: Yes, I know.
L'Engle: The last two adult novels have not been taken seriously. They have been post-Newbery Medal.

Q: I was going to say, "Is it because of the success of *Wrinkle*?"
L'Engle: Yes, and whereas I wouldn't not have won the Newbery for anything, there still is this prevalent attitude that if you write for children, you do it because you're not good enough to write for adults. Now, most of the librarians and teachers I know, it makes their blood pressure rise, too, but it still is a general feeling.

Q: I gather, on occasion, the reverse is true? I seem to recall that E. B. White had a hard time getting *Charlotte's Web* accepted because there was—
L'Engle: Yes, he writes for adults. So, I don't know. I've mentioned this both to my agent and Bob Giroux, and neither of them have turned the idea off. They just said, "Well, yes, maybe, let's think about it." Meanwhile, I'll write the book, and then we'll see.

Q: Thank you, Madeleine.
L'Engle: Thank you, Linda.

Interview 2: Crosswicks in West Goshen, Connecticut, June 15, 1976

Q: The interview of Madeleine L'Engle takes place in Madeleine's studio at her home, called Crosswicks, in Goshen, Connecticut. Crosswicks, a charming two-hundred-year-old farmhouse was once their year-round residence. Now, it's a vacation home, and it's the setting for *Summer of the Great Grandmother* and *A Circle of Quiet*.

Madeleine, again I must ask your permission to use this in the Oral History Collection at Columbia University.
L'Engle: Permission granted under the same conditions as last time.

Q: Fine. Thank you. At the end of the last interview, we were—I asked you about you childhood hero and heroines. We talked about Emily Brontë, but at the time I thought you had more to say. We somehow got sidetracked. Would you like to pick up on that?
L'Engle: Well, I realized that I identified just as easily with men as with women, and that more or less led us on to thinking about sexual pigeon-holing, which I think has been so disastrous, and in a way, women's lib has been pandering to sexual pigeonholing in its more extreme forms" those who don't want any differentiation between sexes or those who really simply want to be men rather than women. We continue to lose our human full-ness, where we enjoy both our masculine and feminine attributes, which does not determine our physiological sexual identity at all. If we limit our-selves only to masculine attributes or only to feminine attributes, we're horribly limited. One result of this pigeonholing has been the chasm that's come between intuition and intellect, and the assumption, thereby—mostly

by men who've been taught through so many generations to repress their intuition—that our intellect is in control of our intuition. I say our intellect is not in control of our intuition. Our conscious minds are not in control of our subconscious minds. I actually heard a man say that his conscious mind was in control of his subconscious mind. Whereas two thousand years ago, Paul of Tarsus said, "The things that I want to do are the things that I don't do. The things that I don't want to do are the things that I do do."

This becomes worse when we try to limit ourselves or dictate ourselves, our conscious mind, which we think is in control. It's not in control, so we become more fragmented and more broken because intellect and intuition are at war instead of at love.

Q: In *A Wrinkle in Time*, you present the naked brain as a symbol of evil, and you talk about the brain uninformed by the heart as being evil. Can the reverse be true, that the mindless passion—

L'Engle: Yes. When everything is repressed down under the water, it does become all nasty, dark, and dirty, as Freud saw everything down there as being nasty, dark, and dirty. It becomes nasty, dark, and dirty by the act of repression, by our fear of calling it up and calling it by our own name. Now, I was talking to a psychiatrist friend of mind (he was, in this chronological order, physician, priest, psychiatrist; he's a very interesting guy) about the necessity for a writer of fiction of memory—that I may not forget what I was like at any age in my life. Otherwise, I can't write out of myself, which is all I have to write out of. He said that most of his patients are afraid to remember what they were like as children or as adolescents because they are afraid to face themselves, to know who they are, and I suppose my profession itself had spared me this very understandable fear. I do understand it, but because I have to draw out of my child self and my adolescent self in my books, I have been—it's been necessary for me to remember exactly what I was like, and I was like all the bad parts of my heroines. I was clumsy. I didn't get on with people. I was all these things that I should be afraid to admit, but because they've been absolutely essential for my books, I haven't been allowed to be afraid that they exist. There they are, and they are part of me and they are named me, Madeleine. The more I'm willing to bring myself up out of intuition so that—oh, the iceberg analogy, of course, is so ancient, we forget it really is true—our conscious mind is just the tip, and our subconscious mind is below the surface. There, I get above the surface; then there, complete, less fragmented, I become.

Q: Do you think that the old custom of keeping diaries and journals served the psychiatric function, if you will, that—?

L'Engle: I very definitely do. Yes. I come from a journal-keeping and letter-writing and memoir-writing family. My ancestors—I'm most grateful to them—wrote their memoirs for their descendants.

Q: Do you have those?

L'Engle: I have them, yes, and I've drawn on them in my books about the South. But I've been keeping a diary—or journal, not a diary, just a book in which I dump what I feel—since I was about ten.

Q: Daily?

L'Engle: No. Sometimes I write daily. Sometimes I'll go months without writing, but it's there when I need it. Since I have been grown and since I have been writing regularly professionally, I don't think I ever go more than a week without writing something in it, but I do think that these—

Q: Tell me, is it something that you intend to keep extremely private?

L'Engle: Oh, totally. These are definitely not for publication.

Q: There are the writers of journals for publication.

L'Engle: Yes, but these are not literary journals. These are, I suppose, where I get rid of the destructive things in my below-the-surface mind. I get them poured out. I can see them, and then they're no longer destructive. I suppose because I have been given the gift of memory and have kept all of the journals, that this is probably one of the reasons why I have not needed a psychiatrist because certainly my life has been as complicated as anybody else's.

Q: Is this the process of naming that you write about in *Wind in the Door*?

L'Engle: I think so. I think, as usual, I was ahead of myself in *Wind in the Door*, and now, I'm coming to understand what it was that the story was about, that I understand things in story first, and then I have to articulate them in my own philosophy.

Q: Tell me more about the journals that your ancestors have—

L'Engle: Well, my mother's great-grandmother, therefore my great-great-grandmother, lived to be a very old woman, known by her grandchildren and great-grandchildren as "Great." Her family came to north Florida from Switzerland, originally from Sicily. They were fleeing religious persecution and growing up in north Florida was an extraordinarily different place from the other pioneering. It was pioneering, most definitely, but there was a cosmopolitan atmosphere to it. In St. Augustine, which was the main port, as you wandered around the docks, you heard every language. You met people from every nation, so, although the life was extraordinarily hard—you had to hack your way through this lush jungle full of insects and snakes and strange creatures—there was an aura of cosmopolitanism to it that my Kansas great-grandparents, for instance, didn't have at all.

Then, Greatie, she never went to school a day in her life, but her parents had a passion for education, and she was taught to speak French, Spanish, Italian, and German. She read—

Q: What time would this have been?

L'Engle: It was early Andrew Jackson. She was a young woman in early Andrew Jackson time because the first time her house was burned out from under her was when Jackson's forces unfairly attacked the local Indians, and the Indians were so furious that they turned even on their white friends. Her father refused to believe at first that his friends would attack him. Finally, one of the servants insisted this was going to happen, and they got the family into a boat and just got off as the Indians arrived, ready to scalp them, out of outrage at what had been done to them by Jackson's men. And it was outrageous, what had been done to them. Her house was burned out from under her seven times because she kept getting caught in other people's battles. The Floridas, as they were called, were being fought for by the Spanish, by the English, and by a group of sort of Mafia-like type people from Georgia, who called themselves the filibusters. One of them was out to become the King of the Floridas, so it was an extraordinarily interesting time. Some day—

Q: And she kept these journals?

L'Engle: She wrote a long memoir, about a two-hundred-and-fifty-page memoir, for her great-grandchildren and descendants. And then, we have letters. They were a marvelously letter-writing, articulately letter-writing, group of people, who, in a day when travel was far more difficult than it is for us, did an enormous amount of traveling back and forth. You would go to spend a month or two with your cousins in Charleston. Then you would go to spend a month or two with your cousins in St. Augustine. Then you would go to spend a month or two with your cousins in Virginia.

Q: Was this the source of *The Other Side of the Sun*?
L'Engle: The story in *The Other Side of the Sun* is totally imaginary.

Q: It is?
L'Engle: Yes.

Q: Even the lynching incident and the uprising?
L'Engle: The uprising was a real uprising, which I came cross in history books. Also, in doing research for this, it was my—I forget how many greats, four or five—grandfather, who was Jefferson's first appointee to the Supreme Court and who was so outraged at the edicts forbidding all slaves to be taught to read and write that he took this to the Supreme Court as unconstitutional. He was several times—he was almost lynched because he was constantly fighting for the right for education for every human being. Now, many people did not think of blacks as being human. They did not have souls, which is one reason soul is so important to blacks now, because you treated your slaves as you treated your horses. If they were good, you treated them well, but you had no moral problem because they weren't human beings.

My family were mavericks. They were like the people in Illyria. They did free their slaves. They did give education to everybody in the household. They did live in what we would now almost call a commune, or a community, which was very—it was God-centered. There were morning and evening prayer, and people were truly concerned for each other. Not everybody. There were stinkers in my family as well as the good ones, but there were the unusual people who had a vision of the inalienable right to freedom for all human beings and who did understand that slaves were human beings and that slavery was bad.

Q: Is this written about in the journals?
L'Engle: Yes, and in the letters.

Q: I loved *The Other Side of the Sun*. It seems to me that you handled a very difficult problem so skillfully. One, in this juxtaposition of two generations, but now, I understand better how you came to that from your own—
L'Engle: I had been around multigeneration groups all my life. I seldom lived only with two generations. There's usually been at least three generations, and here at Crosswicks, we had four summers where we were four generations under one roof. I think this is extraordinarily nourishing, that to limit ourselves chronologically to our own peer group is, again, adding to the fragmentation of modern man. Now, let me make it clear I am using man

generically. Right? It takes both male and female to make the image of God. It takes both male and female to make man, and I am not abdicating my share. I am half of humankind. So are you. When I talk about man, I mean us, too.

Q: Right.
L'Engle: Right—us broken human beings, who are struggling for wholeness.

Q: I was interested in a comment in, let's see, I believe it was *Summer*, about your experience of pregnancy, in being unable, you felt, to create. Let me see—
L'Engle: Oh, yes.

Q: You quote a friend, saying—
L'Engle: A friend of mine who was a dancer and had several children came to me while I was pregnant with my first child and said, "Don't bother to write. You cannot create two things simultaneously." I thought this was absurd because I knew she could not do a tour jeté while she was six months pregnant, but that did not keep me from the typewriter. Now, all I knew is that what I wrote when I was pregnant never came to term. Maybe it was simply happenstance that this—

Q: Have you watched this in other women? Do you think that's—
L'Engle: I have never made a systematic study of it. I think it would be interesting. Certainly, we have enormous changes in our whole body systems while we're pregnant. I have a hunch one could paint. I'm sure one could write poetry while pregnant. It would be fun to do a study of what women have produced during their months of pregnancy. I know the stuff I wrote while I was pregnant, which I threw out, was necessary for what I was going to write afterwards. It was—you can simply go on doing your finger exercises, which you have to do. There's no question about that.

Q: What, then, do you think is the role of career, especially a creative career, in motherhood? You've talked about the conflicts.
L'Engle: I think there is a lot of conflict. I chose motherhood. It wasn't forced on me. I wanted to have my babies. I enjoyed the whole process. I think it's a fabulous thing to create a life. I'm terribly glad that more and more husbands are being with their wives while their children are born. I think this is awfully important. It didn't happen with us until our last child—I know the extraordinary difference it made to both of us—but unless you have an enormous

amount of money, which very few people do, if you want to be a mother, you do lose time, which otherwise would be spent in writing. And I know that when my kids were little, it was impossible for me to realize that I was ever again going to have the kind of time that I had before I had children.

Q: Yes, that's true.

L'Engle: I did not produce as much when the kids were little, partly because of time and partly because I was so tired. Trying to run a big house, help Hugh in the store, and take care of the kids. Many of the things which were most frustrating to me were things which have now been redeemed because I have drawn on them so, in my writing, in my fiction.

Q: Would you be willing to speak for other people and talk about the mother who leaves the home to work in a career? Do you feel that a choice has to be made, especially in the early years?

L'Engle: I think quite often a choice has to be made. Now, my choice was made both more simple and more difficult by the fact that you can write at home, that I did not have to go out to be somewhere at nine. My oldest and closest and dearest friend is a physician, and she had three sons. For various unfortunate and just irrevocable reasons, her marriage broke up, at which point she shifted her career from that of practicing physician to public health so that she would have a nine-to-five job and so she couldn't be called in the evening and things like that. This involved having some-body with the kids during the daytime when they were babies and, also, for when they got back from school when they were older, but when she came home, she was a totally marvelous, warm, loving mother. Her three sons are absolutely marvelous. I think that if you do have a nine-to-five job that you can still make it warm and loving for the kids, but again this does involve spending more time with them in the evening, getting up a little earlier, and being with them for a better breakfast. More and more, as money becomes tighter, more and more women are having to work in to order to support their families, but I don't think this need be destructive for the children as long as the mother is willing to be a mother, too, to double in brass, as the theater calls it.

Q: Do you feel that the women's liberation movement has denied that need, though?

L'Engle: Oh, I think the more extreme branches do. The extreme branches want us all to be androids. No sexuality at all. Well, I enjoy my sexuality, and bearing children is part of the fulfilling of that sexuality. It's exciting. I don't find it degrading at all. Now—I think it was made degrading. I think having babies in hospitals, where women are left alone in labor for long periods of time with nobody there, which is what happened to me with my first child—that is degrading, and that was done to us by science turning into technocracy, rather than technology. So this return to—the Lamaze, having the babies, the whole bit, is good. I had to fight to nurse my children and to have them on demand feeding, rather than "every three hours you give your baby so-and-so," and it was made into a chemist lab kind of thing, instead of something that is joyful and relaxed.

I have a picture on my desk at the Cathedral Library of Josephine and Alan in bed, more or less Alan seminaked, with their five-day-old baby—it was hot—just plopped on his chest, and a friend of mine who was engaged to a woman who already had about, I'd say, a twelve-year-old son, said that she had responded very positively to this picture. She had said, "Perhaps I should have touched my child more," and this absolutely struck terror into my soul because the tactility of parenthood is one of its great joys. When we would wake up in the morning, the first thing I would do was reach into the crib and pull out the baby and throw her into bed with us. And nursing—if you nurse a child, this tactility is there. When the whole thing is bottle and formula and on the hour, again, it adds to our repression of sexuality, our pushing it aside or below the surface or pigeonholing it, instead of the relaxedness of a man and a woman and this creature between them they have given birth to.

Q: Do you think that women, that mothers have abdicated their teaching function in favor of professionals?
L'Engle: Yes. The reason I say this so immediately is I can't tell you how many high school–age kids have come to me to ask about the facts of life. One junior in high school came and said, "How do you know if you're a virgin?" My word, somebody should have told her by then. I think, for some obscure reason, that parents of high school, junior high school kids are embarrassed to tell their children about sex. I simply fail to understand this. I was very fortunate. My mother, very early, told me how babies are born, what the whole thing is about, so I've always taken it as something perfectly natural. And I don't think the kids are rebelling against the attitude of their parents.

Q: When I asked that question, I meant not only about sex education, but about every sort of education. I wondered if one of the reasons women are less satisfied as mothers, in the role of mothers, is because they have given up this important job of teaching, whether it's music lessons or reading aloud to the child at night or sex education or whatever, that now this is all fanned out to other people, so we're rather left in the job of chauffeur.

L'Engle: Right. Well, I do think this is true. I'm glad you read aloud to your kids at night. I'm loving reading to my grandchildren. This is something I think should be shared more by the husband than it is. If you live in a commuter town where the husband doesn't come back until the kids are asleep or gets up before they're awake, it becomes very, very difficult. But Hugh has been marvelous in sharing all of this with me. We've made very conscious decisions. When we were moving back to the city, after a near-decade of living in this little village, we were moving back into Manhattan, with the children seven, ten, and twelve, there was a lot of discussion whether we would move to a suburb for the sake of the children. Jean and Walter Kerr, who are very old friends, live in Larchmont, and they were putting a lot of pressure on us to move to Larchmont. Suddenly, Hugh said to me one evening, "You're not enthusiastic about Larchmont, are you?" And I said, "No, I'm not. Jean can go into the theater with Walter every night. I cannot go and sit in your dressing room. Jean has a live-in maid. We don't have anybody. You would have online in the theater, in the city. The kids and I would have another life in the suburbs. I wouldn't have a husband. They wouldn't have a father. I don't care how rough it is on them living in Manhattan. I think it's better for them to be where I'm happier, and where we have a marriage." And that is what we did. We brought them into the Upper West Side of New York City, which is about as different from this little village as you could possibly get, and we never regretted it.

Q: Tell me something: The little village school in both *Wrinkle* and *Wind in the Door* are not—the village is not kind to Charles Wallace or to Meg. Was this your experience here with your children?

L'Engle: Only to some extent. I've exaggerated. It is also the same village that's in *Meet the Austins*, which is kind. You take a child who is unusual, in *any* school, they're going to have a hard time, but in a city school, there are apt to be more of these little mavericks than there are in a small village. I'm also drawing out of my own childhood where I, being a different child, was handled unkindly by both my peers and my teachers.

Q: Do you think, on the whole, the teaching profession has become more sensitive in these areas?

L'Engle: Yes, I do. I do, but as public education and private education is going down in caliber—and alas, it is, and I don't know all the reasons why; there are thousands of reasons why—teachers get more pressed. They get more tired as they have more children to teach; it becomes impossible for them to deal sensitively with a classroom of forty kids.

Q: Would you like to talk about any of the painful experiences of your child-hood, where you were treated insensitively? You talked about not being good in athletics in our last interview.

L'Engle: Well, I have come to realize that almost all of the experiences which seemed at the time to be totally negative were actually essential for positive results later. I wrote about this experience in *Camilla*, and writing about it helped me, but when I was in fourth grade—the school I'd been to ran only through third grade, so I was in a new school. I was in French class, and I had to go to the bathroom. I raised my hand and asked to be excused, and the French teacher said, "No." I did this three times, and each time, she said, No." When the bell at the end of the class rang, I ran like mad for the john, and I didn't make it. And fourth grade is a very embarrassing time to have wet pants. My mother came to pick me up, and I told her what happened. She went to the headmistress, and the headmistress called in the French teacher. The French teacher said, "Well, Madeleine never asked to be excused. Of course, I would have let her go if she had asked." She was believed, and I was told not to lie about it the next time. It wasn't that bad to wet your pants.

Well, that was my first experience that grownups can lie, and the lie can be believed and the truth not be believed.

Q: And from a teacher?

L'Engle: Yes, and that the headmistress who's supposed to know things believes the lie instead of the truth. It was a very valuable lesson for me. It was my first experience of fallen human nature because my own parents were extraordinarily honorable people who would never, ever tell a lie. It was good for me to learn that they were rather unique, that grownups can lie and be beastly.

Also, at that school, athletics were very important. Any team I was on automatically lost. When you could call out, choose teams, the unlucky team that got me would let out great groans, and my home room teacher accepted the assessment of the other kids in my class and decided I was dumb. Nothing I did for her in the way of homework pleased her, so naturally, I stopped doing it. What's the point of doing homework if it's going to be held up for ridicule, if nothing you do is going to be accepted?

The good thing that came out of this bad thing was that I would go home from school, dump down my schoolbag and think bitterly to myself, "I am the unpopular girl," and then I would move into a deep, interior world. Because there was no nearby library, I couldn't go out and get books. When I finished the few books I had, I wrote books. That was the only way I could get books to read, to write them, and of course, many of them were simply wish fulfillment stories in which my heroine did all of the things that I would like to have done. But I established a pattern of writing and a discipline of work. I wrote vast reams of poetry. Then, my sixth-grade year, there was a poetry contest, and it was judged by the high school English head of the department, and I won it. So naturally, my home room teacher accused me of copying it and said I couldn't have written the poem because Madeleine was not very bright.

So, Mother then brought out all of this poetry and stuff that I had been writing when I should have been doing homework, and they had to concede that Madeleine probably had written that poem after all. But that again was another experience in fallen humankind.

Q: Is that kind of experience essential to the creative process?
L'Engle: I don't know.

Q: Do we put too much emphasis on the well-rounded child, with all the adjustment and—
L'Engle: I have a hunch that the totally adjusted child would be perfectly happy running races, climbing trees, and skipping rope, that it takes a certain amount of pain of one kind or another for the psyche to intuitively heal the pain by getting it out in poetry or in painting—I did a lot of painting, too—that this is an act of healing, and there has to be something to be healed before you need to paint or to write.

Q: Do you think this is related to the inability of pregnant women and mothers of young children to finish their creative effort? That is, that there's such satisfaction in that, that there isn't the urge then to create another way?
L'Engle: It's perfectly possible. I know my fascination with my first pregnancy, with my burgeoning tummy, seeing my belly button for the first time in ages as the baby pushed it out—I was just fascinated. Also, I had the joy of—my friend Pat, as I mentioned, was in medical school at this point, and

she was studying obstetrics and gynecology at the time I was pregnant. She was always coming with her stethoscope, listening to the baby's heart and explaining to me what was going on. There was simply pure physical joy. When we would go to bed at night, and I would curl up against Hugh, immediately the baby would start kicking him. So, already, before this child was born, we had a trinitarian relationship, and I took great pleasure in this. It was very satisfying.

Q: Do you think that not being the natural mother of Maria has had an effect on your relationship with her? Of course, it's had some effect.
L'Engle: Yes.

Q: What did you try to do to make up for that?
L'Engle: How it first worked out so that she became my cub, so that I responded to her in the same instinctive way as I did to my biological cubs—I don't know really how it happened. I just know that when she was dealt with unfairly in her Brownie troop, my responsive rage towards that Brownie leader was exactly as it would have been had it been a biological child, and I then knew that the process of her being my own child was complete. On the day of the adoption, the judge gave a little homily, actually, in which he said that she was now our child as much as though we had given birth to her. When she first came to stay with us, before the adoption, always the last thing at night, I would go around, check the children, see that their clothes were out for morning, tuck them in, and kiss them. And when I kissed her the first night she did not smell like my babies. We underestimate a sense of smell. It wasn't that it was an unpleasant smell in any way, but she didn't smell like my babies. I had to get that smell into my own bloodstream, as it were, so that the smell too then became part of me. Why I'm convinced that my first grandchild, who would not go to very many people when she was an infant, immediately came to me, I'm sure it was because I smelled familiar. I had the smell that was the right smell, the mother-grandmother kind of smell.

So that was a rather staggering thing to me, suddenly to realize that here was a child who was going to be entrusted to me as my child, who didn't smell like my children. I had to be literally like a lioness. I had to get this smell reorganized in my own heart, and it happened so that my feeling for her and I think her feeling for me is totally physiological, as well as intellectual, mother-daughter. It took time, and it took effort. It took tears.

Q: You've written about the effect of your sons-in-law on your work. Have your daughters pursued careers?

L'Engle: Yes. My younger daughter is an artist. She specializes in photography. She and Peter are living in England, and she has had several one-man shows now and is teaching art history to the sixth form, which is equivalent to our first year in college. My elder daughter married when she was not quite nineteen and is now back in college, and then she will get herself organized in the direction she wants to go. She has a marvelous intuitive sense with people, and in a way, she has a team ministry with Alan in that he will very often send people to her for counseling. She does a great deal of simply, quietly listening. I don't think she realizes what a marvelous counselor she is, but she is. She has a great sense of smell for knowing when to speak, when to be silent, and what to say. She's a healer.

Q: Does she have any interest in the priesthood?

L'Engle: No. I think her interest is more scientific. She's a brilliant mathematician, and when she was in college she was studying psychology and sociology, with a particular interest in autistic children, so she may go in that direction.

Q: Have we pursued the issue of sexuality as much as we—

L'Engle: I think could probably get into it a bit more. I'm still very much fumbling in the book which I'm doing final, final revisions on now, which is my first overtly theological book. I finally set down how disastrous I think it is that men have been taught to repress their intuitive side and that we women are very fortunate in that we have been allowed, partly by indifference, to keep our intuitive side alive. Many men who have gone into the fields of art have found trouble with their sexuality, in a sense almost being pushed into being homosexual, because it is assumed that somebody who is tender must be effeminate, whereas I think it takes incredible strength before you are capable of true tenderness. So I think that it's important that men recognize within themselves their feminine characteristics, as part of their whole maleness, and that we women recognize in ourselves our masculine characteristics as part of our whole womanhood. I remember sitting out on a green field in Delphi, talking with a brilliant Greek woman who was saying that it was very easy for her, sitting there in that light, to think of Apollo riding his sun chariot across these and that Apollo is the god of light and of reason and of intellect, and is worth nothing without the earth goddesses of intuition and poetry and music and painting, and that always the oracle is female. She speaks through the male, but the male cannot speak before the female within has spoken. All of this, to me, is mythically talking about wholeness, which has been broken and which must be brought together again. I'm convinced that in bringing together our male and our female selves we do not become androids, but we become more fully human and more fully woman or more fully man. Then a relationship between a man and a woman becomes a much more open and creative one.

Q: So you say this increasing acceptance of the other side of sexuality is changing the marriage relationship?

L'Engle: I'm not sure we're accepting it as increasingly as I would like. A young friend of mine here in the country who had her baby with natural childbirth with her husband right there was in one of those classes when they were talking about breastfeeding. She was practically the only one who was going to breastfeed her child, and one woman said, "Well, my husband doesn't want me to go about with my boobs exposed." I thought, "My God, sexual stereotypes still among this generation." But there are at least a few people who are aware of this and who are seriously trying to break out of it, and seriously, with laughter. If we don't laugh, then we're closed. We're closed. We need laughter for openness and fullness.

Q: We have talked, not in the interview, but just when we were talking, about marriage, and you suggested once that you—at least, this is how I understood it, I have to be careful, that you felt that one should be either single and chaste or married. Are those the two choices that you see?

L'Engle: Oh, I don't think I said that.

Q: All right. Correct me. Say—

L'Engle: I think one should be chaste, either single or married. Chaste does not mean celibate.

Q: All right.

L'Engle: Okay? It's very important that we recognize this. My physical relationship with my husband is intensely important to me and enjoyable, but it is chaste, in that neither one of us is using or possessing the other sexually. We are trying to give the other one pleasure and joy and fulfillment. Many, many relationships, either hetero- or homosexual are possessive and not participatory. Daniel Day Williams, in his marvelous book, *The Spirit and*

Forms of Love, was the one who pointed this out for me: that love must be participatory and not possessive, and far too much love is possessive.

Q: Is it possible to have that participatory love outside of the bonds of marriage?

L'Engle: Well, Linda, I was twenty-seven when I was married, and he was twenty-nine. I'd been living in the theater, living in Greenwich Village. I was not a virgin. Neither was Hugh. We were both very serious about our marriage, and I had found that I could not give myself fully to anybody I didn't have a certain responsibility towards. Sometimes, it was simply the fact that the man was using me. That made me realize, "Uh-huh, this is not going to lead to marriage." Cut. I didn't play around, but I guess I don't think it's bad to know a person fully before you're married. I think once you are married that faithfulness is obligatory, although no two human beings are ever faithful to each other all of the time, and physical unfaithfulness is not necessarily the worst kind. I would find it, for instance, terribly difficult to be married to a businessman who had me in a beautiful, expensive suburban house and who left early in the morning to go to work, stopped in the bar car on his way back, had a couple more Martinis, went to bed, maybe laid me, and then went off to the office to his true love in the morning. I would find that kind of unfaithfulness intolerable because it would be a regular unfaithfulness. We're unfaithful in that we simply don't recognize when there's a need, for example, if I'm preoccupied and I don't recognize Hugh's need, or he's preoccupied and doesn't realize mine. It's out of our response to the little tiny things we do daily to let each other down. It's our awareness of these and our trying to redeem them that a chaste, in its most fully physical sense, marriage is slowly built up. Now, for an actor and a writer to have been married for thirty years—

Q: Is an accomplishment.

L'Engle: Yes. It is an accomplishment, and it hasn't been done easily. There have been lots of times when there's been lots of pain on both sides. I think many marriages break up at the first moment of pain, without realizing that this is a natural procedure, that marriage has to be born constantly and that there is no coming to life without pain, that each new stage in your knowledge of each other, as it is created, has birth pangs. Then you move on to the next level in your relationship, and Hugh and I have very slowly, and in many cases, painfully, naturally, have worked out to a marvelously responsive place where we do talk about everything and share and, very often, share simply in the warmth of silence together. We're able to be quiet together and yet be in complete communion. We'll sometimes, after we've both had a hard day—I'll cook dinner, and we'll sit at the table by candlelight and eat in silence and in absolute comfort and communion.

I used to bore my kids when they were little. I used to say, "Nothing that's worth anything is easy." But it's true. Nothing easy is worth anything, and a good marriage is a marvelous thing to work towards, because when your children leave the nest you want to be sure that you two really know each other. I don't believe in the child-centered household. When there are decisions to be made, if it was a choice between the children and Hugh, I chose Hugh, and I told the children that. For instance, when we moved back to the city, I was trying to get up with the kids in the morning and get them off to school. Hugh was in a play. He would come home at eleven, eleven-thirty at night. I would try to be up with him, have a drink with him, fix him a sandwich and a supper, or whatever, and I was physically incapable of burning the candle at both ends. I plain got sick. So we called everybody together. I said, "Now, Daddy needs me more at night than you need me in the morning, and you're going to have to get up and get yourselves off to school." They were seven, ten, and twelve, and we don't like each other too much in the morning anyhow. We're not a happy breakfast-eating family. "When you come home from school, I'm all yours, but I've got to be able to sleep late so that I can be up with Daddy at night," and that's how we worked it.

Q: And you were able to do that? *You* were able to do that?
L'Engle: I didn't find it easy, but I was able to do it. Now, it was not—on my own, I probably couldn't have. Do you remember in *The Summer of the Great-Grandmother* the character, Mrs. O? The Englishwoman? Well, it was she who said, "This is absolute nonsense. Josephine is twelve years old. My children could take care of themselves when they were that age because they had to, because I was off at work. You're going to get really sick if you do this. The boss needs you at night. Those kids can do it themselves in the morning." She made me realize that if I kept insisting on martyring myself I was going in for this whole false guilt syndrome. And it worked. It was fine.

Dinner, though, was and always has been the focal point of the day. I didn't care when we ate. We'd arrange—if people had things to do, we would eat at any hour, but we would all eat together. We've always eaten together, and by candlelight, so that then the family, the extraordinary unity and diversity, was gathered together. We've been doing that this week here with two little girls, six and seven; a high school senior; a college sophomore, our son who will be—oh, yes, he got a full teaching scholarship at Syracuse, he'll be both teaching and taking—

Q: What is this in?
L'Engle: English. He wants to write, and he is an excellent teacher so he will be teaching and writing next year. Also, his girlfriend, Laurie, who is in medical school at Syracuse and Hugh and me. It's been a very noisy, chaotic, confused, and merry household.

Q: Does Hugh have to go into the city every day?
L'Engle: No. He had to go in to do a show yesterday. He'll be back up this afternoon.

Q: Do they film in chunks?
L'Engle: Oh, no. It takes twelve hours to do a half-hour segment. It's done day by day.

Q: It is? I didn't know. I wondered if they filmed all the sequences.
L'Engle: When they're properly synchronized, if he tapes on Monday, he shows the following Monday. If he tapes on Tuesday, he shows the following Tuesday. Therefore, nobody does five days a week. His contract is for two shows a week, and those two shows even out over a six-week period. So, scheduling is very difficult because he may have a week with no shows; the following week he may have four shows. This week, he has two shows.

Q: Tell me, had you traveled in South America before writing *Dragons in the Waters*?
L'Engle: Oh, yes. The glorious thing about this soap opera is the vacations. Actors don't normally have vacations, but we get great paid vacations. Our very first one, we took a freighter, a Royal Netherlands freighter, which went straight to Venezuela, and the first stop was Maracaibo, and Dragon Lake, Dragon Port is really Maracaibo. I just changed the name. We've gone into the Caribbean via freighter, oh, five times now, so I really had got the smell of it before I dared write the book. Took five trips into that area.

Q: I hope you'll pursue the Quiztano Indians.
L'Engle: Oh, I'm in love with them. There are similar Indians off the far end of Lake Maracaibo. Yes, I would like to pursue them.

Q: Shall we talk about that further?

L'Engle: Whatever you want.

Q: About the book, I had a sense of wanting to get to know those Indians better, which is why I said that I hoped you'd pursue them, and it's perhaps especially in the sense of what we were talking about earlier, this whole issue of sexuality and the roles of men and women, and the effect on the culture of those roles.

L'Engle: Right. I suppose I was idealizing in the Indians, in having a culture where their full sexuality was accepted. I wrote it out at much greater length. I cut, oh, maybe a hundred pages of Quiztano Indian stuff, which I had to write, though, to get to know them. I think the fact that they did have two vocations—the two gifts were the gift of healing and the gift of memory—and in many primitive tribes, the elders, the old people of the tribe, are revered simply because they do have the memory of the past, the memory of this tribe, and I think that's what we're groping towards in our Bicentennial, that we have forgotten our memory and that forgetting our memory leads to things like Watergate. I think, unconsciously probably, in our intuitive area, we've realized that Watergate, the whole chaos in our government, is a result of the loss of the memory of the original American dream. Now we're groping back towards it with the various Bicentennial celebrations.

Q: How successful do you think they've been?

L'Engle: I think the fact that there's an effort at all is marvelous. One of the things that I have learned in my gradually lengthening life is that we don't have to succeed. It was a marvelously freeing thing for me to learn. I do not have to succeed. All I have to do is try. We don't have to answer the questions. We do have to ask them, and how I learned this was in our four-generation summers, when I was trying to succeed at being the perfect wife, the perfect daughter, the perfect mother, the perfect grandmother, the perfect mother-in-law, the perfect everything and failing terribly in all of it, and when I realized that I didn't have to be the perfect anything, that I was free, in order to be alive and functional, to come out here and write in the morning, that I was free to go with the dogs to the brook, that I was free not to fulfill these imposed, unrealistic roles. Then I relaxed and was a much better wife, a much better daughter, a much better mother, a much better grandmother, and the household was merrier.

Q: Something I think you imply in *Summer* is that your failure to be that perfect everything allowed other people to grow and fulfill some of these needs.

L'Engle: Right. I was imposing on myself, through pride; almost I was putting myself in the place of God, who has to run the universe. Well, I don't have to run the universe. It was very refreshing to discover that. Then everybody else was freer to take over responsibilities, which I had assumed, which weren't mine at all, so that we did become, therefore, a—it became a mesh rather than things bumping into each other.

Q: It seems to me that women today are suffering terribly from this need to be the superwoman. The image that's portrayed in the press and so on is the woman who is—you know, has the full career and is also the perfect mother and wife—

L'Engle: Absolutely. And never has underarm odor and her kitchen is always tidy. That's not the way life is. You see, what Madison Avenue does is to set up for ourselves totally false expectations of an unreal world in which we are consumers. Another word for consumers is devourers, and I think that what we're meant to be is providers, nourishers, and we nourish each other out of our own humanness, which means accepting our own failures, ourselves as we are, not this false image set up in front of us, which we can never quite make. As long as we're looking at that, we're not free to be ourselves.

Q: Madeleine, may I ask what your plans are for the summer and for the future, in terms of writing?

L'Engle: Oh, sure. Right now, I'm doing final revision on the *Irrational Season*, which has got to be done by the end of this month, and I'm already about a hundred pages into a novel, which is set in an English cathedral town. That is a very ambitious project. I hope I haven't bitten off more than I can chew, but I'm going to spend the summer working on it. I do have a couple of lecturing jobs and one writers' conference to teach, but other than that, I'm going to be right here enjoying my family. Our son will be home for the first—this will be the first summer he hasn't worked since he was about twelve, and the reason he is not going to work is that he has an incredible amount of reading to do for the teaching he's going to be having to do next year. So it'll be fun having him, and Laurie will be here, back and forth. Josephine and Alan and the children are just twelve miles away, and I just hope to have lots of time to enjoy the family, as well as spending a good four or five hours a day at the typewriter.

Q: Good. Thank you.
L'Engle: Thank you, Linda.

Allegorical Fantasy: Mortal Dealings with Cosmic Questions

Cheryl Forbes / 1978

From *Christianity Today*, June 1979, pp. 14–19.

Madeleine L'Engle won the prestigious Newbery Award "for the most distinguished contribution to American Literature for children" in 1963 for *A Wrinkle in Time*, her first fantasy novel. Since then she has written two others, *A Wind in the Door*, and her latest novel, published last fall by Farrar, Straus and Giroux, *A Swiftly Tilting Planet*. The three books form a trilogy and, as she explains, contain much of her theology in story form. Although she is known as a fantasy writer for children, most of her books have been written in the realistic genre, many of them for adults. She has also written, among her twenty-six published books, several works of nonfiction. (*The Summer of the Great-Grandmother*, for example, is a moving portrayal of the death of her own mother. Anyone who has lost a parent, or who is losing one, should read that book.) L'Engle serves as librarian and writer-in-residence at the Cathedral of St. John the Divine. She lives with her husband, actor Hugh Franklin, in New York City. Many of her manuscripts and papers are housed in the Wade Collection, Wheaton College, Wheaton, Illinois, where she is a frequent speaker. Editor at large Cheryl Forbes interviewed her last fall. The following is an edited version of the transcript.

Question: When did you become a Christian?
Answer: Conversion for me was not a Damascus Road experience. I slowly moved into an intellectual acceptance of what my intuition had always known.

Possibly I was fortunate not to have had the usual formal religious background. My parents were Episcopalians and so were theirs and so on back. My father was ill during my childhood and young womanhood; he'd been gassed in the First World War. Mustard gas slowly and relentlessly eats away at a man's lungs. He worked at night, writing until two or three in the morning. No one got up in time to take me to Sunday school. Now I am convinced that was a great blessing. I wasn't taught things I had to unlearn.

I don't know why I always had a deep sense of the nearness of a personal God to whom I could talk. Perhaps part of it was the influence of a marvelous old English Roman Catholic woman, Mary O'Connell, who took care of me. Mrs. O. was a true Christian saint. Wherever she was, there was laughter and joy, the infallible signs of the presence of God. Yet, she had a terrible life. Her husband was a total alcoholic. She had to take her children's Sunday coats with her to work; otherwise, her husband hocked them for booze. She quite often didn't know where the money would be for the rent. In her later years she suffered with painful arthritis, but she always brought laughter with her. A close friend of mine says that a Christian is someone who's met one. I met one, early.

Q: You indicate in your writing that at one point you were an atheist—or thought you were—and then you decided otherwise. How did that come about?

A: When I realized that I was trying to be a Christian with my mind only, trying to put Christianity in terms of provable facts. My husband left the theater when our children were little, and we moved to a little New England village. I was asked if I would teach Sunday school. I explained to the minister that I didn't really believe in God, but I couldn't live as though I didn't believe in him. I found life intolerable without God, so I lived as though I believed in God. I asked him, "Is that enough for you?" I began teaching Sunday school. I learned a basic thing from my high school students: cosmic questions do not in mortal terms have mortal answers. We learn through analogy, through story. A distinguished writer friend of mine said that Jesus was not a theologian but God who told stories.

My father died when I was seventeen, my last year in high school. That Christmas I had a date with a sophisticated young man—or so I thought. He said that death was death and that was that—that we are our cerebral cortex. We think through it. When it's gone, we're gone. My outrage brought me an analogy. I'm extremely myopic. If I take off my glasses, there are no stars in the sky at night and all faces become vague little pink blurs. I said to him, "I can't even see you without my glasses. Are they doing the seeing? No. I am. I'm seeing through them. My brain isn't doing the thinking; I am. I'm thinking through it." That's analogy. Now, an analogy is never a provable fact. An analogy is something that opens the door or the window and gives us a glimpse of the truth that gives meaning to lives.

Q: Then, what about doctrine and theology?

A: I think that right doctrine is far more often taught in stories than in direct dogma. At least it works better for me that way. I'd like to go back a minute to something you asked about atheism. One of my sons-in-law is an English Anglican theologian priest. He has talked about being atheists for Christ's sake. He means that Christians build up little gods, little temples of Baal. We begin to worship them, and we must tear them down, destroy them. The gods we erect are easier to worship than the creator of the universe. They're more comprehensible. The God *I* believe in is not comprehensible in finite, mortal terms. God is infinite, immortal, and all-knowing. I have a point of view; you have a point of view. God has a point of view. But we don't like having to depend on that which we cannot control, manipulate, or dominate.

In a sense, praying and writing involve the same disciplines. When I sit down with an act of will, either before the typewriter or to pray, I have to let go of my control and listen. I listen to the story, or I try to get beyond the words of prayer and listen to God. Ultimately when I hear, that is the gift, not my act of will, not my act of virtue. It is pure gift. I guess my favorite analogy for the difference between faith and works came from Rudolf Serkin. My husband and I heard him play Beethoven's *Appassionata* sonata better than Beethoven could play it. When the last note faded away, there wasn't a sound. Then, slowly, like the ocean waves, the applause swelled. Later I realized that we had been present at a moment of transcendence, of transfiguration. What did Serkin have to do with that? He practices eight hours a day, every day. I have to write every day whether I want to or not. I have to pray every day whether I want to or not. It's not a matter of feeling like it, or waiting when I feel inspired, because both in work and in prayer inspiration comes during rather than before.

Q: Are you saying that emotions don't count or that they only count after the fact?

A: That's partly what I mean. When we work either with our intellects or with our emotions, that's fragmented. When we're really working well, we work with intuition and intellect together, with heart and with mind. This fragmentation is old. Paul talked about it in Romans. When mind and heart, or intellect and intuition, work together, it's a gift. To sit down to work— whatever it may be—is an act of free will. But then you have to let go.

By and large, that's a frightening thing. You're moving into mystery, into dark waters. When I let go and move into what I call overdrive, any interruption jolts me as though I've been shoved through the sound barrier back into a world that is less real.

Q: Which leads—emotion or intellect?
A: It really isn't a thing of the cart and the horse, or one leading the other. It's a question of true collaboration.

Q: How would you define love?
A: I'm learning that love is not an emotion. God is love, but God is not an emotion. We may not always feel love toward those who are close to us, but that doesn't alter the fact of our love. Love is what we do. One of the great victories of the Enemy is to persuade us that love is a feeling.

Q: When did you marry?
A: I wasn't married until I was twenty-seven. I think that was good. My husband was twenty-nine. He's an actor; I'm a writer. We've been married for thirty-three years, which in our professions is surely unusual. I'd already had two books published. In the middle of my marriage, I didn't have to say, "I want to be a writer." I already was a writer. We knew we would have to divide the domestic chores.

Q: What about children?
A: I had seen other theater wives getting up at six in the morning with their babies and being exhausted when their husbands got home. That didn't make much sense to me. Hugh would go to the theater at night, and I would put the baby to bed. When he got home, I woke the baby up, and we had our evening together. Right from the start, neither of us was being dominant all the time or giving in all the time. It really was a collaboration.

Granted, we've had plenty of rough times. I don't think any good long-term marriage comes free. But I think many marriages break up just on the point of pain when they might begin to grow. Why didn't we break up? Why were we able to stay together? I don't know. Hugh asked me not long ago, "What have we done to deserve this?" "Not one single, solitary thing," I said. It was a sheer gift of grace, and I'm grateful for it daily. Hugh has always been behind me in my work, and I have been behind him in his.

Q: Aren't you saying that you respect each other?
A: Yes. We also love each other. They can be two quite separate items. You can have two people who respect each other but the chemistry is missing, or you can have a wild chemistry but no respect. Neither one is going to

work very well. You really need both. I think we underestimate our phero-mones, that is, our subconscious, intuitive sense of smell. In my relation-ship with my editor, for example, pheromones have to be right. Two editors can tell you exactly the same thing. One you'll hear. The other you won't. I think the same thing is true with preachers. Two preachers will say the same thing. One I'll hear; the other I won't. But, if we all had to hear everybody, what a cacophony there would be. In a sense, that also leads to our ways of approaching Christ. For me, my writing brings me to Christ.

Q: Let's talk about the ten dry years. You'd had five books published. You must have thought you had it made. Then, nothing. What did you do? How did you feel?

A: I felt terrible. My husband had left the theater. We wanted more chil-dren. He thought it was unfair to bring more children into the world with two parents in totally precarious professions. Even with five books, I wasn't making enough royalties to support us.

We had gone through a perfectly terrible year. He'd had a number of jobs, but they'd taken him out of town. We were together two weeks out of the fifty-two. So, he left the theater forever, and during the nine years of forever, we lived in a two-hundred-plus-year-old farm house. And, we bought a run-down general store and brought it back to life.

For the first time in my life I got involved with the institutional church. I found real Christian community. I was beginning to think more about why I couldn't live without God, about why I had to have meaning to all of life. This affected my writing whether I wanted it to or not, or whether I knew it or not. Obviously, even in telling a story, what we're thinking about is going to underlie the story.

It seemed ironic and unfair that just as I was turning closer to God I couldn't sell anything I wrote. Particularly, *Meet the Austins*. It was rejected for over two years because it begins with a death. At that time death was taboo in children's literature. What I believed about the Christian family, about our responsibility to each other, about living and dying, was being denied. I wrote another regular novel, and then I wrote *A Wrinkle in Time*. It was rejected and rejected. I would put the kids to bed, walk down the dirt road in front of the house, weep, and yell at God. I'd say, "God, why are you letting me have all of these rejection slips? You know it's a good book. I wrote it for you."

Q: You were writing. What were you reading?

A: I tried to read German theologians. I thought, "If I have to believe the way they believe, I cannot be a Christian." I found them depressing, though their soporific sentences did help my insomnia. Then I discovered higher math—physics, which is easier than lower math—but higher math asks questions that don't have simple answers. Reading Einstein and Eddington, for example, opened up a world where I could conceive of a loving God who really could note the fall of every sparrow and count the hairs on every head. A book that had enormous theological influence on me was *The Limitations of Science*. In writing *Wrinkle* I was writing about the universe in which I could love and be loved by a creating God. When it was finally accepted, the publisher told me it wouldn't sell. The editors were indulging themselves. When it won the Newbery, everybody was shocked. If my prayers had been answered years earlier, the book might have dropped into a dark pool of oblivion.

Q: Would you have kept on writing indefinitely?
A: I hope I would have had faith in my work, but I'm not sure how much failure the human psyche can take. My agent was afraid that failure would kill my talent. In that decade I was protected by my worst faults—stubbornness and pigheadedness.

Q: That verse where Paul says God only sends us as much as we can bear seems pertinent here.
A: Yes. That verse has been important to me, though I sometimes ask, "God, why are you overestimating my capacity to this extent?" But, always, we're given the strength that we need.

Q: Explain more fully your idea of freedom.
A: Freedom comes on the other side of work. If I want to play a Bach fugue, I must practice scales. If I hope for any transcendent experience in prayer, I have to have just done my ordinary, everyday prayers, which is the same thing as practicing my scales. I have to write every day. Freedom and discipline, rather than being antithetical, are complementary. Permissiveness, either from others toward you or toward yourself, ends up being restricting and crippling. If you choose to be a writer and a mother, you have to be incredibly disciplined. Otherwise, you won't manage. Discipline does not imprison you.

Q: What about failure? Fear of it can cripple even disciplined people.
A: We've got to be free to fail. As Christians we follow a man who, in terms of the world, failed. He listened to his mission, to where the Father told him to go. We seem to have lost sight of that. We live in a world that insists we

be successes. If you're not free to fail, you'll never be anything but mediocre. You must try to do more than you can really do. Sometimes, you *do* do more than you can really do. That's the marvel of it.

Q: Is writing difficult?
A: Yes and no, but basically no. I find getting started every day difficult, but once I'm started, in a sense I find it almost too easy. I love to do it. I've been doing it for so long. I'm convinced that every work has its own life, quite aside from the artist who serves it. Artists of all kinds are servants no matter what the discipline. We bear the work; we bring it to life.

Q: Why do you find the form of a children's book compatible for what you want to say?
A: The fantasies are my theology. In a way, I'm going to say things in my new book, *A Ring of Endless Light*, I said in *Planet*. People who can't understand the earlier book may understand this one, but I couldn't write *Ring* if I hadn't first written *Planet.*

Theologically, I suppose that there is an openness and an aliveness to many young people that ceases in adulthood. Jesus said, "I thank thee Father of heaven and earth that you have revealed these things to children and hidden them from the wise." Maybe I'm still trying to grow up myself.

Q: You enjoy reading children's books, then?
A: Yes. I get bored with depressing novels about discontented women who end up discontented women at the end of the book.

Q: The act of honest work—would you call it a form of worship?
A: Yes. I've called it a form of prayer before, but I think prayer is largely worship. Prayer may be work. Adam worked in the garden. His work was his play. For me that's true. I think the awful thing is that for many people their work is drudgery—neither a gift nor a vocation. Hugh and I are both lucky that we do work we love.

Q: How do you redeem a situation like that?
A: I have a story about work. There was an old woman who ran one of the elevators at Columbia University, when it was an all-male bastion. It was a menial job, but it was her vocation. Those students had to say, "Good morning" and "Good evening." If their clothes weren't straight, she straightened them. When she died, the church couldn't hold the people.

Q: Would you say that art is religious?

A: Whether artists are aware of it or not, art is always incarnational. True art is Christian. Sometimes I know that my work at its best keeps me from straying, keeps my faith intact. Someone once asked me if the fact that I was a Christian affected the way I work. I said, "No, but the way I work affects my Christianity."

Q: Are you a universalist?

A: No. I am a particular incarnationalist. I believe that we can understand cosmic questions only through particulars. I can understand God only through one specific particular, the incarnation of Jesus of Nazareth. This is the ultimate particular, which gives me my understanding of the Creator and of the beauty of life. I believe that God loved us so much that he came to us as a human being, as one of us, to show us his love.

Q: Let's talk further about the relationship between science and theology.

A: Einstein, for instance, was a theologian. He said that anyone who is not in awe at the mind behind the universe is as good as a burnt-out candle. We've lost our sense of awe and reverence in worship.

Q: I don't think we know how to worship.

A: We don't. At our best we must amuse the angels enormously. I read last summer that scientists are closer to the creationists now—that there does seem evidence for a beginning to the universe. This has upset other scientists. I don't see why it should. Galileo upset the establishment enormously; Jesus upset the establishment. Galileo did nothing to change the nature of God. He only changed human thinking. That was threatening. We get things organized, and we don't want to rethink them.

We live in a Newtonian, Euclidian world. Your desk for all practical purposes has to be flat and firm. We know it's a mass of swirling atoms. If we knew how we could put our fingers through it, but for you to work on it, it's got to be Euclidian. Contemporary physics is really mystical. It accepts that time is a creature, created, that it has a beginning, that it has an end. Timelessness is, in fact, still a concept of time. Eternity and timelessness aren't the same thing. The two words I like are "kairos" and "chronos." We live in chronology. Kairos is eternity, which has nothing whatever to do with time. An artist is free to know kairos. The person who prays is free to know kairos. We are literally free from time.

Q: Time seems to be fluid, right?

A: Yes. Yes. It is fluid; it can expand. Sometimes I do more in a day than it's possible to do. Another day, I'll work just as hard, and I won't get nearly as much done. The Mad Hatter in *Alice in Wonderland* says that he quarreled with time last May and ever since then time won't do anything for him. Lewis Carroll was right. Time is a creature we can work with. Time can work against us or for us. Eternity, in which we will live ultimately, has nothing to do with time at all. It isn't endless time. It isn't time going on and on and on. It's a quality that we don't know, because we are in chronos. But we have these fleeting glimpses of kairos.

Q: Time is fluid. What about space?
A: They don't exist without each other. Time exists only when there is matter in motion. If I knew how, I could close my eyes now and move to my star-watching rock in Connecticut.

Q: Perhaps when we dream, our concept of space is altered.
A: In the Bible, God often calls men when they're sleeping.

Q: *The Wind in the Door* deals with space, right?
A: One of the whole points in the book is that to God there's no difference between a farandole and a galaxy. Size is not what matters.

Q: In *Wrinkle* you dealt with time.
A: And in *Planet* I'm back to time.

Q: Well, there I think you've combined the two.
A: Yes, maybe that's the way it's supposed to be. Time. Space. Time and space.

Q: The two have come together in an unusual way. Space is radically different when time changes.
A: Time and space acting on each other. After we first exploded the atom bomb here, many of the physicists who worked on that were converted. Pollock became an Episcopal priest. More and more, scientists are turning back to the church. That's a wonderful thing. Science should help us enlarge our vision: never change it, never diminish it, but enlarge it.

Q: God doesn't need protection?
A: No, and the establishment feels it must protect God.

Q: Yet, God was always shattering images of himself. He did the unpredictable, as with Jonah.

A: We've built up an image of God—a comfortable God. It must be shattered.

Q: God shatters it by various means.
A: All kinds of means. Always particular means, like Galileo, for instance.

Q: Or your neighbor next door?
A: Yes, the greatest shattering of all being with Jesus.

Q: Because who would have thought that God would do such a thing?
A: Born in a stable. Born of a virgin. Died on a cross. Nothing that anybody has been brought up to expect. Totally, totally shattered.

Madeleine L'Engle: An Interview

Ted Baehr / 1980

From *Searching*, the Episcopal Radio-TV Foundation.

Trinity Church presents, direct from Broadway and Wall Street, the program *Searching*. This week on *Searching* we'll be visiting with Madeleine L'Engle, author of the new book, *A Ring of Endless Light*, and author of such great books as *A Swiftly Tilting Planet*, *A Wrinkle in Time*, which won the Newbery Award, and *A Wind in the Door*.

Ted Baehr: Today I have the pleasure of talking with Madeleine L'Engle. My name is Ted Baehr, and this is *Searching*. Madeleine, thank you for coming and speaking with us. *A Ring of Endless Light* is your twenty-eighth book?
Madeleine L'Engle: I've lost count. Something like that.

TB: And you've written a nonfiction book after this, right?
ML: Yes. It's called *Walking on Water*, with the subtitle *Reflections on Faith and Art*. I was asked to write it. I never would have done it otherwise.

TB: Who asked you to write it?
ML: Harold Shaw. He's a very small, very fine evangelical publisher. The evangelicals are just discovering art and that it can, in fact, be Christian instead of sinful. That's a very fine discovery.

TB: It's a great discovery. You can be an artist and a Christian.
ML: It's so nice being an Episcopalian. You're allowed to be an artist from the word "go."

TB: Yes, you don't have to worry about it. I just gave a panel on that. I've been reading your fiction, or at least I've been reading your trilogy. I've just read *A Ring of Endless Light* and must admit I cried frequently.

ML: Glad to hear it.

TB: It's a very touching, very beautiful book. Is this something out of your past history?

ML: Somebody pointed out to me that it is a fiction version of a nonfiction book of mine called *The Summer of the Great-Grandmother*, which was the story of my mother's ninetieth and last summer, and our fourth summer of four generations living under one roof. I hadn't realized that I was doing in fiction much of the same thing that I had been doing in nonfiction in that particular book. I think that artists of all kinds frequently don't realize what they're doing. You listen to the work and go where it tells you to go. It's not that you are off lost in a vague vacuum, but you're so concentrated on what you're doing that you're not thinking of things on either side of it.

TB: Do you look at your fiction as being evangelical? You were talking about an evangelical publisher.

ML: Well, it's kind of fascinating to me that here I am, one of these unusual things, a cradle Episcopalian, and I was discovered by the evangelicals and Roman Catholics long before my own church. I go frequently to Mundelein College, which is Roman Catholic, and I stay with the sisters. I go to Mass with them. Then I go an hour away to Wheaton, known as the Harvard of evangelical colleges, and I say the same things that I said at Mundelein. And I don't change my voice. They are not as far away as they think from each other. In a sense I have inadvertently moved in very ecumenical circles in my speaking, and the last people to discover me have been the Episcopalians.

TB: But you wouldn't call your books evangelical? You would call them good fiction?

ML: I am a storyteller. What I am thinking about in my own life is going to show underneath that story, whether I want it to or not. Emerson said, "What you are speaks so loudly of your head that I cannot hear what you say." So what I am when I'm writing the story is going to show through. I'm always writing, in a sense, what concerns me. I've known for a long time that I was going to write a book about Vicky and the grandfather's death. I was just waiting for the right time. When I started the book I had no idea that I was going to get deeply involved with dolphins. That was the greatest fun I've ever had in research. I had to play with dolphins.

TB: You talked to them? Did you ride them?

ML: No, I didn't ride on them. That was not permitted, but my dolphin did tell me to scratch his chest. There is no question that he could tell me exactly what he wanted me to do. They're wonderful creatures, and we have a lot to learn from them.

TB: I was asking about evangelicals because when I read your works I think of them as being pre-evangelical. I think of them as being something that opens up the miraculous, a whole world beyond.

ML: Isn't that really what the evangelicals ought to be doing?

TB: That's right, preparing people for the gospel.

ML: Yes.

TB: What you really do is prepare people.

ML: I speak a great deal in secular groups, at universities, and state librarian and teachers' groups. Many of these have been alienated from the various churches or synagogues, from faith. They're groping and lonely and seeking, so I've found myself trying to speak to people who've not found a direction. The only way to do it is by sharing my own voyage, as it were. So I'm speaking largely to people who haven't found their answers, but are looking for answers. I'm almost happier with people who are looking than with people who think they have found. I haven't found it all yet. It's a great, wide, marvelous unknown. I'm never going to find it all. All I find is newer questions and more questions so that I'm speaking for the questioners rather than those who have all the answers. The evangelicals' great concern about me is they think I may be what they call a universalist. When I was a student a universalist was someone who thought that Jesus and Buddha and Lao Tzu and everybody were sort of equal and all religions were the same. That's not what they mean. I finally found out what they mean. They think I believe that God is going to wave his magic wand and say, "Whoopee! You're all forgiven! Home free." That's not what I believe at all. However, I do believe that God's loving patience is going to outlast all of our willfulness, all of our disobedience. And the idea that the blessed of heaven are looking down at the tortures of the damned in hell is not my idea of blessedness. It's very difficult for many people to accept that God can forgive people they cannot forgive. I was talking to someone today who said, "I'm being punished." I said, "Well, there's only one point to punishment. Punishment is to teach a lesson. There is only one lesson to be taught, and that is love." That's not what it's about. It's about revenge or retribution, but it's not punishment. We get all of these things confused. I base my life on God's forgiveness. I sometimes wonder about these people who feel that they're going to be in heaven while the rest of us are down there. Why are they so sure they're going to be in heaven? I don't think any of us gets through the day without doing some small, unloving act. I might be too tired to hear somebody, but I never get through a day with the acme of perfection. I don't think anybody does. We're human, and we're flawed.

TB: And the process of sanctification is reliant on the holy mystery, not just thinking of it as a nonmystery.
ML: Oh, it is a holy mystery. It makes life worth living.

TB: That's right.
ML: One of the responses to *The Summer of the Great-Grandmother*, the book about my mother's death, was that I didn't know how to be angry. I have never hesitated to be angry with God. First of all, that's an affirmation. You cannot be angry with someone who isn't there. When I'm angry with God I want him to put his wings around me and hold me. I'm beating against a reality, a mysterious reality but one that sustains me. The other thing that I was working through in that book was real guilt and false guilt. Living in a four generation household is quite a strain. Real guilt is never a problem. It's false guilt where we get hung up on these little marvelous plaster images that the world would like us to be, and then we fail our plastic images. For instance, during our first four-generation summer I thought I had to be the perfect wife, the perfect mother, the perfect daughter, the perfect grandmother. I was awful. It wasn't until I learned that I had to be what I thought was selfish, be totally imperfect, that I had to spend the morning writing, that I had to take an hour away every afternoon to get away from everybody I loved, that the summers began to be easy. As the only daughter of the great-grandmother a lot of the burdens of the summer obviously fell on me as chief cook and bottle washer, too. So I learned that I can't divide my good qualities and my bad qualities. All right, here I'll put all the good ones, and here I'll put all the bad ones because there are times when the bad ones are absolutely essential and the good ones are no good at all.

TB: How would you define real guilt? You've already defined false guilt.
ML: Well, if I am so preoccupied with something that I cannot hear somebody in deep need who speaks to me, if I ignore my husband for instance,

I can wake up and say, "I'm terribly sorry. Please forgive me." When I do something which I know is unloving and wrong, I can say, "I'm sorry." It's when I'm trying to live up to that plaster image. My husband is a television actor who plays Dr. Charles Tyler on ABC's *All My Children*. Commercials on television portray great plaster images of what we ought to be. There is one about a young woman whose mother-in-law is coming to dinner, so she rushes out and buys the right floor polish so her mother-in-law will love her. What if the mother-in-law slips on that floor polish and breaks a hip? It deals with a nonreality, a non-world, and we fall for it. Whereas the world of the Bible, which has been my great storybook, is full of people who are full of faults and flaws. God never used qualified people. In a sense we're all unqualified. It seems that God took great pains to choose the most unqualified people. Moses was past middle age and had a stutter, and he didn't want to do all of these things. He was very rebellious. For me, the message is that if we're qualified, we might think we did it ourselves. If we know ourselves to be unqualified, then we know we do nothing without our hand in the hand of God.

TB: So what you're talking about is real grace as opposed to cheap grace. Very simple. Very beautiful.
ML: Yes. You're putting it beautifully for me, thank you.

TB: What about all the mythological characters in your books? In *A Ring of Endless Light* you have dolphins, which are not as mythological as *A Wrinkle in Time*.
ML: Most everything in there about the dolphins is within reason or within what is being done in dolphin research.

TB: Like the dolphin who asked you to scratch its chest?
ML: Yes, but I read a great deal about dolphins. I talked to people who worked with them about dolphins, so it's closer to fact than fantasy. Gaudior, for instance, the unicorn in *A Swiftly Tilting Planet*—for me, myth is an icon, a vehicle of truth. I don't dream up my mythological characters. They come to me. Sometimes they come in very funny ways. I live on the Upper West Side of New York City. I walk my dog at night on the upper level of Riverside Park. I was reading Ezekiel and some of the descriptions of cherubim, those marvelous wild creatures with many, many wings and many, many eyes, spurting flames. I wondered how unusual it would be to have cherubim with me as I walked Timothy in the park. That was how Progo the cherub in *A Wind in the Door* got created, as it were.

TB: A great, wonderful character.

ML: Characters arrive. The job of the storyteller is to say, "Okay, I recognize you. Hello!"

TB: What's so beautiful about your characters for me is that they give you a chance to look beyond your prejudices, to look beyond your preconceptions and to fall in love with something that's totally indescribable, that's totally beyond what you'd expect in life.

ML: I had a very rational education. I was brought up to believe in pragmatism and that my intellect must be able to comprehend everything. It took me a long time to realize that my intellect alone is a very faulty and flawed organ and that it can't go very far unless it collaborates with intuition, that the mind and the heart must work together. St. Theophon the Recluse, a Russian monk of the nineteenth century, used to counsel his penitents to pray with the mind in the heart. That's what writing is, the mind in the heart, which basically means you let go intellectual domination. I don't control my work. I don't manipulate it. I don't own it. I don't possess it. It is not mine in any definitive sense. I listen to it. When it's going well, I'm able to get out of the way and listen. For me, to listen to a story is the same discipline as trying to get out of the way in prayer, to empty self and listen and then, perhaps, be able to hear something.

TB: Beautiful. There's a great deal of Christian mysticism, a great deal of speculational mysticism. Where does that fit into your theology?

ML: We spent almost ten years living in New England. My husband left the theater for forever, and during forever, which lasted not quite ten years, we managed a general store in a small New England village. There was only one church, the Congregational church. We really had Christian community there that was fantastically good, but I found myself starved for symbol, starved for sacrament in a terribly agnostic period in my life without realizing that not knowing is, of course, where we all are. So I was given German theologians to read to convert me, although I didn't wish to be converted very badly. I would read the German theologians, saying, "Uh-uh. Not for me." So the story came. In a sense, on one level it is a rebuttal of the German theologians. A funny thing about *A Wrinkle in Time* is that I thought of it at the time as being a very heretical book, and of course it's perfectly good orthodoxy. The Holy Spirit has a nice sense of humor.

TB: It's a sacramental book.
ML: Yes.

TB: What do people say to you, the Roman Catholics or the evangelicals, when they confront *A Wrinkle in Time*, wrestling with it?
ML: Two funny things are said over and over again. "Of course, you have had a union analysis," and I haven't had any kind at all. The other, which I think is very interesting, is "Of course, you do belong to the program, don't you?" which means AA or Al-Anon. Of course I have to say, "No, I don't." I see the reason for the second remark in that in my books, particularly the nonfiction, and my speaking, I make myself vulnerable, which is what you do in AA and Al-Anon. You come there with all your faults and you say, "Help."

TB: You have to.
ML: You have to. I think it's what we should be doing in church but don't as much as we should.

TB: So good communication comes from opening yourself up?
ML: When I'm conducting a retreat or lecturing, I simply try to talk about where I am because I'm not the only person who's there. Most people are a little afraid to talk about the things you don't talk about. Really, it was my husband who got me to do this. After *A Wrinkle in Time* won the Newbery Award, my first big invitation was to go out to San Francisco to the National Council of the Teachers of English. I wrote a very witty and self-protective talk, but my husband said, "That's very amusing, dear, but they are not paying you to travel that distance just to make them laugh. They think you've something to say, so stick your neck out and say something." I tore up my talk and stuck my neck out, and it worked. Everything good that happens, I've got somebody to thank for it. For instance, my mother thought of the title for *A Wrinkle in Time*.

TB: Do you read all the time while you're in the library?
ML: I write while I'm in the library. I went to the library to write because I was working in the bedroom at home, and with an actor husband that's not the best place to write. So when the librarian left . . .

TB: You became the librarian for the Cathedral?
ML: Yes, but they now call me the writer-in-residence, which is a much more realistic assessment of what I do. For me there are three things to be

done in that library. One is to write books, one is to listen to people who need to talk, and one is to do the library work. Something had to go, but guess which?

TB: The library work?
ML: Yes.

TB: Does somebody do that now?
ML: I have a wonderful young woman, Andrea Melrose, who gives me a whole day per week. She's putting the place back into shape again.

TB: I remember taking a class there with Canon West, and all your papers were spread out. "Don't touch Madeleine L'Engle's papers!"
ML: Three assistants and maybe four if mine was there while I was away came leaping at you!

TB: Exactly. *A Wrinkle in Time* has been picked up to be made into a motion picture, is that right?
ML: This is a kind of extraordinary miracle. All standard Hollywood contracts have a clause, allowing the producer freedom to change character and theme. I am physically incapable of signing that clause. I cannot do it. My agent says I will never sell a book to the movies, so I'll never sell a book to the movies. In fact, I negotiated this contract myself. It states that they may not change character or theme. The characters may do nothing inconsistent with their development in future books. They must be played by real people, and I must be consulted all along the line. Then they offered me some money, and I said, "That's not enough." They said, "Do you need money?" I said, "No, but unless you double it, I don't believe you're serious. I want the money, so I know you're really serious about this." Norman Lear bought it, but the light behind it is a marvelous young woman called Cathy Hand. Her father was in both the Johnson and Truman administrations, and I think her great uncle was the great Chief Justice Learned Hand. She grew up completely believing that the American establishment was unshakeable, and then when JFK was assassinated her world fell apart. At that moment she read *A Wrinkle in Time*, and she said it put her back together again. It's been her one desire to acquire it as a movie, the right movie. So I trust Cathy implicitly.

TB: She brought it to Norman Lear?
ML: She's his right hand. When he decided to branch out into movies, she said, "This is the first thing you've got to do, Norman!"

TB: Will there be some animation in it?
ML: For special effects, but all of the characters will be real people.

ML: This sounds like a $30-million-dollar movie.
ML: It probably is. I have only ten fingers and can't count that high.

TB: How's the movie doing right now?
ML: I think it's going quite well. They're being terribly nice about talking to me here in New York as they're moving into ideas.

TB: Have they finished the script?
ML: They had to dump the script, as it were, to which we all agreed. It wasn't working out as it should, but that's okay. We're starting again. I believe it's going to be a good movie.

TB: Do you find him easy to work with?
ML: I have great respect for him. I think he's a man of real integrity who cares about human beings and looks to see a cosmic, ultimate purpose in life. He cares about shape, pattern, and meaning. That's good.

TB: Does he have your same theological perspective?
ML: No, but I think it's semantics which separate us because at one point we were having lunch and he looked at me saying, "Are you a very religious Christian?" I said, "Norman, we've got to define a few words. What do you mean by 'religious'? Hitler was very religious. Khomeini is very religious. What do you mean? Do I believe that God's love for his creation is unfailing? Do I believe that the very hairs on our heads are counted? Yes, I do." And we moved further, arriving at the point to where we could talk, but there was a high semantic wall that first had to be knocked down. Norman is Jewish but nonpracticing, I believe. Many words in the world must be redeemed. I am just coming under attacks from the evangelical right. One criticism is that at the end of *A Ring of Endless Light* Vicky turns to the dolphins and not to Jesus. If I had Vicky turn to Jesus, I would have slammed the door in the faces of a lot of people who aren't ready to walk through the door. I don't want to slam doors in people's faces. My idea of the gospel is not that it must be kept with a small group who is already there, but it is to be spread to the rest of the world that isn't there. My own tiny discoveries of light and loveliness are what I want to share, but I want to share them openly, not in a closed or smug "I am there" kind of way.

TB: Yet, the theme of death and resurrection comes through in your book very clearly.

ML: Oh, yes, I have a book called *Dance in the Desert*, which I wrote as an eight-page short story, an epiphany present for Canon West. It is a fully illustrated small children's book. It's about a family, mother and father and small child, crossing the desert with a caravan. During the night all the animals come to dance for the child, and then at dawn the family and the caravan continue their journey into Egypt. I never say that it's Jesus, Joseph, and Mary and their flight into Egypt. If you know it, there it is. If you don't know it, something in the story is there. If I had said that, it would not be picked up by somebody who was not already a Christian. I don't think that makes it any less Christian. I hope that makes it more Christian. The illustrations by Symeon Shimin are absolutely gorgeous. He really got it. They are strong and powerful and joyful.

TB: Has Norman speculated on how to do the special effects?

ML: Oh, yes, there are all kinds of ideas. We're still very much in the dreaming stage, but these are exciting dreams. He's getting excited about it.

TB: Has he looked into electronic animation?

ML: Yes, everything that is brand new we're looking at.

TB: A good friend of mine was one of the three people who designed the New York Institute of Technology animation center. They were the key elements, two physicists and one artist, who made the first computer animator that was later picked up by the networks, and now they've all been hired by George Lucas to do his next movie.

ML: Of course!

TB: They've just been plucked out of the New York Institute of Technology and taken up by Lucas. He's captured these minds whom I've always hoped to work with at some point.

ML: That's marvelous. This isn't really a change of thought, but I find that the modern mystics are the astrophysicists and the cellular biologists. When I want to read the mystics, I read the works of the astrophysicists and the cellular biologists because they are exploring the nature of being itself.

TB: Quarks and quasars and mesons . . .

ML: Oh, yes, I just read a fascinating book called *White Holes* by the English astrophysicist John Gribbin. Actually, I read it quite a while ago. It's full of the idea that time is not linear. It does not move in one direction. Then, of course, there is Jesus on the mountain talking to Elijah and Moses, completely disregarding linear time. We limit ourselves.

TB: Is your primary reading scientific works?
ML: I read *Scientific American,* but one of the wonderful, unexpected fringe benefits has been that readers across the country send me books they think I would enjoy. They are widely diverse. Some are fiction, some Zen Buddhism. They range the waterfront, but I haven't received one I haven't enjoyed. One of my editors just gave me a mystery by Dick Francis, an English ex-jockey who writes mysteries about horse racing. I couldn't care less about horse racing, but he's marvelous. He's a theologian. He has an incredible sense of honor and reality and doing what is right and good and beautiful. The first book I read I handed to Canon West, saying, "Here, it's full of sermons for you," and I haven't been able to get it back from him.

TB: Well, I hope you send me some books down at the foundation when I take over.
ML: I would love to.

TB: What was your last nonfiction book? Tell me a little about it.
ML: You mean *Walking on Water*? It's about the process of creativity. I've already spoken about the job of the artist being able to listen, to get out of the way, to serve the work and not own it. The great artists are the collaborators. For most of us it is our greatest joy to try to serve the work as best we can. At one point I quote the English theologian Harry Williams: "The opposite of sin can only be faith and never virtue," which might be why some artists are so downright sinful. When they are working, they must believe in their work. It's not a very long book.

TB: How long is it?
ML: A couple hundred pages.

TB: Can it be put into movie form?
ML: Well, I don't know. We could see about that.

TB: That's wonderful. I think you're doing absolutely terrific work. You're writing another novel and looking ahead to another 128 books to write.

ML: My son-in-law says that one day I will be found dead on top of the typewriter, and that's certainly how I hope it happens.

TB: I've enjoyed having you here, and I hope we see each other frequently and that we work together. I just praise God for the work you're doing. I think it's absolutely tremendous. Thank you.

ML: Thank you.

"Listen to Your Work": An Interview with Madeleine L'Engle

Connie Soth / 1980

From *Arkenstone* 4.4, July/August 1980, pp. 9–17.

"We've decided that the best way to get together is to pack a picnic lunch and meet you in the University's parking lot. We can sit in the car and eat, and you can get your interview. You won't have any trouble finding us—we'll be driving a white Rabbit, which carries a bumper sticker, 'We brake for Unicorns.'

"Oh, by the way, we have to go on to New York after I talk to the librarians' conference, and we've suddenly thought, 'What'll we do with Max?', so—that's our Irish setter—he'll be in the car, too. It'll take us about an hour to get there from Crosswicks. 'Bye."

Just off the plane after a red-eye flight from Portland, Oregon, via Seattle and Chicago, I stood with phone in hand and listened aghast as Madeleine L'Engle cheerily outlined her plan to meet me on the University of Hartford campus, where I had come to attend a conference of congregational librarians. Madeleine had so generously granted me an interview, even though this would be just before she would be talking to two hundred librarians. For her, that meant almost two solid hours of talking, of expenditure of energy. My feelings of gratitude, confusion, and apprehension churned inextricably—who were "we" and how could I cope with a big dog in a small car while juggling lunch and tape recorder and a sheaf of questions? And with that white Rabbit—feeling eerily like Alice, I mumbled some polite phrase and went out to search for the parking lot, on unfamiliar territory in Connecticut's humid summer rain.

Happily, we did meet, without untoward incident. Madeleine, "with my long legs it's best," climbed into the back seat, leaving me to fit myself into the front bucket seat. Me, that is, plus coat, bookbag, attaché case, tape recorder, clipboard, sandwich, and potato salad, all somehow scrunched around so I could see and talk to her. At intervals, rain pelted my side of the car. Hurriedly, I would roll the window up, the sun would shine hotly through, and I would roll it down again until the next shower.

Hugh Franklin, beaming congenially from the driver's seat, thoughtfully absented himself for most of the interview. Like the Cheshire Cat, his smile remained, except that his left pleasant vibrations in the air. Max, on command, draped himself gracefully, like a silky red rug, across the back window ledge and never moved.

No, it wasn't like *Alice in Wonderland* after all—Madeleine and Hugh made me feel, if not like family (I couldn't expect that), at least like a long-time friend of the family. That "long-time" may be in the future.

Connie: Madeleine, today I'd like to talk about two areas of your life: the theater and writing, with emphasis on how you've experienced them as a Christian.

Madeleine: Well, the theater was a pragmatic way to earn my own living in a way that I felt was compatible with writing. I had no illusions about myself as a great actress—I'm too tall and too clumsy. I wasn't too proud to take general understudies and assistant stage managerships, and I worked—

C: You did act in *The Cherry Orchard*—

M: My first show was a play called *Uncle Harry* and then *The Cherry Orchard* in which I met Hugh. We met in *The Cherry Orchard*, and we married in *The Joyous Season*.

C: Oh, how nice. That sounds like a line you like—you've rehearsed it!

M: I do kind of like it—but one of the other pragmatic reasons was that I'd been ten years in female institutions, six years in Anglican boarding schools, and the male sex was a total mystery to me. I learned in college—I went to Smith—that when we worked in plays with men from Amherst I could talk with them. In any social situation I was tongue-tied and impossible. Well, I thought, "If I work in the theater I'll have time to write, and I'll understand men," which more or less happened. I was fortunate also in working with Eva Le Gallienne and Margaret Webster and Joseph Schildkraut—all marvelous people who taught me a great deal. Chekhov's *Cherry Orchard*—I never got tired of it. I was in it a year on Broadway and a year on the road—I learned something new every night. It was seeing words enfleshed—

C: That's an interesting concept, I think, because we Christians have so encapsulated the word "enfleshed" or "incarnate" we find it very difficult to think of it any other way except spiritually. That's very good—

M: It was very good for me, too, to see that the word is more than what is put down on the typewriter. I also learned in stock and in working with playwrights on new plays that not every word brought forth from a writer's mind is a precious pearl—some had to be thrown out or rewritten and rewritten. I learned the value of rewriting, struggling to cut through to what you are really trying to say. I still rewrite an incredible amount because one thing I learned in the theater: When you're on stage you have to listen—and when you write, you have to listen. I listen to my work. My work knows more than I do, and I listen to it. Listening to work, the techniques of listening to work and the techniques of prayer are identical. It's getting out of the way—

C: Can you expand on that a little? How is it the same?

M: Well, when I say my prayers, and I start and end the day with prayer, I have to pray whether I want to or not—

C: You have to?

M: Yes. If I don't pray daily, when God wants to say something to me, how am I going to hear if I'm not listening? I find morning and evening prayer just a good framework for the day because I lead an extraordinarily busy life. I need, I must have, discipline if I'm going to write. I must have this good structure—it gives me scripture morning and evening and time to stop and think. To really pray is to get out on the other side of the words, to be without words, but you have to go through the words. That's an extremely difficult concept to really convey, but more and more people are interested.

C: Well, the big surge in meditation has something to do with that, doesn't it?

M: But you see, what a lot of people want is instant meditation, and you don't get instant meditation. There's no such thing.

C: Now, referring to your early days of living in Greenwich Village [between 1941 and '48], when you were writing the first of your many books, you also wrote three plays: *18 Washington Square South, How Now Brown Cow,* and *Journey with Jonah.*

M: I wrote *Journey with Jonah* fairly recently. I was directing the spring play at the school my kids went to, and I didn't want to do anything with the high school group that wasn't worthwhile. Here I was, in despair trying to find a play, and I would wake up in the middle of the night—and knowing my body wouldn't let me get back to sleep, I would be wide awake. Suddenly one night I got this vision of Jonah sitting, absolutely furious. The worm had eaten his gourd, and he's furious at the worm and out of the twenty-second Psalm I heard the words, "Well, after all, I am a worm and no man." I began to giggle and that was the genesis of this play, in which Jonah is the only human character. All the other characters are anthropomorphic animals. I think Jonah is not only hilarious, but an extremely contemporary book. I wanted a play we could discuss as well as act in. With every play we got discussions going—we did *Androcles and the Lion*—but the kids got into some wonderful discussions about Jonah, the main point being that it is so much easier to destroy than to forgive. Jonah wanted God to destroy Nineveh—which was the enemy after all, they're not "us"—but God forgives them, and Jonah is absolutely furious. The point is that Jonah is fleeing God—the whale is just part of the flight—the whale has a marvelous conversation with Jonah. God is more forgiving than we are, and we don't want God to be more forgiving than we are.

As for *18 Washington Square*—it is pure fluff, pure wish fulfillment about two girls who come to New York to get into the theater. *How Now Brown Cow* I collaborated on with a friend. Writing plays and working in the theater was very important for me in that I do think that my dialogue is good; I'm sure that's because of my theater background.

C: Did Hugh influence you in the writing of your plays?
M: No, I wrote plays long before we met. Actually, while I was writing plays I would write an act at a sitting; it would take me from twenty-four to thirty-six hours. Once you're married and have children you can no longer do that. Then I became fascinated by the novel—you can put aside the writing of a novel. And about writing, one thing was very important to me: When I was twelve, thirteen, and fourteen, I was in an English boarding school; there, we were allowed no privacy whatsoever, never allowed to be alone. There's where I learned to concentrate in any amount of sound and fury. I wrote my first novel when *Uncle Harry* went on tour. I wrote in trains—during World War II—I wrote in dressing rooms surrounded by other kids. I wrote in hotel rooms I had to share with others because obviously I was getting equity minimum. As long as I am not responsible for noise I can shut it out. I travel a lot, and I write in planes, in airports, in hotel rooms. The only time

I was not able to use my force field of concentration was when I had growing children. When my kids were little I couldn't write until they went to bed.

C: So the very situations which you might have labeled bad or inhibiting or frustrating became the very things that helped you grow.

M: In *The Irrational Season* I said that all of the bad things have been the most necessary. All the most negative things in my childhood, in adolescence, and all through my life have been most important in forming me as a woman, as a Christian, a writer, a wife and mother—maybe that's part of my love for Jonah. Like him, I never hesitated to kick against the pricks, to be furious at God. If I'm angry at God I tell him so. I went through more than ten years of rejection slips—the entire decade of my thirties and into my forties—and particularly when *Wrinkle in Time* was being rejected, I'd get the kids to bed and then walk down the dirt road our house faces. I'd say, "God! Why all these rejection slips? You know it's a good book. I wrote it for *You!*" (It's a very theological book as far as I'm concerned.) Now the fascinating thing was that if *Wrinkle* had been accepted two years earlier than it finally was it might have just died. It came out at what was exactly its right moment.

C: I will have other questions about *Wrinkle* later, but for now, what advice would you give young Christians who yearn for the stage?

M: It's the same for Christians or Jews or Buddhists or Sufis or atheists—and that is: you have to work. It takes incredible discipline; you must have discipline in all areas of your life; you must decide what you can and what you can't do (according to conscience)—I suppose my advice, if you really take it all down the line, would be Christian advice, but I don't put it in those terms because so many people are put off by it.

C: On another subject, you wrote an article for *Commonweal* in 1978 titled, "We of the Broken Body," which I'd like to discuss with you. You said, "One of the many ways in which Christians have managed to avoid the demands of the great Christian story is a way that strikes me as more frightening than the demands themselves. It is the willingness to collaborate in the tearing asunder of life by breaking Christendom into warring denominations and communions, a major victory for the Enemy." What exactly are the demands of the "great Christian story"?

M: That every human being is a child of God, that we must serve each other, that we are faulted and flawed and fallen, that we are not these plastic images of perfection that the world seeks to set up for us, and that we have to accept ourselves with our monsters. As in the fairytales, when the monster is accepted, loved, and kissed, it stops being a monster. We have to accept that God is more forgiving than we are and that our human calling is collaboration with God in the writing of our own story—we do have a say in it.

C: Well, if that's the Christian story in the sense of each one of us finding out what our own story is or living our own story, what about the Christ story? Maybe we ought to differentiate between them. Is there a meshing there between our story and the Christ story ?
M: Say I'm at a point of decision where I'm confused. I must decide between two actions—I try to look and see what He would have done in the situation. I would try to follow. What Jesus did wasn't always what His disciples wanted Him to do—I try to follow the reality of what Jesus did, rather than all the things we impose on Him.

C: But couldn't we say that there's one basic thing—I don't know how else to say it except in the words, "Christ died for me," realizing that we couldn't be reconciled to God by ourselves, that His death makes it possible—would you say that's the essence of the Christ story?
M: We all have to die over and over again.

C: But isn't there something special about Christ's death?
M: Yes, if you're a Christian there's got to be. It's death and resurrection—

C: Okay—another subject: do you know the derivation of the name, Arkenstone?
M: No, I don't.

C: In J. R. R. Tolkien's *The Hobbit* the Arkenstone of Thrain, also known as the Heart of the Mountain, was used as a means of reconciliation. The literary allusion is that Arkenstone seeks to be an analogous jewel of reconciliation to the mountain, which is Christendom. In another part of your article, you described just exactly the kind of thing that alienates Christians from one another and calls to mind our need for reconciliation: "I was shocked in an evangelical setting to hear someone say, 'I couldn't possibly talk to Dr. X about this. He wouldn't understand—he isn't a Christian.' Dr. X is Roman Catholic."

M: Yes, but shocked as I am by this kind of put-down, I'm also fascinated by the fact that I go frequently to speak at Mundelein College, which is Roman Catholic. I go equally frequently to Wheaton, which is evangelical, but I don't change my voice. I don't do anything different in either place. At Mundelein, I stay with the sisters and go to Mass with them. When I'm at Wheaton I usually stay at the home of one of the professors—I'm extremely *happy* in both settings.

C: That must mean that people respond to you knowing that you are not putting on for them, not using the jargon. This is the kind of honesty Arkenstone is seeking to bring forth—
M: I think that Christian unity is going to come about by voices like Arkenstone's, by people discovering they're not as far apart as they have been taught to think they are.

C: We may not understand one another's viewpoint—we do some groping and stumbling—but we must try to be reconcilers as well as the reconciled.
M: Someone called one day, who had read that I thought God was ultimately going to forgive everybody. And I said "Yes, I do."

He said, "But what about the people who choose to exclude themselves?"

I replied, "When you were little, didn't you choose to exclude yourself from your family? And didn't they let you come back when you wanted to?"

Sure, we can choose to exclude ourselves, but I cannot believe that God's loving patience with His creation isn't going to outlast our willfulness. The entire creation is groaning in travail—this is part of it—it is broken. And until all of creation is once again one—which is His plan—we're not whole.

C: Would you say that we're the ones who put limitations on what God is able to do?
M: I know that I tend to make Him anthropomorphic over and over again. It's all right when I know I'm doing it because I can't understand God. He is infinite and I'm finite, after all. I *have* to perceive Him anthropomorphically, but I've got to know that this isn't what is real.

C: Well—what do you suggest that writers who are Christians do to write integrity into their work, to combat bigotry, to be aware of our finiteness?
M: Listen to their work. Don't dictate it; don't control it; don't manipulate it. Listen to it, and go where it wants to go. My book, *The Arm of the Starfish,*

was a good example of this. A character, Joshua, just turned up, uninvited, in the story. My protagonist wakes up and is very surprised to see Joshua just sitting there, looking at him—well, I was very surprised to see Joshua—there was no Joshua in my plot. My choice then was to say, "Out! I won't have you. I don't want to throw out 150 pages and start all over again," or to say, "Well, I guess you're meant," which is what I finally did. And now I can't imagine the book without Joshua, even though he demanded an incredible amount of rewriting. Someone has pointed out to me that Joshua is a Christ-figure. Ha—I could never *try* to write a Christ-figure. I cannot try to write a Christian book. If I do, I will fail abysmally. All I can do is try to listen to what is sent. This becomes more and more clear with each book, that my job is to be a servant, to listen and to be obedient.

C: You said something else that comes right along in that line. You said, "Story is one of the great healing elements in a world that is broken. Story takes the fragments and puts it all together for us."

M: A friend of mine, a writer, said Jesus is not a theologian but is the God who told stories. I love it—and besides, if you look at a lot of the parables they don't make any sense at all unless they're funny. They're hilarious. He was turning away wrath with a soft answer—

C: Speaking of stories, you teach many courses about writing. Tell us about your course at Wheaton.

M: This past June I was teaching a four-point credit course in two weeks—I taught the four-and-a-half hours 8 A.M. to 4 P.M.! What I was trying to get through and finally did is that you can give a Christian message without mentioning Christ. People were saying, "I want to write for Christendom," and I said, "Why? I don't write for Christendom. I don't write for women. I write for people. The point of the Gospel is not to keep it for a little in-group, but to spread it. A small book of mine, *Dance in the Desert*, which was gloriously illustrated—any practicing Christian will know that this is the flight into Egypt, but this is never mentioned. I get letters from non-Christians who love the book. I do not believe the message of the book should be exclusive.

C: Is that published by—

M: Farrar, Straus and Giroux—they are my home. I will do things for other people. I love the Shaws—Harold and Luci—wonderful Christians—they asked me to write a book on Christian creativity; that's *Walking on Water*. Basically, that's because that's what I've been asked to lecture on at Wheaton where they are just discovering that art is not immoral, that story is not a lie. I keep saying that if story is a lie, what do you do about Jesus? He told stories all the time.

C: Well, then, if the purpose of the Christian artist—whether writer, painter, sculptor, musician—is to tell the Christian story, how can they learn from our Lord? He was the world's greatest storyteller, although He never wrote but once, and then in the sand. Has it anything to do with showing rather than telling?

M: Yes, absolutely. He always renders. He does not report. He shows. He does not tell, and He never explains. Also, you can tell the Christian story without telling the Bible story or mentioning Jesus. If you really want to hear a story that mentions Jesus all the time, pick up any porno book. They'll have "Christ" or "Jee-sus" on every page. That is *not* a valid criterion.

Jesus never mentioned "Jesus" in His stories. He talked about people working in a vineyard, about how angry the ones were who worked all day with the ones who came and got the same pay—the message is mighty clear. We don't like it because we always feel the same way. We'd all be angry—we also have within us the Prodigal Son's elder brother, who's mad because nobody killed a fatted calf for *him*.

Then there's another thing that fascinates me: in the Western church in the parable of the Good Samaritan, we see him as the Christ-figure; in the Eastern Orthodox Church, they see the man set upon by thieves as the Christ-figure, which I find much more challenging.

Thus, anybody who is hurt, anybody who is wounded—and that's most of us one way or another—is a Christ-figure. In St. Luke's Hospital in New York they insist that everybody, every patient who enters the hospital, is to be treated as Christ.

C: That's like Mother Teresa who sees Christ in all those poor—

M: If I weren't married and if I weren't a writer, I would either join Mother Teresa or the Little Brothers and Sisters of Jesus. However, God has given me something else to do, so I'll just admire them.

C: Speaking of what you do, Francis J. Molson, in *Children's Writers*, says this about your Newbery Award–winning *Wrinkle in Time*, "The Christian ethos is more implied than explicitly stated and is not preached. The novel is didactic but carries its moral/ethical weight gracefully." Do you feel that you conveyed "Christian ethos"?

M: Well—it was my rebuttal to German theologians. At one time we were very involved in the Congregational Church in our little village—we really knew Christian community. But I'm a writer, I was starved for the Sacraments, and I was in a very agnostic frame because I wanted to know with my mind. So my Congregational minister friends were giving me German theologians to read. I would read them and think, "I don't have to believe this—it's not for me." I finally decided there's one good use for German theologians—that's for insomnia. They'll put you to sleep.

C: Were you reading them in German?
M: No, but they're still the long, German sentences—never use two words if you can use twenty. I was trying to think about a God great enough to care about every atom and subatom and molecule in the galaxies. Then I discovered the great physicists. Einstein, who said that anyone who is not lost in awe—awed rapture, I think he uses—at the power of the mind behind the universe is about as good as a burned-out candle. Now that really got me soaring, too. Magnificent. What I didn't like about German theologians was that they answered my questions—my questions do not have answers. What is God like? We don't know what God is like. We see what He is like in Jesus, but it's not a finite answer. It's an analogy, which is all that God can give us, all we're capable of coping with. So I think it was with *Wrinkle* that I really first began to realize that my job was to listen; it wasn't *mine*.

C: Okay—but the fact is, some readers feel uneasy with your implications about Jesus. That is, they have some problems with it.
M: They do? What are the problems?

C: A specific point: In the story where Meg, Charles Wallace, and Calvin learn that they will be battling the Dark Thing, they find out from Mrs. Whatsit that Jesus is just one of the many fighters of the Dark Thing.
M: No—He is the first. You see, I was on my way, at that point, myself. I still hadn't come to full acceptance. I didn't want to turn myself off; I didn't want to eliminate all the others God used. In other words, we are all in incarnation; Jesus is number one.

C: The thing that they were most disturbed about, I think, is that they weren't hearing you say Jesus is unique.
M: Number one is always unique. We know that all things work together for good to them that love God, to them who are the called according to

His purpose, for whom He did foreknow He also did predestinate to be conformed to the image of His Son that He might be the first-born among many brethren.

C: Oh, so that's what you were talking about—the "First-Born among many brethren" . . . as one who comes from another branch of the church, do you find it stimulating to be in dialogue with a lot of evangelicals?
M: Yes, and fascinating. One of the gifts God has given me is to be articulate. Now, as you can see, I have biblical precedent for doing what I did. What has struck me as so amazing in both the Roman Catholic and evangelical groups is all the talk about the Bible—but how few of them have read it. I've always been a Bible reader; I love the stories. Another thing—they don't seem to remember that God *never* chose qualified people to do His work. He looked for the most unqualified—because if you're unqualified and know it—you know you didn't do it yourself.

C: Then what you're saying is that if parents or teachers who are concerned about what children will learn from *Wrinkle* would read their Bible more faithfully and then, say, take that passage about Jesus being number one and explain it to the child so he or she would understand it better—
M: I don't think the child is up to that passage, really, but . . . children will ask everything they're capable of understanding. We tend to answer more questions than they ask.

C: Talking about Jesus reminds me of something you said in *The Irrational Season*, that you'd had trouble with the Second Person of the Trinity more than either of the other two—
M: Any artist can understand the Holy Spirit. That's simple: Anything we do that's good we don't do ourselves. That's perfectly simple. I had a father I could honor and respect. I don't think of God in terms of sex, but I don't mind the father/daddy concept because it means something honorable and loving and concerned. But that the Power that created the galaxies could come into being as a little baby—could be exactly like us? The thing that really turned me off was saying that Jesus of Nazareth was exactly like us, except sinless. I said, "Very funny! He's not like us at all, then! That's absurd!"

C: Contradiction of terms, huh?
M: Yes, but then what really reconciled me to it was that tragic flaw of pride. The church falls for it all the time—the three temptations in the wilderness

were temptations of pride, and Jesus is the only one who never said, "I am God," and therefore He was. He always said, "Not me—my Father; not me, but my Father through me." We all try to play God—He didn't. So I'm condensing something I'd really like to spend an hour on—

C: I feel the same way—

M: Some of that may be in *Walking on Water*. And about *Wrinkle*, people should remember that I wrote that in 1960, and I have made some development since then. With artists we don't stay in one place—we move; we develop; we grow. I know a lot more, or I have been told a lot more—more has been revealed to me than when I was writing *Wrinkle*. If we don't move, we might as well dig a six-foot hole.

Madeleine L'Engle and Studs Terkel in Conversation

Studs Terkel / 1980

From Studs Terkel Radio Archive, Courtesy Chicago History Museum and WFMT Radio Network. Used by permission.

Studs Terkel: For a long time, publishers have regarded children who read books as a special species: someone you patronize, someone you write the little, ah, what—
Madeleine L'Engle: *Dick and Jane.*

Studs Terkel: *Dick and Jane* books for. Madeleine L'Engle has come along, and she's revolutionized writing for—she's been writing and has won the Newbery Award for *A Wrinkle in Time*, a beautiful book written for people who read—in that case, young people. It won, well, the equivalent of the Pulitzer Prize. And since then her writing has been recognized as writing for people who like to read books about subjects that are thoughtful. She's my guest today, with her most recent work, *A Ring of Endless Light*, and Farrar, Straus and Giroux are the publishers. Of course we'll talk about that whole attitude toward young people as readers and her approach to it, and of course this very beautiful book that I call a celebration of life. So in a moment, Madeleine L'Engle, my guest, and *A Ring of Endless Light.*
Madeleine L'Engle: [reading from Henry Vaughan's poem "The World"]

> I saw Eternity the other night,
> Like a great ring of pure and endless light, All calm, as it was bright;
> And round beneath it, Time, in hours, days, years, Driv'n by the spheres,
> Like a vast shadow mov'd; in which the world And all her train were hurl'd.

Studs Terkel: Madeleine L'Engle, the author of the book, reading one of the verses from seventeenth-century poet Henry Vaughan. Following a couple of verses from the song Shakespeare used in *Twelfth Night*. Alfred Deller just sang a part of it, "When that I was a tiny little boy." These two bits of art are related, aren't they, as far as you and your book are concerned?

Madeleine L'Engle: Yes, very definitely, because I think the artist and the great scientist have to retain the open imagination of the child. We're not free to shut our doors and our windows; we have to be able to let the boat rock a little bit.

Studs Terkel: As you're saying that, the heroine of your book, Vicky, is about . . . not quite sixteen, and she is, even for her age, naive. And yet the discovery she makes—I read, you know, last night and this morning, finished it, and I was very moved by it. What attracted me was the directness of its style, the simplicity. I thought it was a book for adults to read. You tell me eleven-, twelve-, and thirteen-year-old kids read this book. Now, we have to talk about this a bit.

Madeleine L'Engle: Well, first of all, I'm often asked why I write for children, and I never write for children. I write for myself. I'm a grown-up and a mother; I'm a grandmother. My ten-year-old granddaughter read this book in manuscript; she read it in galleys. She's now read it three times in the printed book, but I've already begun to get letters from college students, from people nearer my age. I don't believe that books should be slotted and pigeonholed and stuck into age levels. They're for people who like to read. If they're about the human predicament, if they're about what people are concerned with, then there isn't any age limit.

Studs Terkel: When did you first read, say, *Three Musketeers*? I remember when I first read *Three Musketeers*. Or Dickens? What was it—was it *David Copperfield*, or was it *Bleak House*, I forget, pretty—I think Dickens probably felt the same way.

Madeleine L'Engle: Yes, Dickens wrote for people. I read *David Copperfield* when I was eight or nine and Oscar Wilde's *The Canterville Ghost*, along with my regular fairy tales. I just went from my bookshelves to my parents' bookshelves.

Studs Terkel: What happened? When you start writing in this vein, the L'Engle vein, whatever that might be, the way you write—

Madeleine L'Engle: Disaster happened.

Studs Terkel: Oh, how?

Madeleine L'Engle: Well, I started writing regular novels. You have to say "regular novels" because when you say "adult novels" that means porno, so I started writing regular novels.

Studs Terkel: Hey, wait a minute. Let's stick with that. When we say "adult novels" today, or adult movies, that means porno.

Madeleine L'Engle: It means porno, which is terrible. So I started what I was—what I considered to be at that time, novels for grown-ups, I mean, books. When I wrote *A Wrinkle in Time*, I thought I was making a giant step in my ability to write, that I was learning to listen to the work, to go where it wanted me to go. I wasn't thinking about writing for any age level. I was writing about some things that fascinated me, and I thought it was a terrific book. I was not prepared for two years of rejection slips.

Studs Terkel: By the way, I thought it was a terrific book, too; in fact, you were a guest on this program—

Madeleine L'Engle: I was.

Studs Terkel: You point out to me, and I'm a little stunned, thirteen years ago, it was?

Madeleine L'Engle: 1963, yes.

Studs Terkel: Seventeen years ago.

Madeleine L'Engle: Seventeen years ago.

Studs Terkel: Wow.

Madeleine L'Engle. Wow.

Studs Terkel: What happened? Here was *A Wrinkle in Time*, a beautiful book for people who read, some of whom happen to be young. And what happened with the publishers?

Madeleine L'Engle: Well, the publishers—first of all, it's a rather difficult book for many grown-ups. So these tired old editors would read it and couldn't understand it, and therefore they would assume that children could not understand it. So two years—you name a publisher; they rejected it. I had to dig out the rejection slips to prove to some publishers that they really did reject it, after the fact. When my present publishers, Farrar, Straus and Giroux, finally took it, they assumed it couldn't be read below high school level. They said, "Dear, now we do not expect this book to sell well. We're doing it as a sort of self-indulgence. We don't want you to be unhappy when it doesn't sell." So when it took off like a skyrocket, they were totally bouleversé by it. My kids were seven, ten, and twelve while I was writing it. I was reading it to them at night, at bedtime, and they'd say, "Oh, Mother, go back to the typewriter." So I knew kids could understand it. But there's this incredible misconception on the part of grown-ups—

Studs Terkel: But the editors couldn't understand it, and they were certain that little children, or children, could not.
Madeleine L'Engle: Yes.

Studs Terkel: It's this patronizing idea again—
Madeleine L'Engle: The assumption that kids cannot understand concepts. Now a kid doesn't want a naked concept, but if you have a good story, a good storyline—and storyline was good enough for Shakespeare; I don't mind trying to tell a good story—then underneath it you can say anything you want. This is based on Planck's quantum theory, on Einstein's theories of relativity, on post-Newtonian physics, and therefore it baffles some adults.

Studs Terkel: This is Madeleine L'Engle, the author of *A Ring of Endless Light*, which is part of a trilogy, and so we begin: it deals with Newtonian physics, it deals with theology, and it deals with science. It deals with pseudoscience as well, for one of the characters, Zachary. It begins at a funeral of a guy who was killed, perhaps unnecessarily; he died trying to save some idiot boy who was one of these derring-do, devil-may-care kids, who seem to be bored with life. And Vicky, who is the central figure, is about . . . not quite sixteen. It begins with a funeral, doesn't it?
Madeleine L'Engle: It begins with a funeral because it's a book about life, and we can't live until we've faced death. We just don't know how to go about our living, and so Vicky has to learn to live. She's naive for her years; she's intellectually sophisticated. As far as living in the world is concerned, she doesn't really know anything, and she's asking all those cosmic questions, the whys: Why am I here? What's it about? Why did this guy die?

Studs Terkel: You know, it's so funny, just at the moment—you don't mind if we freely associate—because in a sense your book deals with that too. Lillian Smith, remember Lillian Smith?
Madeleine L'Engle: Oh, yes.

Studs Terkel: Wrote *Strange Fruit* and *Killers of the Dream*, marvelous woman of the South. She remembered asking about why she could no longer play with her little black friend. This is a number of years ago. She's from Georgia, and her mother tried to explain to her. Very gently, she says, "You know, when you're old enough you will understand." And the question, it went gently unanswered. And [Ms. Smith?] began, "I was rather a funny little girl, asking, 'Why? Why are you my moth—? Why?'" Asking all these questions—and this is Vicky, too, isn't it?

Madeleine L'Engle: Yes. Only, fortunately, Vicky's mother doesn't say when you're old enough you'll understand because first of all, we never will understand. We just need to go on asking more questions. The point is to find the right questions to ask and not be limited by finite, rigid, tight little answers.

Studs Terkel: It's a certain moment in Vicky's life where death surrounds her; this friend of the family is dead. Her grandfather, whom she was—this minister, a rather enlightened guy, is dying, and so she's surrounded by this. Something's popping; that doesn't terrify her, but she wonders what it's about. And that's how the book begins.

Madeleine L'Engle: And also with her meeting three young men.

Studs Terkel: And there're three young men.

Madeleine L'Engle: Vicky, who has always been unhappy because she hasn't dated; the kids call her up about homework but not to ask for dates. Suddenly, there are three radically different young men, all interested in her, so it's a summer full of growth and surprises. Then I think, of course, one of the most important things is she gets involved in a serious experiment in nonverbal communication with dolphins.

Studs Terkel: Yes, the three young men—we'll come to the dolphins in [a moment]. One is—this is the smooth guy, Zachary. He's the easy—

Madeleine L'Engle: The catnippy guy.

Studs Terkel: He's the what?

Madeleine L'Engle: The catnippy guy. As Vicky's little sister Suzy says, "Zachary is catnip for somebody like you. You can't resist him."

Studs Terkel: Yes, he's smooth and very attractive, but he's kind of a—he's the one who says he tried to kill himself, bored with life. He's the one who was in a sense responsible for the death of this man, this funeral, that's being attended at the beginning. Suppose I read Zachary, and you're Vicky in this thing, just to give you an idea of a kind of—he's one of the three guys. Why don't you set the scene?

Madeleine L'Engle: They're horseback riding, and Vicky says, "We started off side by side, on a wide, woodsy bridle path. The trees were their fresh, early-summer green without the dusty look they get later on. I sniffed the lovely island smell of green growing things and silvery salty breeze. Neither of us spoke, and as the silence stretched out, and it was not a peaceful or companionable silence, I knew that I could not be the one to break it. Zachary hadn't answered my question, and until I knew the answer, nothing could work between us. Finally, he spoke. He turned toward me and his face was white and his eyes dark, and I hadn't noticed before how bruised-looking the shadows under them were. The reflection of the leaves gave a greenish pallor to him. 'I'm not sure why I needed to see you, Vicky. I'm not good for you.'"

Studs Terkel: Oh, that's him.
Madeleine L'Engle: That's you. Sorry.

Studs Terkel: And you say, "I looked at him and waited." And I'm Zachary: "I tried to kill myself."
Madeleine L'Engle: "Again the silence stretched out like a rubber band. 'Why?'"

Studs Terkel: "I'm bored with life."
Madeleine L'Engle: "Bored?"

Studs Terkel: "Bored. So bored it hurts like a toothache."
Madeleine L'Engle: "Why?"

Studs Terkel: "It's a lousy world."
Madeleine L'Engle: "Would being dead be less lousy?"

Studs Terkel: "Sure. It would be nothing. A nice quiet *nada, nada, nada*."
Madeleine L'Engle: "So how come you're still here?"

Studs Terkel: "Well, some Boy Scout Coast Guard foiled me by rescuing me." And then it comes out it was this guy. We get this guy, and later on he's talking about how the world really is lousy. He says, "What's the point?"

And so we get this pseudophilosopher, this bored kid, whom she finds physically very attractive. Now, there's another kid, Leo, whose father is the one who died, and Leo is sort of the ungainly, awkward one.

Madeleine L'Engle: Leo's the guy that Vicky always thought was a slob, and he turns out to be not as much of a slob as she thought. So she's again, she's—Everything's turned upside down. Leo and she cry together. That's a terribly intimate thing for two people to do, and she's not ready to be that intimate with Leo.

Studs Terkel: And then we come to Adam.

Madeleine L'Engle: Adam is a young scientist. He's a marine biologist, and his project is to work with wild dolphins and to work on nonverbal communication. I'm convinced that when we do communicate with dolphins, that's how it's going to be done because not only is our vocal equipment so totally different, but our way of thinking is different. We think differently from dolphins because we have hands, because we pick things up and look at them. Our whole way of conceptualizing the universe has got to be totally different, so we can't do it on a verbal level.

Studs Terkel: So Adam works with—he's working on some marine biology, and Vicky comes along to work with him. He makes a discovery about her, and she about herself and about dolphins and humans. When you said hands—and somewhere in this book you've got a marvelous sequence about how humans have hands. I think Vicky's grandfather is explaining it to her, isn't he?—about how the hands can create such beautiful things. And the dolphins don't have these hands. But hands also carry the gun and the knife, and drop a bomb.

Madeleine L'Engle: Yes, they can play Bach fugues, and they can destroy. They're a blessing, and they're a bane. They're a curse, and they're marvelous too. We have them and—you see, the dolphin was a land animal. The dolphin's flipper is not a flipper. It's got the bone structure of an arm and a hand, so it was a land animal that chose somewhere in the remote past to return to the sea. One thing that has always fascinated me is, when I'm working on a book, something terribly important that I need and don't have is simply handed to me on a silver platter. I knew I couldn't describe what a dolphin feels like, until I had felt a dolphin. Now, I live in New York City, and there are not that many dolphins around the island of Manhattan [laughter]. I just got to that point where I couldn't avoid that scene any more, where Vicky first goes out and meets Basil the dolphin. There I was flying out to

San Diego to teach at a writer's conference. I went to Sea World, and I spent the day playing with dolphins.

Studs Terkel: Where was this; was this an open zoo?
Madeleine L'Engle: Yes.

Studs Terkel: You say world?
Madeleine L'Engle: Sea World, yes, it's one of the—

Studs Terkel: Oh, Sea World, Sea World, yes.
Madeleine L'Engle: One of the conference people got the idea that it would be nice for me to get in a little deeper, so they called the Sea World people to see if I could have some pictures taken with dolphins and were met with hostile indifference. Finally, this bored voice said, "Well, what has she written?" The first one of them said, "Well, *A Wrinkle in Time . . .*" "*A Wrinkle in Time* is my favorite book! Bring her right out!" So the doors were opened, and I played with dolphins. Vicky's description of what Basil feels like is exactly what dolphins feel like.

Studs Terkel: So, you played with dolphins. You said you played with dolphins; you didn't say you worked with dolphins. You played with dolphins.
Madeleine L'Engle: Well, I think work ought to be play and play ought to be work, and it's a sad thing we've made it drudgery, isn't it? My work is my play. It's hard, hard work, but it's my play. And I played with dolphins.

Studs Terkel: But in putting yourself into the mind of Vicky—this intellectual girl—she's talking about family, Bach music and folksongs, and Shakespeare; the grandfather's an enlightened minister; the father, a doctor; and mother plays piano [or] guitar. At the same time, she's very naive about relationships to people outside, particularly the males of the species, but here she is open. And the dolphins are open.
Madeleine L'Engle: It just occurred to me right now—it never had before—that Vicky is a poet, and artists tend to be very slow developers. Maybe I'm saying that to comfort myself. I was an extremely slow developer, and I remained a child, a naive child, long beyond the permissible chronological level. I think that happens with artists. Now, it's a known fact that when a wild dolphin responds to a human being they respond more quickly to children than to grown-ups, and this dolphin responds to Vicky immediately.

Studs Terkel: Is that so?

Madeleine L'Engle: Yes. Oh, I had a wonderful time doing research. That was work; that wasn't play. I did a lot of research.

Studs Terkel: Where'd you do the research?

Madeleine L'Engle: Oh, I read and read and read and read and read. Before I had done most of the reading, I had played with dolphins. I was leaning over the public petting pen one day. Most of the kids come, they pat the dolphin on the head, and they go away. I was just staying there and thinking at the dolphins, "Come on; tell me where you want me to scratch you." And one dolphin came over and said, "Scratch my chest."

Studs Terkel: You knew he said that?

Madeleine L'Engle: Yes, and I scratched his chest. This went on: I'd try to stop; he'd come back and say, "Hah, come on; scratch my chest." And some of the kids said, "Hey, that dolphin really likes that lady!" You do establish an incredible rapport, a real relationship.

Studs Terkel: So there is that communication without words.

Madeleine L'Engle: Yes.

Studs Terkel: It's something, not written communication. It is that—what is it? What's the sound, the supersonic . . . what's the sound, the dolphin—

Madeleine L'Engle: Most of the dolphin sounds are supersonic. When they talk with themselves, it's above the level we can hear—sort of at the level where a lot of birds sing—but it's beyond that. I've been married to an actor for thirty-four years, which is kind of, in our professions, unusual. We'll sit down to dinner, with the candles lit, and we will eat dinner. We won't speak, but we are communicating. We don't need—we've got to the point of knowing each other so well that we don't need to say it aloud, and we each know what the other one is thinking.

Studs Terkel: You are dolphin-like.

Madeleine L'Engle: Well, yes [laughter].

Studs Terkel: There's something, a feel of some sort, I suppose. Also there's an intelligence at work, isn't it? The dolphin's brain is larger than the human brain, isn't it?

Madeleine L'Engle: It's larger than the human brain, and it's just as complicated. Now, in work on some other books, I've done quite a lot of research into ESP. It's a fascinating thing that you have it more with some people than you have it with others. It isn't anything that's just as along a level. For instance, my husband and my mother had it incredibly with each other—far more than I did with either of them. Here they are, totally unrelated, yet each one could go into his room and pick up where the other one was without any trouble. So it's a gift with variabilities, just like musical variabilities.

Studs Terkel: You're not putting down extrasensory perception?
Madeleine L'Engle: I'm putting up extrasensory perception.

Studs Terkel: Yes, I know. You think there is an aspect—
Madeleine L'Engle: But I don't believe in dabbling in it, in playing with it.

Studs Terkel: No, no.
Madeleine L'Engle: It's very dangerous. It can, like any kind of power—it is power, and power can destroy if you are careless with it.

Studs Terkel: At the same time, you show here in all your books, of course, a tremendous respect for science, but it's a certain kind of scientist. We're going to come to that now, aren't we?
Madeleine L'Engle: Yes. The scientist who is the artist. The scientist, like Einstein, who grasped something and then has to go back and work out the mathematical formula to prove it. If you remember, Einstein wasn't that good a mathematician. He made a mistake in his formula proving his first field theory. He didn't really like it when it was pointed out to him that one of his equations was wrong, but he finally had to accept that it was. The scientist who sees a vision—in the world of science, almost every great discovery has been made simultaneously in more than one place by people who don't know each other.

Studs Terkel: You realize you are echoing, or perhaps he was echoing you, Jay Bronowski. Bronowski was describing the scientist whom he respects, the true scientist. He says he is a poet. He is an artist. There is a leap of the imagination—
Madeleine L'Engle: Yes.

Studs Terkel: With the sciences, as much as there is with Bach, as much as there is with Picasso, as much as there is with Shakespeare. There's a leap of imagination. It's the technician, or somebody else, who goes one step at a time without too much imagination. The how-to guy.

Madeleine L'Engle: He's stuck with using his intellect alone.

Studs Terkel: Yes.

Madeleine L'Engle: The scientist uses intellect and intuition, and he knows that often ideas, I mean the great ideas, will come when we let down our guard. In the morning just as we're waking or walking with the dog, when we're not really thinking, suddenly, the subconscious mind will flip something up to the conscious mind. The conscious mind has to be good enough to grasp it, but that's how most of the great scientific discoveries have come, with this sudden flip up, this leap of imagination, and then they have to say, "Oh, yes!"

Studs Terkel: This is one of the threads in all your books, isn't it, in a way? One of the threads that children or young people get immediately, don't they?

Madeleine L'Engle: Yes, because they're not afraid of the new science. I find that higher math is so much easier than lower math. I find lower math extremely difficult, but higher math I find exciting because it deals with the nature of being itself. I love to read. I've read a marvelous book by the astrophysicist John Gribbin, an Englishman, called *White Holes*. White holes are the reverse of black holes. Some of that has come into Vicky's conversation with John, about the incredibly poetic names that the astrophysicists have.

There's a special kind of white small star, which is known as a degenerate white dwarf. Then there's another star with a helium-burning core, which is the red branch—red giant on a horizontal branch. How much more poetic could you get?

Studs Terkel: You know what's marvelous about what you do? You take a theme some would call highly complex, or highly, a misused word, "sophisticated," and you say it's for children. Because again we come to the poet, there's a child in the poet. Dylan Thomas spoke of the dead child and the poet.

Madeleine L'Engle: Yes.

Studs Terkel: There's a child in the poet, and that is a child in the best sense. The air of wonder in the scientist, too—the air of wonder, the air of discovery all the time, is what you're talking about, aren't you?

Madeleine L'Engle: Yes, that you don't lose that, and so many adults lose it. When I discover something that I think is really exciting, then I have learned to put it in a book that's going to be marketed for children because they will understand it is too difficult for the grown-ups.

Studs Terkel: Too difficult for the grown-ups?
Madeleine L'Engle: Yes.

Studs Terkel: One moment ago, I think, you pointed that out. The editors said, "We can't understand this . . ."
Madeleine L'Engle: Yes.

Studs Terkel: But the kids, they immediately . . . [laughing]
Madeleine L'Engle: The kids have no problem, whatsoever. First of all, they're interested in the story.

Studs Terkel: It's the story. Yes.
Madeleine L'Engle: And as long as the story carries them on. . . . I was in Denver, Colorado, this autumn with a group of children's writers, and one of them, a young published—they're all published writers—said, "When I was about ten, I read *A Wrinkle in Time*. I didn't understand it, but I knew what it was about."

Studs Terkel: That's funny.
Madeleine L'Engle: That's a marvelous way of saying it. The kids know what it's about.

Studs Terkel: They know what it's about because there's a story there. Madeleine L'Engle is my guest. "A ring of endless light" is the line from the seventeenth-century poet Henry Vaughan. How does that go again? You opened reading it.
Madeleine L'Engle:

> I saw Eternity the other night,
> Like a great ring of pure and endless light

Then another theme from another of Vaughan's poems, "There is in God some say a deep but dazzling darkness," and that's the other theme, that all of the things that happen to Vicky that summer, they're pretty dark things. It's hard for her to see the dazzle; the light is there. You can't live to be as old as I am without having gone through a lot of life, a lot of tragedy, a lot of darkness. And it's not always easy to see the dazzle, but it's important not to let it go out.

Studs Terkel: We're talking about both the duality, and, also of course, life and death, and mortality.
Madeleine L'Engle: Yes.

Studs Terkel: Intimations of mortality, and here you say, also, I would guess, intimations of immortality. Now, we come to something—we're going to pause right now—to the grandfather; the daughter; this guy, young guy Zach; Adam; throughout, the dolphins; throughout also, music; and the air of wonder of somebody growing up. It's called *A Ring of Endless Light*, Farrar, Straus and Giroux, the publishers. We'll resume in a moment after this message with Madeleine L'Engle.

Studs Terkel: So resuming, Madeleine L'Engle. It's L ap—used to be, I suppose originally, L apos—it is apostrophe!
Madeleine L'Engle: Yes.

Studs Terkel: So, Madeleine the angel!
Madeleine L'Engle: That's right!

Studs Terkel: We come to *A Ring of Endless Light*. We began with the funeral, the grandfather who is one of these theologians, this minister who is also interested in science. He loves science because he speaks of that as a kind of theology, too, doesn't he?
Madeleine L'Engle: He finds that the great scientists are the theologians of today, and they're the ones to whom he goes for theological insight. He's a wide open person, not a closed-in person.

Studs Terkel: In contrast, well, she's bringing up the subject of her friend, Zachary, who's from a rich family, and they're interested in cryonics. You know by the—we live in a certain time too of a great deal of pseudo-everything—pseudoscience and religion today, don't we?
Madeleine L'Engle: Lots of plastic.

Studs Terkel: Okay, so, cryonics. We've heard of that. Cry—
Madeleine L'Engle: Yes, it's real; it happens.

Studs Terkel: All right, what is cryonics?

Madeleine L'Engle: Cryonics is freezing, deep-freezing a body immediately after death—very, very expensive. It's done in California.

Studs Terkel: Are there people doing them?

Madeleine L'Engle: Oh yes, and they're put into incredibly secure vaults, on the assumption that in several hundred or so years, a more enlightened scientific age will be able to thaw them out and revive them. What disgusts Vicky about this—this is what Zachary has done, and his father has done with Zachary—

Studs Terkel: They're called "the Immortalists" [laughter].

Madeleine L'Engle: Yes, the Immortalists. Here they are, dead, frozen, deep-frozen like fish or green beans, and Vicky's friend was just buried in good solid rich island earth. It strikes her that is somehow more realistic than deep-freezing somebody.

Studs Terkel: Yes, and she tells her grandfather, and he says, "If that's immortality, I'll take vanilla." I'm paraphrasing, but there's one—perhaps his comment about—he believes in something called the resurrection, but in a poetic sense.

Madeleine L'Engle: Yes.

Studs Terkel: A different kind, he says, I believe, "a different kind of resurrection." Would you mind expanding on that?

Madeleine L'Engle: Well, Grandfather is very specific about not being specific, as I am specific in not being specific in this book.

Studs Terkel: Yes.

Madeleine L'Engle: I think it comes out most clearly when Vicky and Adam are talking at the beach, and she's very distressed. One of the dolphins has a baby which is born with a damaged heart, and it dies. Vicky is very upset about that, and she says to Adam she's afraid of nothingness; she's afraid of annihilation.

Instead of answering her, Adam says, "When are you most you?"

And she finally says, "Well, when I'm with Basil, the dolphin."

He says, "Are you thinking of you?"

She says, "No, I'm thinking of Basil."

And he says, "But you're really being you, aren't you? I think that's more what it's going to be like. When we're not thinking about ourselves, but we are really wholly ourselves. It's not going to be anything we can define right now."

And then Rob, her little brother, says to Vicky, "There's probably lots of other planets besides ours with life on them."

And she says, "Sure," because she realizes he's very serious.

He says, "Well suppose there's a planet where nobody has any eyes."

And she says, "Well, they'd probably compensate," and the little boy—

Studs Terkel: The dolphin has no hands.

Madeleine L'Engle: Right. And he says, "Well, if they didn't have any eyes, we couldn't describe a sunset to them, or a people, person's face, we couldn't describe what sight is, could we?"

"Well, no," not knowing what he's getting at.

And he says, "Well, maybe, when we die, then we're going to get something as important as sight, but just as we couldn't explain it to a planet where nobody has eyes, nobody could explain it to us here because we don't have it."

Studs Terkel: You know, it's funny you say that. You know Arthur C. Clarke's work, of course.

Madeleine L'Engle: Oh, yes.

Studs Terkel: Well, Arthur C. Clarke was saying he's convinced there is life on other planets, but they probably are—

Madeleine L'Engle: Oh, so am I.

Studs Terkel: Well, he said they are, probably in some cases, superior to us humans. He's sure on some planets there are species who do not make war on each other. This is a self-liquidating proposition, of course, utter lunacy, so there are some creatures who probably are superior to us.

Madeleine L'Engle: I don't have any doubt, and they're probably very different from us. We don't all—I mean, why should creation be identical? There may be planets where you have chlorophyll instead of blood or some form of creature which can live in a frozen world or a purely liquid world. Why should we be the only kind of thing?

Studs Terkel: We speak of people—we, of course, are a prime case— all these powerful countries are ethnocentric. That is, we're it. We are the center; we are it; we're solipsists. We're what the world is all about—we Americans or Russians or Chinese, certainly— we're what it's all about. The same kind of thing can apply to the human species. We're what it's all about on earth.

Madeleine L'Engle: We're the center of the universe.

Studs Terkel: Yes, we're not really, are we? [laughter]

Madeleine L'Engle: No, we're a minor star off the edge, off the far edge of an ordinary galaxy.

Studs Terkel: How many years ago was it, now, that Copernicus, and then Galileo, discovered it? And still, we haven't discovered it yet.

Madeleine L'Engle: What was great about Copernicus's discovery was you can prove mathematically that the Ptolomaic theory of the universe is true. It can be proven, but the equations are ugly. Copernicus didn't like ugly equations, so he set about finding something that was aesthetically pleasing. He comes up with the totally unexpected discovery that the earth is not the center of the universe.

Studs Terkel: See; it was aesthetics.

Madeleine L'Engle: He didn't like the ugly, yeah.

Studs Terkel: There was something aesthetically rotten about those Ptolomaic—

Madeleine L'Engle: Those ugly equations.

Studs Terkel: He was seeking beauty, then, wasn't he?

Madeleine L'Engle: Yes. I think I go along with Keats—truth and beauty can be equated with each other.

Studs Terkel: So we're talking . . . there's another time when Adam, who is the one who becomes closest to Vicky at the end—the guy—says, "When are you most? When you're writing poetry." We come to that again. "Where are you when you're writing a poem?"

She says "In the loft."

"I don't mean that, I mean, when you're writing a poem, when you're in the middle of it?"

"I'm not sure. I'm more in the poem than I am in me. I'm using my mind, really using it. I'm not directing the poem or telling it where to go; it's telling me."

And he says, "That's the way it is with science." And of course that's what Bronowski was saying, as you were saying.
Madeleine L'Engle: Yes.

Studs Terkel: That's the way it was with Einstein and Niels Bohr and Isaac Newton.
Madeleine L'Engle: Yes.

Studs Terkel: That's what we're talking about, isn't it?
Madeleine L'Engle: Yes, and the ability to let yourself go and get surprised.

Studs Terkel: Now, of course, this is all in this book we're talking about, and it was astonishing to me since, I suppose, I have this air of being a patron to younger people without realizing it. I'm astonished, and I shouldn't be, that people who happen to be twelve, thirteen, fourteen read this book, understand it, and are moved by it.
Madeleine L'Engle: There is nothing in it that—

Studs Terkel: But it's also a person of sixty-four can read it and like it, too.
Madeleine L'Engle: Oh, sure. Yes. Well, the characters range in age from Grandfather, who is eighty-odd, to Rob, who is, what, seven. I like to have a multi-chronological list of characters so that you're not stuck with any chronological slot.

Studs Terkel: As you're talking now, —again, we don't digress because it is all one road, really, but it has many avenues that go into it. You like all generations, and I'm thinking what we do today, the categorizing, you know, these suburbs—
Madeleine L'Engle: Yes.

Studs Terkel: Certain ones that have people of the same certain economic stratum, same color, of course, also same age. There is—
Madeleine L'Engle: Yes.

Studs Terkel: Many of my friends who are members of the Gray Panthers, the embattled older people, they say there's a great segregation going on, of age.
Madeleine L'Engle: We had in my family. We had four summers when we were four generations living together under one roof. Now, they were, in a sense, difficult summers, but they were marvelous. I wouldn't have given

them up for anything, but we did a lot of discussing about chronological segregation and about what we do to the old people. In a book called *The Summer of the Great-Grandmother*, also published by Farrar, Straus and Giroux, I have written my mother's ninetieth, and last summer, and how we kept her at home and how my kids and their friends took care of her, and then how in the end she died in her grandson's arms—a good death in this day and age.

Studs Terkel: On that subject, you speak of the grandfather here, who is dying, and it's a question of moving him to the hospital, or among people—
Madeleine L'Engle: Yes.

Studs Terkel: Whom he loves. His own family. We've come to question death with dignity, aren't we?
Madeleine L'Engle: Yes.

Studs Terkel: Or death with delight, perhaps that isn't the word, death among those close to you. We know in many societies, it's at home.
Madeleine L'Engle: Yes, I think—as far as I know just off the top of my head—we're the only society that has isolated death. That has pushed it off where it can't be seen, and I think that's a terrible thing. We need to be with people. We're not born alone; we have to be with people when we're born. Just as a dolphin is a communal people, and a dolphin has to have a midwife—can't deliver a baby alone—we can't do that either.

Studs Terkel: So there is the dolphin here, throughout, Basil and his other colleagues, dolphins.
Madeleine L'Engle: Yes.

Studs Terkel: "Colleagues," I said; that's interesting. Yes, colleagues are the undercurrent throughout: Vicky, her discovery of her growing up, her discovery of life and death, the intertwining of the two, that there is no one without the other, and the value of life, appreciated more because of the awareness of death. There's something—the grandfather would like somewhere . . . nothing fancy, kind of something, a pine . . . the cryonics—
Madeleine L'Engle: Yes.

Studs Terkel: The phony theory of Zachary and his people. "A pine box," he said, and I'm reminded, this is connected with you, with your—what's good about a book such as yours: it brings back, it evokes a number of other thoughts seemingly unrelated yet related. I knew a man; his name's Joe Matthews. He was sort of nonsectarian, I guess, Methodist but—Joe Matthews, I remember, his father died at the age of ninety-something, and there were about twelve kids. They were in different parts of the country, and they all came back to New England to bury the old man. They asked him, Joe, since he was a preacher, to say a few words over the old man's grave, and Joe goes to the funeral parlor that night—

Madeleine L'Engle: Yes.

Studs Terkel: And there he sees his father in a coffin. He says, "That's not my father." He says to the funeral director, it's called a funeral director not an undertaker, the euphemisms, you know.

Madeleine L'Engle: Yes.

Studs Terkel: He says, "I want a sponge and some hot water and some soap, right away."

"I beg your pardon?"

"I want it right away."

"What are you doing?"

He said, "I want to take all this junk off you've got here." He was rouged—

Madeleine L'Engle: Yes.

Studs Terkel: Looked like a baby doll, and he spent hours wiping all the stuff off his father, and then his face, the old man's face sank and the wrinkles appeared, and he said, "Now, that's my old man. Those wrinkles are part of him, and those wrinkles mean—we made those wrinkles; my eleven brothers and sisters and my mother, made those wrinkles. Those wrinkles mean we are alive in him. And so then I said a few words over the old man."

That is not unrelated to what you're talking about.

Madeleine L'Engle: Yes, I remember; at the funeral at the beginning, there's a phony carpet, a phony green grass over the earth, which you see in most cemeteries, and the grandfather says, "Take it away." So four of the coast guard men take it away. Then they hand him the vial of phony dirt, and he moves that away and picks up the real dirt because this is real. Dirt is real, and grass is real. Plastic is not real. I suppose one of the things that I care about in this book is an affirmation of reality, that which is really real, without which we can't love, we can't be, we can't live. We just become zombies.

Studs Terkel: Zombies. Plastic people.
Madeleine L'Engle: Plastic people.

Studs Terkel: But this is Vicky's discovery. What have been the reactions, so far, among—aside from critics who like this book very much, I mean—but young people reading your book?
Madeleine L'Engle: Well, the thing that has pleased me most has been, when they get through to the end of it, over and over again, they say, "But this is a book about life." Now this book is loaded with death, it's true, but this is a book about life. And they get it. One young man, twenty-four, said, "I've never seen so much light in a book." That's very, very important: they see the dazzle in the darkness, that dazzling darkness.

Studs Terkel: A ring of endless light.
Madeleine L'Engle: Yes.

Studs Terkel: Since we're talking about dolphins and the experiments, Adam is a young scientist—
Madeleine L'Engle: Yes.

Studs Terkel: Who becomes Vicky's closest friend, toward the end, whom she [unintelligible]. She's working with him in the water, among the dolphins and all, and something about the use of dolphins, how the military and others try to use dolphins. Perhaps we could talk a little about that, too, because you mentioned hands, that we have and dolphins don't have. Hands can be used for good and bad and so, of course, can experiments by the technicians.
Madeleine L'Engle: Dolphins want to please; they're like children. They want to make us happy, and they will do what we want them to do. There have been discussions of training dolphins to carry torpedoes in a kind of kamikaze act, to torpedo enemy submarines, which I think is one of the most horrible things I have ever heard of. Jeb Nutteley, the head scientist says, "Never." Now, for a dolphin to perhaps find a ship in distress, that's something else again.

Dolphins have incredibly sensitive sonar, far more sensitive than our scientific instruments. A story I would have liked to have used but couldn't work into the book: a woman who had a friend who was a sensitive took her to a dolphin pen, at a time when visitors were not there, to meet some of the dolphins. And the woman told her friend, "The dolphin says that his trainer has something growing inside, and he better see about it." Now, it was not strange really that the dolphin could sense a growth because the dolphin's sonar really will reach right through a body, but that he was able to tell the friend, to communicate nonverbally, that this was happening. The man did go to the hospital. He had a very large benign tumor in him which would have caused a great deal of trouble if not removed, and it was removed.

Studs Terkel: Well, the dolphin, then—
Madeleine L'Engle: The dolphin was able to communicate with this woman who was extremely sensitive what was wrong,

Studs Terkel: Yes.
Madeleine L'Engle: And she was able to explain it.

Studs Terkel: You know, the sequence here with the dolphins, when—it's not a Pollyanna book, either.
Madeleine L'Engle: No.

Studs Terkel: Nature can be rough, too. Suppose you read this sequence?
Madeleine L'Engle: Okay.

Studs Terkel: This is with Adam and with, I think—
Madeleine L'Engle: With Suzy, Vicky's little sister, who is extremely pretty, and that's Adam. You want to start with that?

Studs Terkel: Yes, because this deals with other aspects of nature.
Madeleine L'Engle: So you read Adam.

Studs Terkel: [Reading] "Yes sir, but this summer," oh, "This summer I've been asked if I could do a special project."
Madeleine L'Engle: "Suzy asks, 'Are the dolphins in pens?'"

Studs Terkel: "For a while. Jeb, that's Dr. Nutteley, my boss, never keeps them penned more than six months. Then he lets them back out to sea."
Madeleine L'Engle: "You mean so they won't be corrupted?"

Studs Terkel: "Well, this is Suzy, down on humanity," says her brother John.
Madeleine L'Engle: "If humanity can clobber a thousand innocent porpoises to death, you wonder I'm down on it?"

Studs Terkel: She's a tough little, very bright little thirteen-year-old.
Madeleine L'Engle: Yes.

Studs Terkel: Yes, and "I saw Adam wince." This is Vicky thinking, "And I knew he felt as terrible about the porpoises as Suzy did." And then John, her brother, says, "Nature isn't all that pure and noble."
Madeleine L'Engle: "Isn't it?"

Studs Terkel: "Nature is red in tooth and claw."
Madeleine L'Engle: "Who says?"

Studs Terkel: "Alfred, Lord Tennyson, and it's true."
Madeleine L'Engle: "That still doesn't excuse clubbing porpoises and being greedy about oil and wars and murder and pollution and everything people do."

Studs Terkel: By the way, you have a marvelous little endearing figure in Suzy, who's indignant as a child, and then righteous and very funny. And very bright.
Madeleine L'Engle: She ends up being a good orthopedic surgeon, by the way, later on.

Studs Terkel: She does—oh, in a forthcoming—
Madeleine L'Engle: Yes.

Studs Terkel: "Now Adam looked at her thoughtfully. 'There have been and still are some pretty good people, Suzy.'"
Madeleine L'Engle: "A few."

Studs Terkel: "It's those few who make it worthwhile. Like my boss this summer for instance. The marine biology station is loosely connected to the Coast Guard. But Jeb Nutteley isn't having anything to do with experiments which would manipulate dolphins or use them in ways that are contrary to their nature."
Madeleine L'Engle: "Like what?"

Studs Terkel: "And Adam paused, as though deciding what to say. 'Well, not by the Coast Guard but other agencies. There've been experiments in training dolphins to detect submarines, which maybe is all right. But there've also been experiments in training dolphins to carry a bomb to an enemy submarine, to blow it up like a kamikaze act.'"

Madeleine L'Engle: "Suzy let out a yelp of outrage."

Studs Terkel: "'It's vile,' Adam agreed. 'And Dr. Nutteley won't have anything to do with that kind of thing. Experiments in using dolphins to save a life is something else again. If a dolphin can lead us to a ship in distress, or a lifeboat with people in it who need to be rescued, that's okay.'" And, so of course, here we have the manner, don't we, in which something quite marvelous, can be used for something quite destructive.

Madeleine L'Engle: Yes, and we forget because we have turned technology. I'm all for technology but not when it's turned into technocracy. In the first book that Adam appears in, *The Arm of the Starfish*, which is also Farrar, Straus and Giroux, and Dell in paperback, he's working in regeneration with starfish. Now, did you know that in England, right now, that if a small child accidentally severs a finger, what they do is leave it alone, and it grows back. The younger the child, the quicker the regeneration. Here we've been stitching it off, if the finger has been lost, or trying to sew it back, but it will grow back in a small child.

Studs Terkel: A limb regeneration. I suppose the younger the child—

Madeleine L'Engle: The younger the child, the more quickly it grows back, and the older the child—it doesn't always happen. But here we have been ignoring the body's own ability to heal, to regenerate.

Studs Terkel: That's part of it. On the subject of starfish, you have a book—here's something here, too; there's something about the starfish, the power of science, and then also I started thinking, the power of science can also be used, misused. I was thinking of the possibilities of DNA experimentation.

Madeleine L'Engle: I'm frightened about that, yes.

Studs Terkel: You are, aren't you?

Madeleine L'Engle: Do you know that there was a discussion of DNA? Somebody was saying there was a woman who had had four children, all of whom had birth defects of one kind or another, and she was pregnant with the fifth. What do you think we should have done? The students all said the child should have been aborted. The teacher said, "Well, then, you would have aborted Beethoven." Beethoven's mother had had four children who were not—who had some kind of birth defect.

Studs Terkel: Yes, but, you know, the genetic—I know it's a dangerous thing to oppose it; at the same time, there are men like George Wall, who are terrified by it.

Madeleine L'Engle: I know a geneticist who is terrified by it.

Studs Terkel: So we come to that aspect, too, and we always—throughout, there is life and discovery, and Vicky herself discovering, as her friend Adam does, her rapport, she has a special rapport now with dolphins.

Madeleine L'Engle: Yes, she does have, as Adam says, a very special thing going with dolphins. I understand that so completely because they are marvelous creatures. I have a strong suspicion that if I had been able to carry the book and the experiments further that Vicky could have communicated with the dolphins from great distances, that they are not bound by time and space as we are.

Studs Terkel: There is still much to be done, isn't there?

Madeleine L'Engle: There is still much to be done. I just want to say I am not against technology. I am so grateful for all of those little children with defective hearts who, because of our marvelous heart surgery, have normal life spans. But I am against its misuse, its abuse.

Studs Terkel: Of course. By the way, something you speak of, of dolphins and bumblebees—the law of thermodynamics. What do you mean by that?

Madeleine L'Engle: Technically, the bumblebee defeats all the laws of aerodynamics. The bumblebee cannot fly! But it flies. The dolphin flies through the water, swims faster than the laws of hydronomics would admit, and yet it does it. We still do not know why a bumblebee is able to fly. It's a total mystery to science; they haven't figured it out yet. We know a little bit more about dolphins. They shed skin very, very rapidly, so they don't have the skin pressure against the water that we do when we're swimming. But that doesn't explain quite how they're able to go as quickly as they do.

Studs Terkel: Do all your books deal with this theme, touching upon science and life, in one way or another?

Madeleine L'Engle: Yes, because it's what fascinates me and I like to write about what I'm fascinated by, what I'm interested in, what I'm reading, what I'm talking about. I have a—one of my sons-in-law is a physicist who sends me science fiction to read. I have a lot of friends who are involved in medicine, and my daughter-in-law is a young doctor. She's in her first year of internship. One of my sons-in-law is a theologian, and we have a lot of fascinating dinner-table discussions.

Studs Terkel: And here you are, theology and science around the table.
Madeleine L'Engle: And it doesn't conflict.

Studs Terkel: There's you, doing these books that deal with theology and science for eleven-, twelve-, thirteen-year-olds—
Madeleine L'Engle: Having cooked the dinner first.

Studs Terkel: As a theme, we began talking—in fact your book begins with a funeral, and it ends with another death. Again, themes of guilt—oh, that subject, of course—I am responsible because of an [incident] one way or another. Vicky has a problem overcoming a sense of guilt that she has, and Adam and others explain and show her that it isn't that at all.
Madeleine L'Engle: It's really only Adam, who said you can't dump a load of guilt on somebody. You can't hindsight because we can always say, "Well, if this hadn't happened it would have been all right." We go around carrying loads of false guilt, and false guilt is a terrible destroyer. Real guilt, where you know what you've done, is never a problem. You can say, "I did it. I'm sorry." It's false guilt that Adam is trying to free Vicky from.

Studs Terkel: Returning to Zachary a minute, there is this very fascinating young guy—he's bored—whose family is into cryonics, who tries—who, by the way, is wholly irresponsible and does endanger other people's lives with his self-indulgence as an almost–plane crash there—and then her discovery, *her* discovery—she was drawn to him, of course, very much—that he's really not worth it. Her discovery that this guy is a pitiful guy.
Madeleine L'Engle: And then at the end, when she needs him, he walks out on her.

Studs Terkel: So, he who courts, so he says, death—
Madeleine L'Engle: Yes, he—

Studs Terkel: Runs away from life.
Madeleine L'Engle: Yes, you're right.

Studs Terkel: That's what it amounts to.
Madeleine L'Engle: He's terrified of life. He's had too much money all his life, he can buy his way out of almost anything, and he doesn't know how to

live. I think that by the end of the book, Vicky is growing up. She is learning how to live, I hope, with panache.

Studs Terkel: Yes, it's there. At the very end there was this discussion she had with this other guy that Man is basically no good. That's what Zachary is saying and towards the discovery that Man is a combination of everything. She wonders, "Is humanity worth it?" at the end, when she has this guilt because of a certain situation there. Discovery. [laughter]
Madeleine L'Engle: But if we can have Bach and Beethoven and Shakespeare and Einstein—

Studs Terkel: You know, as a friend of mine—perhaps before we end this, some thoughts of yours before we say goodbye for now, the book is *A Ring of Endless Light*. Madeleine L'Engle is my guest, and she's won all sorts of awards. By the way, I think a Pulitzer should be there, too, but she's won the Newbery Award and others, Farrar, Straus and Giroux the publishers. A friend of mine, Clifford Durr, once—the late Clifford Durr—was the Federal Communications Commission under Roosevelt, and then he quit because he wanted no part of any loyalty oaths or anything of that. Clifford Durr was describing something at the time of the Selma-Montgomery march. There was hope, and there was fear. He's a southerner for generations, and he says, "Man? I can't figure Man out." He says, "The Psalmists say about Man: And he created the stars and the heavens. And there's Keats and there's Beethoven, and yet, there's Auschwitz and Hiroshima and My Lai." He says, "Oh boy, there's Man. He's both of them, isn't he?" This is what you're talking about, too, in a way, aren't you?
Madeleine L'Engle: Yes, that there's both and also that we do have some choice in which direction we go. Are we going to tolerate the Auschwitzes, or are we not? Are we going to try to save more heart-defective babies? Are we going to try to feed the people who are starving, or are we going to be destroyers? We do have the choice of being creators or destroyers.

Studs Terkel: So, choice, that's what you're talking about.
Madeleine L'Engle: Yes.

Studs Terkel: There is a choice.
Madeleine L'Engle: And that's what makes us human.

Studs Terkel: Yes.
Madeleine L'Engle: We do have the ability to choose.

Studs Terkel: Madeleine, any other—before we end with a song, I think one—we opened with "When that I was and a tiny little boy"—
Madeleine L'Engle: Yes, I loved it.

Studs Terkel: We opened with that because in the book Vicky's mother is singing it. Because here, that song of Feste the clown, in a way, also says the same thing.
Madeleine L'Engle: One of my great roles in the theater was Sir Andrew Aguecheek in *Twelfth Night* in school. We used the Shakespearian music. I loved those songs. I sang them to my kids and my grandchildren.

Studs Terkel: Any thought comes to your mind now, before we say goodbye.
Madeleine L'Engle: I think it's a good book, and I hope a lot of people are going to read it.

Studs Terkel: [laughter] It is indeed. *A Ring of Endless Light*. Madeleine L'Engle is my guest, and Farrar, Straus and Giroux the publishers. It's available. Thank you very much.
Madeleine L'Engle: Thank you, Studs.

Interview with Author Madeleine L'Engle

Katie Pauley / 1983

From *Family Life Today*, May 1984, pp. 12–18.

Madeleine L'Engle's imaginative stories have taken thousands of readers—young and old—on fantastic journeys through time and space. Perhaps you and your children have traveled with L'Engle on some of her excursions from everyday places to soaring through the stars or even riding on a microscopic cell. If so, you've discovered that woven into Madeleine L'Engle's beautifully spun tales is the reality of God, the wonder of His universe. And always there is the challenge: choices to be made between good and evil. There's a C. S. Lewis quality about many of L'Engle's writings; a second level of meaning, a larger truth hidden within.

A few months ago I mentioned to the editors of *Family Life Today* that not many people are acquainted with Madeleine L'Engle the devout Christian, or with L'Engle the busy family person (wife, mother, and grandmother).

"Introduce her to us and our readers," they encouraged.

That is how it happened that Madeleine L'Engle and I sat talking together at Mundelein College in Chicago last fall. For a time we shared memories about years before when I was a freshman at Wheaton College and she spoke at the student body chapel. That day she talked about suffering and community . . . how her marriage worked on the willingness to win through the hard times . . . and the not-always easy commitment to the community called family.

Soon we were talking about her present views of family and marriage.

FLT: Before we talk about your writing, what do you enjoy most about being a wife, mother, and grandmother?
L'Engle: I love the whole bit. I love just the physical affection among people I'm bound to by blood. It's wonderful. Just last Monday we spent the day

with our fourteen-year-old granddaughter, Charlotte. The grandparenting relationship is marvelous because of the biological remove—the generational space—it's very helpful. My children told my mother things that they'd never tell me because they were protecting me. We tend to protect our parents but not our grandparents.

FLT: You and your husband have a strong, good marriage, and your love has stayed truly alive. Such a relationship doesn't just happen. What do you feel is the foundation of your good marriage?

L'Engle: I think it is very important that we were married in church and important that we made vows before God that we would stay together—in sickness and health, for richer or poorer; for good things, bad things. Simply making those promises in front of God makes a difference for us. It's the absolute opposite of the world today that says, "If it hurts, quit." We have been married thirty-eight years this January, and there have been bad times as well as good times. Nowadays, when people get to a bad time, they often quit instead of working through it and getting out on the other side.

We are both volatile, dominant people. We have arguments. Loud ones which are rather fun. But a good long-term marriage does not come free. You really do have to work at it. This is particularly true during the earlier years when you may grow at different rates. One spouse may spurt ahead of the other for a while, and the one has to wait for the other to catch up.

There were times we weren't sure we would be able to pay the rent or get clothes for the kids. It was not all easy. Often the promises that we made before God have been what sustained us and our marriage.

FLT: In your book *The Irrational Season* you say that love is participation, not possession. Would you explain what you mean?

L'Engle: A lot of people, when they get married, seem to think that they own each other. They want to possess, control, manipulate. Whereas, in participation we share in what the other one is experiencing. We don't try to control it. That's really a thought from Daniel Day Williams, a minister who taught at Union Theological Seminary. It has had a profound effect on me and my understanding of love and my own marriage.

FLT: What kind of advice would you give to a young person looking forward to marriage?

L'Engle: Before I married Hugh, a cousin of mine who is about old enough to be my mother, said to me, "Sex is about a third of marriage, a very important third, but only a part. You've got to be sure that you've got enough going in the other two-thirds of your life to make a good marriage."

I think that is very, very good advice. Sex is lovely, but you have to have companionship too. You have to like the same people. You cannot be in radical divergence politically and remain good friends. Friendship is a very important part of marriage.

You need to want to come home to your spouse at the end of the day, knowing you're going to sit down at the dinner table, light the candles and talk. So, you've got to have something to talk about.

FLT: How did you and your husband meet?
L'Engle: Hugh and I were both working in the theater. We met during the play *The Cherry Orchard*, and after a while we were married while we worked in *The Joyous Season*. Subsequently, I became pregnant. That is when I decided to leave the theater and go back to the typewriter.

FLT: Did you move out to the country at that time?
L'Engle: No, we didn't move to the country until about a half-dozen years later. We enjoyed our child and wanted more children, but Hugh felt it wasn't fair to bring more children into the world with both parents in precarious professions. It takes a writer a long time to make enough money to make a difference.

So Hugh took over a rundown general store in western Connecticut, and we built it up. After it was a success he became bored with it. By that time all three children could put on their own snowsuits, so we decided to go back to the city. Hugh is a good actor, and he's been steadily employed as an actor ever since.

FLT: Does being married to another creative person encourage your own creativity?
L'Engle: I'm sure it does—although our fields are very different. We both have lived lives where there is a good deal of precariousness. We don't have the kind of fixed income that comes with a nine-to-five job. It's taking it day by day and trusting, having faith that God will open the way.

FLT: Has that been difficult? Or has it strengthened your marriage?
L'Engle: Both. Coping with difficult times does develop understanding and strength.

FLT: Is that what you mean in *The Other Side of the Sun* when you say that on love's terrible other side the lion and the lamb abide?

L'Engle: Yes. You can't live as long as we have without having difficulties and tragedies. Now a tragedy will either make or break a relationship. You will either fall apart or grow closer. Somehow, we've managed or been given the grace to grow closer.

FLT: Speaking of difficult times, thank you for the touching story *The Summer of the Great-Grandmother* and the glimpse it gives of your family.
L'Engle: That summer—mother was ninety—was a time we all grew close. It was my kids who made it possible for my mother to die at home. She died in my son's arms.

FLT: Tell us a little about your family's life today.
L'Engle: We're back into multi-generational living in that our son and his wife are living in Crosswicks, our Connecticut farm house. She's started her medical practice in the village, and he is teaching at a nearby university. There we are, two generations living together again and enjoying it. We try to give each other lots of space, but dinner is a time when the whole family gets together. That has always been for me the important moment of the day, gathering around the dining table and having a meal together. When you're away from each other, going in different ways all the rest of the day, then getting together for dinner is very important.

Our eldest child, her husband, and our three grandchildren live in New York where we have to be a good bit of the time because of Hugh's work. Our younger daughter also has a job in New York, so we do all see each other often.

I was a very lonely only child without much of the normal family life. Perhaps that's why this being with family means so much to me.

FLT: Would you encourage people and their families to cultivate that kind of extended family relationship?
L'Engle: I think you have to want it. It could be very artificial. I don't think we cultivated it; it just happened. We always kept our doors open so that at Thanksgiving and Christmas we had a large extended family around the table. The family together is important to us.

FLT: Much of your writing deals with fantasy. As you've lived with your family, your children and grandchildren, how have you come to feel that fantasy affects children?
L'Engle: Oh, without fantasy we'd wither, shrivel, and die. One of the problems with the present-day world is we've been lured into thinking of fantasy as being false. Instead, it is a vehicle of theology, of truth, of seeking for God.

FLT: Are there any dangers to fantasy?

L'Engle: There is unhealthy fantasy as well as healthy fantasy. In your own daydreaming you can tell the difference between healthy daydreaming and unhealthy fantasy. Is it bringing you closer to God? Is it bringing you closer to people you love? Is it making you more open, less judgmental? Then it is healthy. Of course, where there is good, in comes Satan at a hop, skip, and a jump to try to muck it up, but that does not alter the original good.

FLT: Has your Christian faith changed in the last ten years? Have you gone through any major changes or gained any major insights?

L'Engle: I have learned that I cannot understand Christianity with my intellect alone—that it is not a cerebral faith. Because I am a writer, I think in terms of writing. For example, fiction is never general; it is always specific, particular. It is about particular people. Therefore, when God wants to reveal Himself to His creation, He has to do it in a particular way. In the early days, the idea that God would come as Jesus was called a scandal of particularity. I like that phrase. So I can understand God through this particular Jesus.

FLT: What particulars to live by do you glean from the Bible?

L'Engle: I am a daily reader of the Bible—both morning and evening, and I have been most of my life. It's a marvelous book about complex human beings, as we all are, somehow or other listening, learning to listen to God.

They don't have to be good people, either. Jacob was not very good, yet he saw God. Paul says, "God is no respecter of persons." That's one of the chief messages of scripture. Check out the people Jesus chose. They were never qualified people. I think that's because if you are qualified you think, "I did it. Me, myself, and I did it."

If you are unqualified you know you didn't do it. You know you did it only with your hand in God's.

And the Bible teaches love. You can have all the qualifications and moral precepts in the world and yet be a cold, unloving person. That's unchristian.

FLT: How did your story *A Wrinkle in Time* come to be?

L'Engle: Basically, it was because of where we lived—in a tiny village. Even the theology was limited. I wanted a bigger God. I was looking for a freer universe created by a loving God. So the book was a kind of theological enterprise.

Also, I had discovered the new post-Newtonian sciences: higher math, quantum mechanics, astrophysics. What they affirm is the absolute unity and total interdependence of all creation, and that struck me as being very close to God's kingdom.

FLT: Why did you write the book for children?
L'Engle: I didn't. I don't write for children, and I never will. But you have to market this kind of book for children because it is much too difficult for adults. Children haven't shut their doors and windows. They're not afraid of new ideas, and the new science is radically new. It has a great deal more to it than just splitting the atom. It's a completely new way of looking at what God did and does.

FLT: In a recent article concerning our writing, Emilie Griffin speaks of the "intensified reality of Jesus Christ" in your work and then comments, "It seems fair to call her a Christian writer. But L'Engle states firmly she doesn't write 'for Christians.'" Why is that?
L'Engle: As I understand scripture, we're supposed to spread the Good News, not keep it for a small in group. I feel if what I write is going to exclude those who aren't Christian, how am I going to be evangelizing?

FLT: Can stories evangelize? Can evangelizing stories be good stories, not propaganda?
L'Engle: Yes. I don't know how, but they can. I think if they are propaganda they are not good stories, but I do know there have been people who've turned to Christ because of my work. That's a very terrifying, humbling thing. A book can plant a seed of understanding that grows.

FLT: You write about the stars so often. The stars seem to be real friends to you.
L'Engle: They are. They're very important to me. I go out and look at that glory. I see pattern, and I see interdependence.

I worry when Christians isolate themselves from any other part of creation as though God created Christians and nothing else; nobody else really matters.

God created all, all of creation. All of the stars. The Psalmist says God calls all the stars by name. I find it very exciting to be even a tiny part of such a gorgeous, enormous, glorious pattern.

An Interview with Madeleine L'Engle

James S. Jacobs and Jay Fox / 1987

From *Literature and Belief* 7, the Center for the Study of Christian Values in Literature, Brigham Young University. Used by permission.

The following are responses to questions posed by James S. Jacobs and Jay Fox on February 25, 1987, at Brigham Young University.

James S. Jacobs and Jay Fox: What did you believe in as a child?
Madeleine L'Engle: I guess my belief as a child was very simple, and it was kept simple by the fact that because of my father's illness—he had been mustard gassed—I was never taken to Sunday school because my parents slept late. My father worked best in the afternoon and evening, so I didn't get what a lot of kids get—a lot of bad teaching. I went to the scriptures straight. I went to God directly. I was always very conscious of the presence of God in my life, and I did a great deal of reading of myth, fantasy, and fairytale. I read the scripture the way I read anything else: for story and insight. So as a child, I lived in a world where God was a loving creator with a plan for perfecting a very imperfect planet—at least our part of the universe is not perfect. I had a hierarchy of angels, archangels, cherubim, and seraphim.

JSJ and JF: Of your own arrangement or from your parents?
ML: From scripture mostly. I don't think any mother would believe that her baby could live to be two without a guardian angel. The notion of a guardian angel is a very necessary part of my belief. I've met so many people who have had to spend their adult lives unlearning bad teaching about a forensic God, a God who basically looks like Moses—Moses in a bad temper at that—and who is so unloving and punitive that basically Jesus Christ had to come to save us from God the Father. That's pretty bad theology, but it's what a lot of people get as children and seem stuck with all of their adult lives. I had a question yesterday from a girl who wanted me to talk about

judgment and punishment, and I said what I truly believe: that there is only one purpose for punishment, and that is to teach a lesson, that there is only one lesson to be taught and that is love. Otherwise, it is not punishment but retribution or revenge, and that is not God.

JSJ and JF: You said belief was simple as a child. Is it different today?
ML: Not terribly. I think it is still simple, but there is also a deep awareness that my faith involves an acceptance of paradox and contradiction.

JSJ and JF: Could you talk more about that?
ML: Can I tell a story? I went out to speak at a very evangelical college in Missouri. During the question-and-answer session, one young man got up and said, "Your books do seem to imply that you think of God as being forgiving." I said, "What an extraordinary statement!" Then he qualified his statement and said, "No, I think what I mean is that you seem to imply that ultimately God is going to forgive everyone." I heard myself say, "I don't think God is going to fail with creation. I don't worship a failing God. Do you want God to fail?" He said, "But there's got to be absolute justice." And I said, "You're maybe nineteen, twenty, or twenty-one; if you die tonight is that what you want, absolute justice? Don't you want the weensiest, teeniest bit of mercy? Me, I want lots of mercy. Don't you feel you need any mercy at all?" Well, he'd been saved and that had never occurred to him. So he began to quote scripture, and I said, "Look, I probably know scripture better than you do and what I'd like you to do is go back to Genesis 1, and read straight through to the end of John's Revelation with a big pad and jot down God's loving, mercy, tenderness, and forgiveness as opposed to the angry passages. See which comes out on top." There's no question, the loving, mercy, forgiveness, and forbearance are overwhelming—all through the Old Testament, too. The God of the Old Testament is not like Moses either. People complain about God, saying He is too quick to forgive. Whenever I meet anybody who is in a terribly unforgiving mood, I tell them to read Jonah. Jonah did not want God to forgive the Ninevites. Jonah wanted Nineveh nuked, and he was furious with God for being so forgiving. I think that the lack of forgiveness is basically in us. The one thing that really upset Jesus was coldness of heart, hardness of heart. He was much more tolerant of sins of love than sins of coldness.

JSJ and JF: Can you give me another example of paradox?
ML: I think I was setting the stage for what I believe. I believe there is a pattern that has to be perfected but that it is not a pattern that is already

finished; the design is not completed but is still being woven. It is like last summer when I saw my new grandson, tiny, perfect, complete, but not finished—anything but finished. I see creation like that tiny baby—complete, perfect, but not finished. Part of our job as human beings is to co-create with God in the perfecting of the plan. I feel very strongly about free will; we are not human if God has not given us free will. And yet there is the paradox of the fact that there are times when God appears to come into the story and do something about it, and other times when He doesn't. And we don't know why. There are times in my own life when I have had no miracle, and there are other times when I have had. I don't know why in one case God chooses to act and in other cases stays back. I assume it is something that I will know ultimately but not in this life.

JSJ and JF: How did you get this resolution that is clear and quiet now within you and that seems reassuring? Was it automatic for you?

ML: I think it was always there because it is there in scripture. I've been a great reader of scripture because it is a wonderful storybook. One of the most consoling things about scripture is that all of the people that God chooses, that God asks to do something, are people that are singularly unqualified. In a sense, not one of us is qualified, but it seems that God goes to great pains to choose the most unqualified. Would you choose a one-hundred-year-old man and a woman beyond menopause to start a nation? The disciples were not really very qualified, and they let Jesus down pretty badly and deserted Him. Gideon said, "But I come from the least family of all, and I'm the least of my family," yet Gideon was chosen to save the nation. Moses stuttered. Heaven knows that if Paul came up before a church calling committee he would never get chosen. So it's been very freeing to me in that I don't feel I have to be qualified. I have to try. I have to do my best. I have to do my homework, but I don't have to be qualified. And I don't have to be perfect.

JSJ and JF: Have you ever been dissatisfied with the Bible?

ML: I have been very dissatisfied with teachings about the Bible and with teachings about Jesus. I think we have tried to do what Peter did at the Mount of Transfiguration. He wanted to put boxes around Jesus, Moses, and Elijah and make them safe and comprehensible. A lot of dogma has left me very cold in my struggle to understand the incarnation. I was doing a lot of reading and was told that Jesus Christ is exactly like us only sinless. Well, if He's sinless, He's not exactly like us, and that doesn't make any sense at all.

Actually, the best theology of incarnation came from a small child who said, "Jesus is God's show and tell." I think that is marvelous theology. That made a lot of sense to me. Jesus did keep saying that if you don't understand like a little child, you can't come into heaven. He wasn't saying don't grow up. He was saying grow up but keep the simple, open faith that you had as a child. I had a letter from a twelve-year-old asking how she could stay a child forever and never grow up. I wrote back and said, "I don't think you can, and it wouldn't be a good idea if you could. But what you can do, and what I hope you will do, is to stay a child forever and grow up." That's what I think we're all supposed to do.

JSJ and JF: Why don't you like to be called religious?
ML: "Religious" often means fanatic, narrow-minded, hard of heart, cold of heart, intolerant of everyone else—wanting everybody else to be in hell.

JSJ and JF: Then how do you describe yourself?
ML: I'm a searcher in love. I love God. I trust I'm loved, and therefore I have to take that love and try to spread it.

JSJ and JF: So it's hard for you to really put a title on yourself?
ML: Sometimes. I was asked to join a group of Christian writers, and I said, "I'm not a Christian writer. I'm a writer who's a Christian." That's a very different thing. If I understand the Gospels, we're supposed to spread the good news and not keep it for an in-group who's already there. If I were a Christian writer, I would lose the very audience I most need to reach.

JSJ and JF: How did the group respond to that?
ML: It was a group of highly intelligent, very interesting people. Richard Foster, the Quaker writer who wrote *Celebration of Discipline*, and Walt Wangerin, who wrote *The Book of the Dun Cow*, were part of the group. These were people who were open and willing to hear. The question was, "Should we form a Christian writer's group?" I said, "No, the minute you get organized then powerplays can start. It's wonderful to get together to share and talk. I'm currently the president of the Author's Guild of America. Do you all belong?" They did, so we decided not to become a formal group but to get together once a year just to share.

JSJ and JF: Would you say something about why you write? There are other authors who could describe themselves as searchers. Your searching is slightly different; at least it feels different to an examiner. There is a side to your writing that isn't present in someone who is simply exploring.

ML: It's theological searching; I will have to admit that—theological rather than religious because theologians are looking for a word about God. That's what theology means. I'm constantly searching to understand what it's all about. The questions that the adolescents all ask, and maybe we should never stop asking, are "Who am I? Why am I here? Is there a purpose? Is there a meaning? Does anybody care? What is life about?" Those are the nice big questions that we all keep wanting to ask, but when people feel grown up they think they shouldn't ask those questions anymore. I think we should, and I do ask them in my books. One reason that I make many of my protagonists young adolescents is that is the age at which the questions are most openly being asked.

JSJ and JF: Have you ever received any critical comment because of the theological underpinnings in your books?

ML: Only from the extreme evangelical right.

JSJ and JF: Not from the left?

ML: No, the leftists don't bother.

JSJ and JF: They cross you off?

ML: If you're theological, they just don't bother with you, while the right want you to do it their way, which is rather cold-blooded. They would wipe out all of you guys [Mormons] and all the Roman Catholics and most of the world. They're reading books for key words. They're not reading for content—and they're terrified, absolutely terrified. They're terrified of what they call the "new-agers" who seem to be rather starry-eyed. If their faith were really as strong as they say it is, why are they so afraid? Why are they reading books looking for things to put down instead of reading books looking for things to enlarge themselves and give them more hope, more courage? I think they're coming out of fear.

JSJ and JF: How do they respond to that?

ML: They don't give you a chance, really. Actually, there was a pair of parents in a school in the South who wanted *A Wrinkle in Time* taken from the shelves and burned because it deals with witches, crystal balls, demons, and the power of the mind. The principal of the school refused to have the book removed. There were editorials written about why I was such a terrible person, and I actually got a phone call from a reporter. So I said, "I don't know where they got the demons from, and I don't understand what they mean by 'the power of the mind.'" The reporter said, "Well, Meg does think powerful, loving thoughts." I replied, "Is there something wrong with powerful, loving thoughts?" She said, "I don't think so, but I'm an Episcopalian." I still don't know what they mean by the power of the mind. What I think they mean is man-centeredness, the anthropic principle without God.

JSJ and JF: How do you feel about the state of affairs in contemporary literature? Do you worry about it at all? Is it a cause for concern?

ML: I think it's a cause for concern. The literary establishment has always tended to denigrate work which is accessible and hopeful and to like stuff which is obfuscating and cynical. That's been true for as far as I know, even back to the fifteenth century. Shakespeare was not considered very important in his own day. He was far too easily understood. He was too popular and too hopeful—even in such plays as *The Winter's Tale* and *King Lear.* In the year that one of Thoreau's books, one of Hawthorne's books, and one of Emerson's books came out, none of them sold. I think that the state of literature is perhaps exaggeratedly the way it has always been. I don't like reading books about discontented women who think of things to be discontented about which they don't really need. I think that they are inventing problems for themselves. I don't like to read books about antiheroes. I don't want to be left depressed and cynical at the end of a book. I want to be opened, enlarged, given hope and courage, so I don't read a lot of contemporary literature unless it's been around for a while.

There are a few small books which are gems, such as *I Heard the Owl Call My Name* and *To Kill A Mockingbird.* A book which made a big splash in England and made no splash here at all is *Incognito* by Petru Dumitriu, which is a Dostoyevskian book in scope. It is called a post-Christian book, but to me it is a very Christian book. Dumitriu, like his protagonist, was a Romanian. Romania fought first with the Nazis and then with the communists and he had been through all of the ideologies and was trying to get rid of all the incrustation and come out with something clean and new. That is one of the great books of this century. I like Robertson Davies' *Deptford Trilogy (Fifth Business, The Manticore,* and *World of Wonders),* because he too has a Dostoyevskian sense of compassion for the human being, and even his most despicable characters you pity. He doesn't just wipe them out. He gives you a kind of understanding. But I am way behind on a lot of contemporary literature.

JSJ and JF: You mentioned that you didn't want to read books about discontented women. What's your feeling on feminist criticism and this movement?

ML: I have just been asked by *Ms.* magazine to write an article on feminine spirituality in the year 2002. This is an assignment I couldn't resist. I think that a lot of the feminist movement has been in the wrong direction: it's been women wanting to be men. My feminism is wanting to be more fully woman, more fully female. I think that women throughout the centuries have been allowed to remain in touch with the intuitive, with the nurturing, with the numinous, and that society has forced most men to limit themselves to the rational and provable. Rather than being so brutal about men, women should be very tender and very gentle with them and help them back to an understanding of their fuller selves that they have not been allowed to have.

My feminism would be a desire to make human, to make whole. Your president Jeffrey Holland used the example of the root word of *hale* as in "hale and hearty" being the root word for *heal, whole, health,* and *holy.* If you're healed, you're healthy; and if you're healthy, you're whole; and if you are whole, you are holy. And that's all that being holy means.

We live in a very fragmented, broken society, and one of my first intuitive efforts to become whole and holy was when I was in an English boarding school where we were numbered. I was number 97. At that time my passion for being known by name began. We were not allowed any privacy at all. Privacy was suspect. We were allowed no time for daydreaming. We were totally scheduled from when the morning rising bell rang until the turn-out-the-lights bell rang at night.

In the spring, we were given garden plots to cultivate and were allowed to bring the produce of our gardens in for tea. Therefore, most of the kids planted lettuce, tomatoes, radishes, cucumbers, watercress, and things like that. This was in the early thirties when it was possible for a twelve-year-old to be naive in an area that no twelve-year-old is naive in today. My garden partner and I planted poppies; that's all we planted, nothing but poppies. Since our illegal reading included *Bulldog Drummond* and *Fu Manchu,* we learned that opium comes from poppies, and opium gives you beautiful dreams. So we had poppy-flower sandwiches and poppy-leaf sandwiches and poppy-seed sandwiches, and we went to bed at night with dream books and flashlights under our pillows. We learned very quickly that we didn't need our poppy sandwiches for our dreams.

What we were doing with the dream books was rebelling, intuitively rather than consciously, against the limited world of provable fact and moral virtue that is in the realm of rational proof in which the English schoolchild was being forced to live. We were being taught basically that man was perfectible by his own effort—plagiarism taken to the extreme—that all that was needed for a perfect planet was for us to be morally virtuous, good, obedient, and unemotional, to never cry, to do it ourselves, and to never ask for help— all of those good Anglican virtues. Everything was going to be fine.

Well, everything was anything but fine. Hitler was already in Germany. In England during the holidays, I saw the great arms of the antiaircraft lights sweeping the sky as Britain prepared for war. All of this wasn't working, so what we were doing with our dream book was trying to reconcile intellect and intuition. I think that's what great art does. It is the reconciliation of the broken parts into a whole again. That's the response that I feel when I listen to great music or see a play of Shakespeare's or read a great book or see a great painting. It's a feeling that I am being healed and made more whole. A lot of contemporary literature doesn't do that for me.

JSJ and JF: Is there a threshold that you wouldn't cross over in putting something violent or sexually explicit in your writing? Are you a self-censor on that?
ML: I think we are all self-censors. I once bought a book called *Lolita* for a friend because I thought it was about a dancer. I read it and decided I wouldn't give it to her. I don't see any point in reading stuff that is pornographic, but there is a great deal of difference between genuine, healthy eroticism and pornography. I am afraid that a lot of contemporary literature is on the wrong side. Shakespeare, for instance, is bawdy but never dirty— and there is a lot of difference between bawd and dirt. I don't mind good bawd. It's healthy and a good thing to be rejoiced in and never to be used as an object. Eroticism deals with the human being as a subject, but in pornography the human being is an object to be used and defiled. I would not knowingly choose to read a pornographic book.

JSJ and JF: How would you decide where that line is between healthy, erotic literature and pornography?
ML: It's largely intuitive. One easy way of making a decision is to remember that there's much too much published for anybody to be able to read all of it. There are certain writers I will always read and certain writers I just don't see the point in reading much more of than one book—although with modern music, I will listen to a piece ten times before I decide I don't like it. After I have heard it ten times, sometimes I really do like it; sometimes I

don't. In literature, I don't want to read about gratuitous violence. One time I was speaking in Ithaca, home of Cornell University, and in the question-and-answer period someone said to me, "In most books of fantasy and science fiction, the hero or the heroine ultimately turns to the fist, the sword, the bow and arrow, or the gun, and you don't. Is this deliberate?" And I said, "Well it hasn't been up till now, but it will be."

JSJ and JF: Do you visit elementary schools? Do you work with children at all?

ML: I go occasionally into elementary schools but not below fourth grade because below fourth grade I don't get read.

JSJ and JF: Do you have anything to say about the successful separation of church and state? You commented that you believe strongly in free will. A number of other people say they believe strongly in free will, to the point that they believe children are not to be confused by someone's particular world view or ideology.

ML: I think that my world view is going to come across whether I am overt about it or not.

JSJ and JF: Even if you were a teacher today?

ML: I think a child knows if the teacher is an atheist or if the teacher is a believer. Whether the topic ever comes up or not, the child is going to know. Emerson said that what you are speaks so loudly that I cannot hear what you say. I think that is true. Children are taught by teachers, and teachers see children rather than subjects. Even if Christmas and God are never brought up, the child is going to know the teacher's world view—you can't hide it. I am happier when I am allowed to be overt about it, but it's going to come across anyhow.

JSJ and JF: What if you were in a situation where you were forbidden to be overt?

ML: When I go to a school, I'm not there as a teacher. I am there as a visitor. Therefore, I have freedom that the teachers don't have, and if a child asks me a religious question I will answer it.

JSJ and JF: Does that ever happen?

ML: Yes, frequently. I just say what I believe. I will not try to proselytize, but we proselytize by our very being whether we want to or not.

JSJ and JF: You didn't go to Sunday school when you were a child, and yet you had the scriptures. Did your parents give them to you?

ML: I am not sure which books my parents gave me and which books god-parents and other friends gave me, but I was in a house full of books where reading was a normal thing to do. My parents read aloud to each other every night of their lives, so reading was a natural activity.

JSJ and JF: Was there a family circle where you shared scripture together?

ML: No, it was just me. I really didn't have a family life. I didn't eat with my parents. They ate at eight o'clock, and I had a tray in my room with a book on my chest. I was gloriously happy. My mother said that when I ate with them on Sunday we didn't know what to say to each other. It took my mother nearly twenty years to produce a live baby. They really wanted a child terribly, and she kept losing them. I was the only one who lived, but by then their lives had a pattern. I wasn't really a part of it. My father was slowly dying, so I was left to myself a lot. I had marvelous parents, people of total integrity. They would never lie to me. If they didn't know the answer to a question, they told me they didn't know, and they would try to find one if they could. When I would say to my father, who was coughing terribly, "There won't ever be another war will there?" he'd say, "Yes, there will." He would not lie to me. They were wonderful parents in many ways, but they were very different from what we ordinarily call parenting. I didn't get much parenting.

JSJ and JF: I don't sense that you feel deprived.

ML: No.

JSJ and JF: You said those childhood experiences you thought of as hardships at the time were really, as you reflect on them, part of your character building.

ML: When I was in fourth grade, I was put into a girl's school in New York City which was a very good girl's school. In that school, it was very important to be good at athletics. Any team I was on automatically lost. If we were running relay races and we had to pass the stick, I dropped the stick. I tripped over my feet, and my homeroom teacher for some reason decided that since I wasn't good at relay races I wasn't very bright. I soon learned that there was no point doing homework for her—absolutely no point whatsoever. She was going to put it down or hold it up and ridicule it. I would go home and dump my books and think, I am the unsuccessful and unpopular one. Then I moved into the real world, where I wrote, played the piano, painted, dreamed, read, lived a very interior life, far too interior. But I built up a body of work that I never would have done if I had been happy and popular with my peers. Also in fourth grade I discovered the perfidy of the adult world, and I discovered it in French class. I needed to be excused. I raised my hand, and the teacher wouldn't let me go. Three times I raised my hand, and three times she wouldn't let me go. When the bell rang, I ran for it, and I didn't make it. You know in the fourth grade to wet your pants is really pretty awful. When my mother came for me, here was this little wet mess, so she went to the principal. The principal called in the French teacher, and the French teacher said, "Well, Madeleine never asked to leave the room. If she had raised her hand, of course I would have let her go. She's just ashamed of wetting her pants. A big girl like that—tell her not to lie about it next time." So there was an adult lying and being believed, and I was a child and wasn't being believed. That made me determined I never wanted to be like that French teacher. I wanted to be on the side of truth, no matter how much it hurt. When something happens that really gets me in here, I can't heal it until I have written it. Usually I simply write the fact out in a journal, and then it comes into a book sooner or later. This incident finally got into a book called *Camilla*. Once I had it written out, I had it in me to feel sorry for that French teacher—maybe not terribly sorry.

JSJ and JF: Was that the Miss Pepper or Miss Salt?
ML: Yes. I don't know whether I had three teachers in fourth, fifth, and sixth grade or one teacher because in annihilating me they annihilated themselves. I don't remember them. Then I went very briefly to a school where my homeroom teacher was on her first teaching job, and she was the first person to see any potential in this shy, unsuccessful child. She gave me extra work to do, and I remember exactly what she looked like. Her name was Margaret Clapp. She went on to become the first woman president of Wellesley College, a great teacher. I had great teachers in college who were marvelous—what we now call role models.

JSJ and JF: Except for the one who destroyed Greece?
ML: Oh, yes! I didn't have him for long, you see.

JSJ and JF: President Holland has just had a conference here at BYU on what the university's role ought to be in teaching morality to students. Do you think we have any responsibility at the university level to teach character and values, or should we be more academically and intellectually neutral?

ML: I don't know because I have as much trouble with the word *morality* as I do with the word *religion.* Jerry Falwell and his moral majority, which as the bumper sticker says, "Is not moral nor majority," is imposing standards of behavior on people without any intrinsic understanding of why the standards have been chosen. I suspect that simply by your own attitudes in the classroom and in your own lives you are going to be teaching moral values. I had a professor at Smith College who was a very charming, very brilliant professor, but he also loved little girls—I mean the Smithies. I learned a lot about what I didn't like from his behavior. From some of the others, I learned a lot about what I did like—faithfulness, commitment, and forbearance. I don't think you can help teaching it.

JSJ and JF: Maybe you are saying that you don't overtly teach morality, but that it is observed in you by your students.
ML: I think that it is observed by the students just as much when they are in college as when they were in lower grades; you observe the lives of your professors, and you learn from them.

JSJ and JF: So docs that put any responsibility on the professors?
ML: Sure does! I remember saying once to my husband, "Isn't it a good thing we don't want to get divorced because we couldn't," since I have come out in my writing about what I feel about marriage and commitment very strongly. The role he was playing on television was a man of intense moral integrity, and we often laughed together because we were so pleased that we didn't want to get divorced, because we couldn't do it. I get very upset when people write something with which I agree totally, and then they go ahead and act inconsistently with what they have written. I think we have a lot of responsibility to teach consistently with what we are and to be consistent with what we teach.

JSJ and JF: Does that mean a professor could be promiscuous in his sexual habits and write about it just so he is consistent?
ML: No, but we should try to make our actions consistent with our beliefs.

JSJ and JF: Robert Browning is often quoted as believing he was going to be reunited with his wife after death. Do you have that kind of faith about your own husband?
ML: I don't know. I don't know. It's a mystery. All I know is that I don't believe God creates us and then abandons us. I believe that my husband is in some way doing whatever is next that God wants him to do, but I don't know how.

JSJ and JF: Do you look forward to an afterlife?

ML: Indeed I do, but I don't know how it will be. It needn't necessarily even be in human form, but I have a lot of things to learn that I haven't learned. I have got a lot of questions that God is not going to leave unanswered forever. When I was very little in the early grades, I used the analogy of wanting to go all the way through school and learn everything. I still want to go all the way through and learn. I don't think God created us to ask questions and then drop us unfinished. That's not consistent with a God of love. I don't have to know how. When we have to know how, I think we get into all kinds of problems—like the crusader who lost a leg in the crusades and when he was dying ordered the leg cut off one of his peasants and put in the coffin with him because he thought he would need the leg more in heaven than the peasant would on earth. It's only recently that the Roman Catholic church has begun to believe that God could do anything with ashes—the old belief of a literal rising from the tomb. My grandfather would not want to be 101 again; he really would not. I think that when we try to define the mysterious we get into trouble. I think that I am so convinced of God's love and faithfulness that I know Hugh is being taken care of and that I will be taken care of too. I don't have to know how.

JSJ and JF: I heard a student yesterday say that you impressed her as a woman of faith and that faith seemed to give you your peace of mind. Does that seem accurate?

ML: H. A. Williams, the English theologian, said, "Faith is the acceptance of doubt." Faith is not, as most people think, the repression of doubt, and I think that doubt is part of faith because what I believe in is so incredible and so marvelous that how can I believe in it all of the time? Think of the parents in Tennessee who want the textbooks removed because they might stimulate the children's imaginations! It takes every possible leap of the imagination to conceive of the power that created all the galaxies willingly limiting itself to the form of a tiny baby. That boggles the mind. Without imagination, you couldn't begin to believe that God cares so much, that God came to be with us, to be one of us, to say, "Here I am. I'm with you. I care." I guess that I felt God's care so much during the four months of my husband's illness that I never felt abandoned. Everything went wrong. The doctors thought they could cure him. They discovered his cancer presymptomatically and were very optimistic, and then everything went wrong. I knew it was going to, and that was a very strange thing.

JSJ and JF: You knew it even from the beginning?

ML: Yes. As a matter of fact, I knew before we went to China. When we came back, after a wonderful time in China, I was anxious underneath. I thought that I must have been wrong and then within two weeks . . . It was a strange thing of knowing what was going to happen to him and yet of knowing that God was holding me by the hand the whole time, holding both of us.

Luci Shaw—
Madeleine L'Engle Interview

Fay Lapka / 1991

From Oxford '91, a C. S. Lewis Summer Institute Compendium on the Christian and the Imagination. Reprinted by permission of the C. S. Lewis Foundation

Part I

This summer, Madeleine L'Engle and Luci Shaw were speakers in England at Oxford '91, a C.S. Lewis Summer Institute Compendium on the Christian and the Imagination. Fay Lapka, a participant at Oxford '91, enjoyed the following conversation with the two long-time friends. This is Part I of their conversation.

Fay Lapka: How did the two of you meet, and how has your friendship changed and grown over the years?

Madeleine L'Engle: We met at Wheaton College—

Luci Shaw: Yes, about twenty years ago at one of Wheaton's Writers' Conferences. Madeleine was a speaker—I was just a participant—but I bought her book, *A Circle of Quiet*, and then you signed it for me, Madeleine. I asked you if you had any poetry you wanted published.

ML: I told you that *Lines Scribbled on an Envelope* had just gone out of print and that Harold Shaw Publishers could republish it.

LS: And I said, "Maybe you could add some more." You added several new poems, and Shaw brought it out as *The Weather of the Heart*.

ML: Actually, I dumped a whole lot of poems on Luci . . .

LS: Right! And our friendship continued with much correspondence over the years.

ML: We have been more involved with each other's lives I think than each of us realize.

LS: Right. It's been a long-term friendship. The other aspect of our involvement with each other came about as Madeleine began to write nonfiction books. Then we had an editor-author relationship. We would have lengthy, and quite candidly, fights about theological points. I would be speaking for Harold Shaw Publisher's market—the evangelical church bookstores—and I would say, "Madeleine, you just can't say that to these people, or they're not going to hear whatever else you have to say because it's a red-herring. It's going to throw them off balance!" So, Madeleine would prove to me why she could and should say that! I think it was a learning process for both of us; to battle through some of these things and look at the Bible and see what it actually says.

FL: Who usually won these fights?

LS: We usually came out on the same side. I remember one wonderful three days when you were at Wheaton, Madeleine, going through an entire manuscript. Was it *And It Was Good*?

ML: We worked together on four nonfiction works. We started with *Walking on Water*, then *And It Was Good*, followed by *A Stone for a Pillow* and *Sold into Egypt*.

LS: Plus the two books of poetry.

ML: Yes, but it was interesting that with each of the Genesis books we had less to fight about.

LS: Right. But after one session of editing for three days almost nonstop, going through a lot of turmoil and finding resolution, finding ways that these things could be said that both of us felt comfortable with, and that we didn't think was going to set off some sort of revolution in the evangelical market, we suddenly stood up and sang the doxology!

ML: Just the two of us.

FL: Do you see more of an acceptance of the arts in the evangelical community?

LS: I see a polarization. I think that there is a widening in some areas of the church, and a clamping down in other areas.

ML: Fear makes people clamp down—God can be a bit too wild or exciting . . . he leaves a few too many untidy loose ends. I didn't know that the whole evangelical, or fundamentalist world, existed until I was in my mid-forties when I was at Wheaton College for the first time. So it was a whole new experience to me, and I think I have learned an incredible amount. I value enormously the ability to pray for whatever is needed, but what I hadn't seen before, and what frightens me, is the exclusivity. The "only we are saved" attitude—that shocked me.

LS: I think that writers have a prophetic function to the church, to speak into these situations of fear and exclusivity and judgmental attitudes in the church—words that may shock or sting but bring people to an awareness of whatever it is they need to know.

FL: Madeleine, you've chosen to publish, for the most part, in the secular book market; Luci, you have chosen the Christian marketplace. How did you arrive at these decisions?

LS: For a poet to get published at all is a miracle! It wasn't a choice of one over the other. For Madeleine, as an essayist and fiction writer, it's a different story.

ML: I didn't even know there was a Christian market when I began publishing . . .

LS: I'm hoping to submit my next poetry collection through a university press. I know that I could have it published as I have before, through Harold Shaw Publishers, but I need to take that risk because I don't want to take the safe road. And maybe I won't find a publisher. There is an enormous surge of good poetry being written today.

FL: In your writer's workshops both of you urge students to listen intently for what is within, to write honestly from your heart without allowing our in-built censors to edit, or alter, the truth. Madeleine, you express it as "Listen to your story—it knows more than you," and "Write, don't think." Luci, you use different language, but I think you're saying the same thing when you talk about allowing the child within us a voice through our writing—the part of us that sees, hears, feels, and blurts it all out without the adult grids of fear, shame, guilt, pride. There is a fear in allowing this complete abandonment to your heart. I've heard it expressed by students here, and I've struggled with it myself: how can we trust all that comes bubbling up from within? We are all "bent" people: a mix of both sinner and saint. How do we know when our work is trustworthy and safe to be listened to and when it is not?

ML: We never know 100 percent. That's what is so scary about writing.

LS: You do take a risk when you put pen to paper, when you allow your imagination to go to work.

ML: It is dangerous—

LS: But anything worthwhile has risk attached to it.

ML: Yes. If you want to avoid all risk, you might as well find a hole and crawl in it.

FL: But anybody can say, "This is my work, my honest appraisal of the human situation, and therefore it is valid and good." Is there any kind of grid we can use, or measuring rod, as a check on our work?

ML: I have one measuring rod to tell me whether the story, or book, I'm writing is from the Holy Spirit: Does it have in it for me any of the three temptations that Satan offered Jesus? If it does, I won't go on.

FL: You don't mean that all your characters need to be saints . . .

ML: No, I mean, am I writing while thinking, "What's in it for me?" "Is Madeleine going to look good?" "Will this sell on the marketplace?"

LS: Those are temptations that come to an artist, especially a published artist who wants to continue to write and be published. It is a great temptation to continue to write what you know your audience is going to accept and applaud.

ML: When I wrote *A Wrinkle in Time* I wrote something absolutely different than anything else I had ever written before. It was a risk, and it almost didn't work out. It almost didn't get published.

LS: Fay, I believe the scripture that says that as a Christian I have been given the mind of Christ, and I'm learning to trust that mind, which is at work within me. Part of that is being attuned to what the Bible says because that is the authoritative word of God. You do have to test what you're writing against scripture—that is the standard. I'm learning more and more to listen to my own response to what I write, and you learn by experience what is true and what is false. Not that it's all in terms of black or white—there are lots of shades of gray. Another thing that I'm trying to do, and this is also true of Madeleine, I'm not just writing individual works, I'm building a body of work. A body of work that reflects who I am, and the poetry moves in and out of light and shadow as my own life does. I don't want anyone to test me, or my theology, on the basis of one or two poems. Just like you can't know the mind of God from reading only one book of the Bible; you need to read the whole spectrum of scripture.

ML: We had a series of serious questions from the Wheaton students about what I think about the Bible. "That it is true," I answered. "But what about inerrancy?" someone asked. And I said that I believe everything in the Bible is *true*; I don't need to believe that everything in it is factual. It is hard for some people to see the difference between what is true and what is fact: you don't live and die for a fact; you live and die for truth. Luci and I are building up the truth of what we live for.

LS: I love the phrase C. S. Lewis uses in his poem, "The Birth of Language." He talks about "truth" shrunk to "fact." We have this multitude, this enormous diversity of facts about the world. Facts come and go, but the foundation underneath, the rock, is the truth.

Part II

The C. S. Lewis Summer Institute, Oxford '91, was held in July in England. The conference was entitled "Muses Unbound: Transfiguring the Imagination." Madeleine L'Engle, Luci Shaw, and a host of other writers, poets, artists, dancers, theologians, and scientists attended and took part. This is Part II of a conversation between Madeleine L'Engle and Luci Shaw with Fay Lapka that took place at Oxford.

FL: Bishop Lesslie Newbigin in his lecture here at Oxford quoted the phrase: "Our society has technological optimism and literary despair." How do you react to that statement?

ML: I think there is a lot of stuff being published in the secular market that is despairing, but I don't think that's all of it. Unfortunately, there's not enough literature with hope that is coming out to combat it, although I think there is more and more. Strangely enough, what is not recognized, is that some of the most realistically hopeful literature is coming up in the world of young adult novels. You're writing it yourself, Fay.

FL: Do you think our voices are being heard? Are we making a difference?

ML: I get over a hundred letters a week: Yes. That's enough of a statistic for me.

LS: People are being moved and their thinking is being changed. Not always in a flash of light, it's usually more like wearing away a stone with a drop of water. Truly hopeful literature reclaims those huge areas of human need. Every redemptive poem or story or novel that is written has effect. Madeleine is the exemplar of the butterfly effect, that we do effect the people around us and the people far away from us. I think it's a great miracle that the words, the thinking, of a writer from a thousand years ago have been preserved. We can pick up a book and join that writer across geographical and chronological space, rethink his thoughts, and creatively add our own response.

ML: Last summer I reread Dostoyevsky's *The Brothers Karamazov*, not only a great work of fiction, but a great work of theology. To read it in Russia, where it was forged. . . . But it's also dangerous, and a responsibility, to know that our work can have that kind of effect.

LS: It gives you a sense that you have to guard your tongue. You cannot broadcast unthought-through ideas. It forces you to be more thorough in your own thinking and praying. You were talking about "technological optimism and literary despair." I think that the overarching emphasis today is on the "fact" that science is supposed to be able to solve our problems.

ML: Although the scientists are the first to admit they can't.

LS: But we, particularly in the Christian realm, can contribute to that false notion if we are not allowing our imaginations to be baptized and irradiated with the light of Christ. The imagination has been allowed to atrophy in too many segments of the church.

ML: I also think we contribute to despair when we dwell on hate, and judgement, and anger, and exclusivity, wiping out other people who are not the same as we are. I think that adds to despair far more than the secular world does.

FL: Yes. I think we've all experienced that despair at one time or another. Luci, you have made the move into the Episcopal church, into a liturgical, sacramental style of worship. Madeleine, you have in the last few years grown more familiar with the evangelical community. Have you noticed a difference in your writing as a result of your friendship and individual spiritual journeys that have brought the two of you to "meet in the middle"?

LS: I think I've been able to be far more honest and not write poetry the way I hoped life was but the way I really saw life, and to admit some shadows. And some bruises.

ML: Your poetry changed a great deal with the illness of your husband, Harold.

LS: Yes. Harold's illness forced me to face issues of life and death. It's true for all of us—I call it the crucible effect—when the heat is on things either melt or they harden. The things that melt are too trivial to worry about; the things that harden are the eternal things that we need our lives to be founded on. I became a more whole person because I was forced to examine things for myself, not simply through the lens of my husband's theology and his sensibility. In a sense Harold had been a buffer for me. When you don't have the buffer anymore, you get some bruises, but you feel the excitement of the wrestling. Jacob wrestled with the angel, and he was crippled as a result. But the crippling was a constant reminder to him of the presence of God in his life.

ML: And if you are touched by God, you will forever bear the wound.

FL: Luci, in *God in the Dark* you state that you have always been a wrestler, a doubter. When Harold became ill and died, did this increase the questioning?

LS: I was forced to recognize that there were doubts. There was not a great deal I could do except honestly acknowledge the doubts and wait. I have to wait for God—if he is there—to show himself to me. The ball is in his court. There was a great sense of relief in knowing that I could stop trying to make God real. I had been trying all my life to manipulate my image of God into reality. Dr. James Houston from Regent College said to me, "You've been through a long, dark tunnel. When you see light at the end of the tunnel you'll come out onto the edge of a cliff. At that point you have to throw yourself off the cliff and trust that God will catch you." This was spoken without preamble, and almost without context, like a prophetic word to me, and I recognized that it was true.

FL: When did the cliff occur?

LS: Well, then the question was, what does this mean? How do I throw myself off this cliff? What is God asking of me? That very day I lost my journal—which, as you know, is very important to me—but that journal was found by my friend, Karen Cooper, in the middle of the UBC campus, on University Boulevard, in a puddle. She was driving, and she saw this notebook, actually stopped the car, got out, picked it up, and saw my name on the cover, and knew where I was. I was at a prayer group. On the way to the prayer group I had realized that this was part of the "how" of relinquishment. God was saying, "Are you willing to relinquish this symbol of your whole life, your journal? Will you let go of it all and trust that I am there to catch you?" What can I do in a situation like that? I have to say, "Yes." I can't say, "No." So I did say, "Yes." I got to the prayer group, opened the door, and they said, "Karen Cooper just called to say she found your journal." I can't explain it any other way: God was assuring me that if I relinquished my life to him, he would give it back to me. It is that sort of thing that you remember in the dark phases of your life, and you can say, "Yes, God is in my life."

FL: Madeleine, how have you seen your writing change as a result of your spiritual journey?

ML: Sheila, my assistant, has noticed a deepening of my theology in my writing, but I'm too close to this new book to see or describe it. I know it changed as I wrote and rewrote it.

FL: What's the name of the new novel?

ML: The name of the book is *Certain Women,* from St. Luke, "Certain women made us astonished," and King David and Abigail's response to him, "I am certain." It's a play on the word *certain.* There are twelve chapters, each with the name of a woman, each beginning with a quotation from scripture, and then scenes from a play about King David and his wives. The main body of the novel is a twentieth-century story about accepting each other, not as we would like each other to be, but as we are. In response to your question of my writing changing, I found out what I wanted to say as I worked on the book. As the protagonist is working out her relationship with her father, who had nine wives, and her husband, and many half-siblings, what she really had to work on was acceptance. Acceptance of herself as she was and the men as they were. To some extent it follows King David's story.

FL: The novel was a long time coming, wasn't it? When is it going to be available?

ML: It took about three years to write—longer than usual. It will be out in spring of '92.

FL: Luci, you have two books coming out soon.

LS: Yes, I've just finished a book on journal-keeping, to which Madeleine wrote the introduction. It's called *Life Path*s and will be published in October '91 through Multnomah Press. Then, the text of a new book called

Horizons, which is poems and essays—forty-four readings—will be done by Zondervan, next summer, with illustrations by Tim Botts. It's really meant for people who haven't been in the habit of reading poetry, with stories and commentaries as bridges into the poetry. I'm hoping that Christians will begin reading poetry again!

FL: Yes! When you think of the centuries of literature that have come from the church, it would be wonderful if all the church community returned to a full acceptance of the arts. Madeleine and Luci, thank you for your continued work in providing us with honest, truly redemptive literature and poetry.

The Story as Teller: An Interview with Madeleine L'Engle

Gary Schmidt / 1991

From *ALAN Review*, vol. 18, no. 2, Winter 1991. Reprinted by permission.

Schmidt: Let's begin by thinking of the genres your books participate in. Do you consider your books to be written for a specific audience, say, children or a YA audience?

L'Engle: Certainly some of my books should not be read by children; they're for high school and up. But I write fiction. I don't think about those categories. I don't write for an audience. I write for the book. I listen to the book. If I'm thinking of an audience I'm not thinking about the book, so the audience is an arbitrary decision on the part of my publishers.

My book *Camilla* was first published by Simon and Schuster as a regular trade novel. Then it was republished in the sixties as a YA by Crowell and in the eighties as a YA by Delacorte. It was not written as a YA. I did take out two small scenes for the reissues, not so much for the kids' sake as for the librarians' sake. I decided if they weren't that essential to the book they shouldn't be in there anyhow.

Kids read for content; they read for story. They read for meaning and truth. Parents and teachers tend to look for something they don't like, and that's a bad way to read a book. The terrible mistake is they assume that books written for children are different. They are not really books in their view because they're written for children. They're different, and so they go through them to see what they don't like. But they're not different; a story is a story. Fairy tales were not written for children. They were written to express the needs of a people of a community. I still read fairy tales and science fiction, and I read myths, which are blue prints for the human psyche.

Schmidt: For the child audience your best known books are the fantasy series beginning with *A Wrinkle in Time*. Once called the Time Trilogy, I suppose you would call it the Time Quartet now.

L'Engle: No, I don't think of it as that because the Time Trilogy is Meg and Calvin and Charles Wallace and the twins are totally peripheral. Now this is the twins' book, and the others are peripheral. They are not a continuation. I don't think of *The Arm of the Starfish* and that whole group as being part of the Time Trilogy because Meg and Calvin are grown, and it's about their kids. If you want you can look at it as a chronological continuation of what happens to the family.

Schmidt: Though you can understand parts of *Many Waters* better by knowing the Time Trilogy.

L'Engle: But you can read *Many Waters* without reading the Time Trilogy, too. I don't think a book should be dependent upon another book, like series books. I don't see these as series books, but as companion pieces, and I don't write in chronological order. The fourth book actually occurs between the second and third of the Time Trilogy.

Schmidt: You are often labelled a fantasy writer, but you don't write in the same genre as, say, Richard Adams, who moves into the animal world, or Lloyd Alexander, who evokes a medieval world, or Ray Bradbury, who uses the future in his science fiction.

L'Engle: I also like all those writers.

Schmidt: You use a different kind of fantasy.

L'Engle: Well, it is science fiction. I'm basing the stories on the new way of looking at the world since we opened the heart of the atom.

Schmidt: Though that opening is seen in a negative way by one of the seraphim in *Many Waters*.

L'Engle: Everything good can also be bad. That doesn't make the original good any less good, but we misuse that original good. We turn technology which I'm all for into technocracy which I'm all against. We have had a new understanding of God's universe as being far more complex and demanding far more imagination because of the sciences.

Some of the terms in astrophysics suggest this. There is a star known as a degenerate white dwarf and another known as a red giant on the horizontal branch. So we get a picture of the degenerate white dwarf trying to get the red giant off the horizontal branch. You have subatomic particles with charm, and it's a whole different meaning to the physicist. Particles spin, but one physicist said we shouldn't say that they spin but that they gyre, and that's out of "Jabberwocky." Scientists are discovering a world of such incredible, simple complexity, and such total interrelatedness, and that is what seems to me to be so theological about it. Everything affects everything else, so I have never seen any conflict between science and theology. All science can do is open up to us more of the wonder of creation, and then of course we can use it disastrously as we do with bombs.

Schmidt: When you wrote the first volume of the Time Trilogy, did you consider it to be part of a series? That is, did you have the other two in mind yet?
L'Engle: Heavens, no! Heavens, no! I must have written hundreds of letters saying I'd never write another book about Meg and Calvin and Charles Wallace. So along, ten books later, comes along the idea for *A Wind in the Door*. When I finished *A Wind in the Door*, I realized that Charles Wallace's life had been saved twice, and I had to find out why. So I wrote about five more books, and then the ideas began to solidify for *A Swiftly Tilting Planet*. By then it had occurred to me that the twins probably ought to have their own book and that I'd been ignoring them. Because the twins in *A Swiftly Tilting Planet* were so important to each other, I realized that that's why they didn't need Meg and Calvin and Charles Wallace; they had each other. So it took me a long time before that book finally worked itself into a write-able stage.

Schmidt: In a sense the twins are always kything back and forth between themselves.
L'Engle: Yes, yes.

Schmidt: Though they don't have the abilities of Meg and Charles Wallace.
L'Engle: They have different abilities. One of the important things in *Many Waters* is that they have to learn that they're separate people. It's the first time that they've been separate people. I got a very good review in the *New York Times* with one exception which I'm sure must have been a typo, and that was that in this book the twins were eighteen. If the twins had been eighteen this would have been a very different book. They're not quite sixteen and that's very important.

Schmidt: In your writings you talk about your role as a storyteller, that you are a teller of stories. You focus on the importance of that process, suggesting that that is what makes us human, that story is a vehicle for truth.

L'Engle: Yes. Once there was a man who had two sons. He asked them to go work with him in the vineyards. One said, "Yes, of course, Father," and didn't go. The other said, "I won't!" and then he went. That tells us an awful lot.

Schmidt: Does that mean that when we come to the Time Trilogy, that when we talk about the narrator, we can never separate the narrator from Madeleine L'Engle? That you do not set up a construct but that your voice is the dominant one?

L'Engle: No, I don't think so. In that it is the story itself that is the narrator, and I listen to the story. It does things I don't expect. I have to follow the story, and that's why I said that to have the audience in mind is disastrous because you're not able to listen to the story if you're thinking about the audience. Almost all writers I know agree that the story does things they don't expect. The story has its own integrity, and the job of the storyteller is to listen to that story and try to tell it. But it's the story that is the narrator. Of course, I have to tell it. I'm the vehicle that this particular story has chosen, and my job is to tell it as honestly and truthfully as I can. I don't think any of us does it totally well. Jean Rhys, whom I quote in *Walking on Water*, says that the job of the writer, the storyteller, is to feed the lake, and the great storytellers (Shakespeare, Dostoyevsky) are the great tributaries. Many of us are just little trickles, but that doesn't matter; the important thing is to feed the lake.

I do not control, own, or dominate my stories. I serve them, and for me they are truth. When I am writing, so often I am given what I need. All I have to do is to recognize it. I listen to what happens and then set it down simply because that is what happened.

Schmidt: You begin *A Wrinkle in Time* with the narrator telling an inside joke: "It was a dark and stormy night."

L'Engle: Long before Snoopy did it.

Schmidt: Yes. It's from Bulwer-Lytton.

L'Engle: Well, it's an old English chestnut. It's been around in England for hundreds and hundreds of years, even before Bulwer-Lytton. It's one of those primordial images like the fire of roses, which I use in *A Swiftly Tilting Planet*. T. S. Eliot refers to it in "Little Gidding," and Dante uses it in the

Inferno. But I suspect it goes way beyond that. One of the things that the human being has done probably back in the caves and the trees is to start a story: "It was a dark and stormy night. I was sitting up in my tree."

Schmidt: It seems to me that one of the things that is going on in *A Wrinkle in Time* is an affirmation of a universe which is in trouble but which is essentially a secure universe. We know that the story is already written and that there is affirmation and joy and love and security in the end.
L'Engle: It's not that the story is already written but that I trust the author of the story to be the one to finish it.

Schmidt: The narrator of *A Wrinkle in Time* seems to reflect this security since there is a very strong control throughout the novel. For example, when Meg goes to see IT, she thinks that nothing could possibly be worse than the present situation. But then the narrator comes in to say, "Oh, no? Wait!"
L'Engle: But I think of that as Meg's subconscious mind as saying that, not mine. You know, sometimes in my own life when things have been terrible, I think that nothing could be worse. But then I think, "No, I better not say that." So I see that as Meg, not me.

Schmidt: It seems that in both *A Wrinkle in Time* and *A Wind in the Door*, Meg and the narrator are often allied.
L'Engle: Well, I'm Meg. I mean, I don't know anybody else better than I know myself. People say, "Do you write about your children?" No! I have all of Meg's problems. I made her good at arithmetic and bad at English, and I was good at English and bad at arithmetic. I was an only child. I wanted brothers, so I have her three brothers. I had all of Meg's problems in school. I am very nearsighted; I wear contacts. I never could do anything with my hair. I always thought of myself as an ugly duckling. It took me a long time to grow into myself. I have gone through everything that Meg has gone through, and that's why our voices are the same voice. I'm also Vicky Austin. I'm not Mrs. Austin. Mrs. Austin is the mother I thought I ought to be and certainly wasn't. There is always a "me" character so that the voice is indistinguishable. When I write about Meg in *A Wrinkle in Time* when she is fourteen, I have to be myself, the way I was at fourteen, and also with the scientific knowledge I had acquired in the intervening years.

Schmidt: That's not necessarily true in *Many Waters.*
L'Engle: Yes, I moved into the twins.

Schmidt: It's striking that the narrator of *Many Waters* is not nearly as present as the narrator of the *Time Trilogy*. Most of the meaning of the novel is conveyed through dialogue.

L'Engle: The reason that the narrator isn't as present is that the twins are far more objective. They work far less from intuition and instinct. They are the objective kids who have made it good at school. Therefore, that precludes a certain amount of self-searching. This is the first time in the world that they have been out of this sort of dual security. Their relationship isn't something that they have ever articulated. They have never needed to articulate it, and so the narrator isn't as present.

Schmidt: The narrators of *A Wrinkle in Time* and *A Wind in the Door* never seem to be surprised at the extraordinary things that happen in the novels. For example, Mr. Jenkins is multiplied three times, but the narrator never seems to blink an eye. It is sort of like a fairy tale narrator in this sense.

L'Engle: Extraordinary things happen all the time. They are not what's surprising.

Schmidt: Does this mean that the narrator is pushing us as readers and forcing us to ask one of the central questions of this book: What is real?

L'Engle: I'm not trying to push anything, except myself. I believe that if something is necessary for me to learn, then probably a lot of other people share that same need. But I'm not worrying about the other peoples' needs because that is to get out of it, and control and manipulate and dominate, which I don't think a storyteller ought to do. I'm trying to learn and grow through listening to the story, so the story is the teller.

Schmidt: Would it be accurate to say that the narrator is constantly asking us, "What is real?"

L'Engle: Yes, and that more and more, as I read more particle physics, is the question that physicists are asking, "What is real?" Old Bishop Berkeley started it in the nineteenth century when he asked, "Are the stars there if I don't see them?" And this seems to be the point of view of the Nobel laureates. The human being, and I'm quoting, is called to "serve and contemplate." Sounds more like a theologian than a scientist, doesn't it? And we've blown it. We've not done a good job of it, of observing and contemplating and making real. That's part of the job of the storyteller. We make real. We look for truth, that truth which will set us free.

Schmidt: This, then, explains why the unicorns in *Many Waters* are real only when they are believed in.
L'Engle: There are particles called virtual particles, and they have a tendency to life. One physicist says that the world is far more imaginary than we had originally thought. Now when you put this in the context of science alone, it's pretty awful, but when you realize that it's held in God's mind—this is God's thought—it makes a lot of sense.

Schmidt: *A Wind in the Door* came substantially after *A Wrinkle in Time*.
L'Engle: Ten years and ten books later.

Schmidt: Like Maurice Sendak. Each of the books in his trilogy was separated by ten years.
L'Engle: Yes, it takes about that long.

Schmidt: You did a great deal of research in cellular biology for this novel. Was there any particular biologist you studied?
L'Engle: The first one I read, the first time I encountered mitochondria, was in an article by Lewis Thomas in the *New England Journal of Medicine* before he published any of his books. My oldest friend is a physician, and she would feed me things she thought would interest me. It was just like WHAM! I better learn cellular biology, so I just went and got some plain classic textbooks at Columbia. I had to know a lot more about cellular biology than is actually in the book so that which is in the book is accurate.

Schmidt: The world of *A Wind in the Door* seems to be more up for grabs than that of *A Wrinkle in Time*. Unutterable things are happening here; the sky is being torn. When I look at the narrator of this novel it seems that the controlling narrator who controls the structure of *A Wrinkle in Time* isn't there. It is much more Meg, a weaker character who is not really in control all the time, and that seems to mirror the kinds of things that are going on. Would that be accurate to suggest, that this is a much less controlling narrator?
L'Engle: Well, Meg is that much older, and the more you grow—if you're willing to grow—the less you know, the less certain you are. Meg in *A Wrinkle in Time* is still young enough to believe that daddy could fix everything. That was one of the big things she has to learn, and that's one of the things that many young women who marry too early tell me has been so hard in their lives, to understand that daddy couldn't fix it all. Meg has learned that lesson, so we move into a world of unknowns. We don't know what's going to

happen each day. We should treasure each day in a marvelously conscious and joyous way because we don't know what's going to happen.

Schmidt: It seems that this narrator periodically gives a hint that there is some knowledge beyond the bounds of this plot. We hear, for example, that Charles Wallace is crucial to the whole galaxy, that this one death might cause irremediable harm. But we don't find out why until *A Swiftly Tilting Planet*; he saves the world from nuclear war.

L'Engle: He also has to let go his own strength, his own pride, and his own power before he can do that. Now it's fascinating to me that my books tend to come true. I take real comfort in the fact that nuclear war is prevented. I had a letter from a woman asking about mitochondria because something was wrong with her son's mitochondria. In *The Arm of the Starfish*, Dr. O'Keefe regenerates a child's finger. I'm being fed articles, mostly from English medical journals, where, now if a very small child accidentally severs a finger or toe you keep it clean and you leave it alone and it grows back. I was speaking out at Ohio State, and this came up in question-and-answer. A young woman said, "Our baby cut off her finger. Our doctor gave us *The Arm of the Starfish,* and we watched it grow back."

There's a fairly early age cutoff when the body remembers it's forgotten, but the younger the child the more complete the regeneration, fingernail and all. But in moving into a technocratic world where we've limited ourselves to our minds alone, we've lost abilities that are innate in the human being. My theory in *Walking on Water* is that whatever Jesus did while he was alive we should be able to do too, but we've forgotten.

Schmidt: You speak of this also in one of your journals, when you recall that you used to be able to float down stairs as a very young child.

L'Engle: Oh yes, and I cannot tell you how many letters I have had that say, "I've never dared tell anybody this before. I did it too." Or, "I was walking across the field, and I found I was walking a little bit above the ground. But I told my parents, and they said, 'What a good imagination you have, dear,' or 'Don't lie!'" So it's beaten out of us. You go to school, and it's beaten out of you, this world of marvel. And there's fear. I'm just so convinced that if our own true faith is thoroughly grounded in God's love we needn't fear.

Schmidt: That seems to be one of the basic messages of the entire Time Trilogy.

L'Engle: Yes, it is. But I didn't write the message; the story did.

Schmidt: Yes. At times you seem to manipulate the text.
L'Engle: Oh, I hope not.

Schmidt: Well, I don't mean manipulate in the sense of contort. Instead, I mean in terms of the way the sheer words are placed on the page. This appears in both *A Wind in the Door* and *A Swiftly Tilting Planet.* You don't worry about sentence structure or punctuation or matters like that.
L'Engle: Yes, but I'm not doing it; the story is doing it. The story needs to do that. Okay, let me give a marvelous example of faith and works. I went with my husband one Sunday afternoon to Symphony Hall in Boston to hear an all-Beethoven concert, with Rudolf Serkin playing, and he played the "Apassionata" sonata better than he could play it. I mean, it was absolutely an incredible performance. I thought to myself, "What does he have to do to have the spirit fill him like this?" The answer is really very simple: he practices the piano eight hours a day every day. If he didn't practice the piano eight hours a day every day, the music couldn't come through his fingers. If I didn't work on writing, on poetry, on language, then that passage couldn't have come. I couldn't have written it, so my part in it is to keep my finger exercises, my technique, so that if something like that comes, I am able to set it down.

Schmidt: So that passage comes principally . . .
L'Engle: Because the story needs that. When you have partial sentences with no periods, there is a sense of rapidity, a sense of urgency that the straight periodic sentence won't give.

Schmidt: That's what makes them so appropriate for *A Swiftly Tilting Planet*, especially when they are used in connection with the attacks of the echthroi. They simulate the chaotic events.
L'Engle: Yes. I do play the piano and music is very important to me. I think that's why these sort of semimusical forms come out.

Schmidt: Let me ask you about *A Swiftly Tilting Planet.* This strikes me as the most complex of the novels.
L'Engle: It is. We had a terrible time of cutting it because it was at least twice as long as it is. I had gone into each episode much more deeply.

Schmidt: Each episode could function as a separate novel, particular that with Matthew Maddox.
L'Engle: The funny thing was that when I first set the novel down I didn't

have that. It was all a flashback from Beezie and Charles, and my editor said, "Madeleine, you really need to think about that scene." I said that when I wrote it, it didn't work. The reason that it didn't work was that I had made a Bran-like character, but that was all. And suddenly the idea of Matthew Maddox came to me. And then Matthew Maddox had to be weaved into the whole book.

Schmidt: One of the reasons that *A Swiftly Tilting Planet* seems so complicated is the narrator refuses to coddle us. The narrator does not help us with family relations. The narrator does not clue us when Charles Wallace makes some wrong connections between Madog and Maddog Branzillo.
L'Engle: I think Gaudior said, "Watch out!" or something like that.

Schmidt: Yes. "Watch out for your own strength."
L'Engle: It was a really important lesson for me to learn that in our society, and particularly in our church, we are so dependent upon our own version of strength. But Charles Wallace had to let it all go when he went into Chuck. Also, one of the things that I have been trying to become more clear about is intercessory prayer. So this is really about intercessory prayer. When Charles Wallace limits himself to somebody else's limitations, he is moving with compassion into somebody else's problems, letting his own go.

Schmidt: One of the things that seems to be happening in *A Swiftly Tilting Planet* is that the narrator and the reader are merged. Our perspective and that of the narrator are always the same. Whenever we watch Charles Wallace, we look through Meg's eyes because she is seeing it as she holds onto Ananda. In a way, this stance of the narrator leads us to simulate kything. We kythe with the narrator and Meg as they kythe with Charles Wallace.
L'Engle: That's what I want when I read. I want to read about somebody into whose adventures and thoughts I can enter and I hope be enlarged and more courageous when I'm through.

Schmidt: When we come to *Many Waters*, it seems that a deep sadness pervades this book. At the end of the Harcels episode in *A Swiftly Tilting Planet* there is that same feeling: we have lost so much. But here it goes through the entire novel, particularly at the end.
L'Engle: Yes, there is that. Human beings have experienced incredible loss, but one of the things that brings some of that back is story because story is a vehicle for truth. And truth and story is what connects human beings with one another.

A Mind in Motion

Betsy Hearne / 1998

From *School Library Journal* 44.6 (1998), pp. 28–33. © School Library Journal.
http://www.slj.com. Used by permission.

Madeleine L'Engle, author of the Newbery Medal–winning *A Wrinkle in Time*, is the 1998 winner of the Margaret A. Edwards Award recognizing an author's lifetime achievement in young adult literature. The award is given annually by ALA's Young Adult Library Services Association and is sponsored by *School Library Journal.*

The Edwards Award Committee cited two of L'Engle's series for recognition: the Austin Family series and the Time Fantasy series. Chair Jeri Baker said that L'Engle was chosen for her ability to tell "stories that uniquely blend scientific principles and the quest for higher meaning."

A lifelong New Yorker born in 1918, L'Engle began her career in theater, where she met her husband, Hugh Franklin. After publishing her first book in 1945, L'Engle devoted the fifties to raising two daughters and a son, but she found the urge to write too powerful to resist. It's an urge that has driven her to publish fifty-three books to date.

L'Engle, who lives on Manhattan's Upper West Side, near Columbia University, will receive her award this month at ALA's Annual Conference in Washington, DC.

Hearne: Let me ask you about your perseverance in getting published. Can you tell us what kept you sending out the manuscript for *A Wrinkle in Time* through so many rejections?

L'Engle: My first manuscript was easy. I got letters from several publishers—from stories I had sent out to literary magazines—asking if I had a novel, which of course I did. I sent it to the first publisher who wrote, it was published, and it did extremely well. My first half dozen books I had no problem with. Then when I began to grow and change in my writing, nobody wanted it.

Hearne: And that was *A Wrinkle in Time*?
L'Engle: Yes, and also *Meet the Austins.* That mild little book took two years to find a publisher. It began with a death and children were not supposed to know about death. But we had more or less the same thing happen in our family. Two of our friends died, and we inherited a seven-year-old girl. So again I was writing out of my own experience, and my children were certainly part of that experience.

Hearne: Many of your characters, male and female, integrate a passion for work with a dedication to domesticity. Could you talk about the way you balanced family and work when they may have presented conflicts of time and energy?
L'Engle: They presented great conflicts. Jane Austen didn't make the beds, Emily Brontë didn't do the cooking—but I didn't want to give up either writing or children, so doing both was a choice that I made, not an easy one. I know there have been many women who stopped writing during their childbearing years. I would have gone mad. I was slowed down, I didn't write as much, but I did write. I basically wrote *Meet the Austins* as a Valentine's present for my husband. He loved it! I do have several books on the shelf which never got published. I could probably have them published at this point, but that's not where I am now. They were good, but they were further ahead in the YA field than the book world was then.

Hearne: As a teenager I read and loved your early realistic novel *Camilla.* Do you have your own favorites, or books that were easier, harder, or more satisfying to write?
L'Engle: Not really. If I don't love them there's no point in my trying to work on them. *Camilla* was first published as an adult novel. Did you read about her in *Live Coal in the Sea*? Camilla's probably in her sixties there, a professor of astronomy. That book looks back at how she's gotten to the more or less peaceful place where she now is. I knew I wanted to know more about Camilla, just as when I finished *The Small Rain* I knew I needed to know more about Katherine. But I had to wait until I was old enough, so I waited lo those many years till I wrote *A Severed Wasp.*

Hearne: So it's a lifetime illumination process, and that may be why your characters keep growing.

L'Engle: The amazing thing is that they grow behind my back. When I finished *The Small Rain*, Felix was a second-rate violinist and a fairly second-rate person. Then in the beginning of *A Severed Wasp* he's a bishop—and he's a good bishop! I never thought he'd turn out that way.

Hearne: Let me ask you about the characters in the two series for which you've been cited. There are lots of parallels between the Murry and Austin families. Do these characters reflect your own family, and if so, how did you let the models go and the fiction grow?

L'Engle: I don't see them as being that alike. The Murrys are far more intellectual. The Austins are more like us, just regular people. Of course, I used my own family model because it was the only one I knew—I guess my family would come halfway between the two.

Hearne: How did you manage to keep sequels and prequels and companion books straight? Was there a master plan to the series, or did you take them step by step and trust a subconscious pattern?

L'Engle: There was no master plan. If I plan them, they can't grow. If I listen to them, they tell me what they are doing. I never anticipated writing another book about Meg after *Wrinkle*, and, in fact, I think there are ten books between *Wrinkle* and *A Wind in the Door*. I don't write the books in chronological order. *Many Waters* chronologically comes before *A Swiftly Tilting Planet*, but I wrote *A Swiftly Tilting Planet* long before I wrote *Many Waters*.

Hearne: The family trees in your fiction connect, through an intergenerational cast of characters, across books and whole series. Did your characters just start to cross paths?

L'Engle: Yes, and they are far more crossed now than when we started! Somebody suggested that we should have a genealogical tree, and I thought it was a good idea. I'm not good at that kind of thing, so I asked if a young writer, Charlotte Weaver Geltzer, would do it. I think she did it for $100.

Hearne: A lot of the characters in your books are famous, either as scientists or artists; does that reflect your own circle of contacts, or did you deliberately select world-famous figures because of our culture's obsession with superstars?

L'Engle: None of them are superstars. They are not people you would see on television. They are people doing good solid work. In the book I'm writing now, Meg is explaining to one of her kids that the reason they don't have much money is that Calvin is working alone. He's not with a university getting grants, so I see them as people who are important in their own right but don't fit the media patterns.

Hearne: The parent/grandparent figures in the Murry and Austin families seem almost too good to be true sometimes. Did you perceive of these matriarchs and patriarchs as hero figures? Do you think the ideal strength and security they model is one of the attractions for young readers who are insecure in their own, often fragmented families?

L'Engle: I think grandparents are very, very important. It was important to me to have grandparents and to be a grandmother. I think the grandparent relation is less stressful than the parent relation. You tell your grandparents what you don't tell your parents. You protect your parents, but you don't protect your grandparents.

Hearne: What about villains? Is Zachary Gray a kind of perennial trickster/stranger/tempter figure who will always remain dangerously elusive, or do you think he could eventually grow and change in the positive directions he keeps promising to take?

L'Engle: Most of us have had a Zachary in our lives. People keep saying, "You have got to redeem Zachary!" When I started *An Acceptable Time*, I thought I was going to redeem him, but instead he hit bottom. Then when I started the one in Antarctica, *Troubling a Star*, I thought he was going to be there. He never got in! I will try to redeem him sooner or later.

Hearne: Where did saintly super-sleuth Canon Tallis come from?

L'Engle: My elder daughter and I were playing duets, and we played a canon. I love the hymn "Tallis Canon." As we played the canon I thought, "Oh, turn it around; make it Canon Tallis." So it really came from something as silly as that, but I did have a friend here at the Cathedral [of St. John the Divine] who was in a way similar to the character.

Hearne: So there was a model?

L'Engle: The character came first, and the person who modeled it came later. He liked being Canon Tallis.

Hearne: How do you decide on voice? You wrote *Meet the Austins* as a first-person narrative and *A Wrinkle in Time* in third person. Is one more comfortable for you? Or do you just simply follow your ear?

L'Engle: I think first person has become more comfortable than it used to be. In the book I'm working on now, which is about Meg in her fifties, she's speaking in the first person. All the others are speaking in the third person.

Hearne: Do you think kids will continue relating to Meg even though she's fifty and your readers are still twelve?

L'Engle: She has seven children. She's in the voices of all those children, too.

Hearne: Let me ask you some questions about writing style. Dialogue seems more prominent than narrative in unfolding your plots, and chapters often end in dramatic moments that heighten the reader's attention. Has your interest in theater influenced your writing techniques? And is music and poetry as integral to your life as it is in your literature?

L'Engle: I'm sure that's all true. The fact that I was married to an actor and that I started work in the theater certainly has had its influence. My parents, who were very literate people, read to each other every night. So poetry and music—they adored music—have always been part of my life. I love getting letters saying, "I've just learned this nice music from hearing about it in your book."

Hearne: What process or person has been the most important in shaping your style?

L'Engle: I can't think of any one person or process. I've written since I was five. When I was in college I kept trying on styles the way the other girls tried on clothes and finally came to what seemed to me the simplest style, the one that fitted me best. It was trial and error.

Hearne: What about themes? Yours reflect two dominant aspects of US history—the religious conviction that led many to found early settlements here, and the scientific technology that some claim has rivaled or even replaced that religious fervor. How and why do you so specifically seek to reconcile these sometimes conflicting beliefs in religion and science?

L'Engle: Well, I have never seen any conflicts. It seems to me that anything science can uncover simply gives us a wider view of the universe and of the Maker. Conflict is where you cling to an idea without allowing it to change or grow.

Hearne: There has been some backlash, from both the left and the right, against your fantasy series. Some left-wingers object to your "mysticism," as in love overcoming all problems of the universe in *A Wrinkle in Time*. Some right-wingers object to your witch figures or "demonology," as evidenced by the nephilim [a Hebrew word meaning giants] in *Many Waters*. Have you had direct or indirect interactions with such critics, and if so, what have these interactions been like?

L'Engle: Well, mostly it's been very, very good. Not much protest has come in the mail. It has come when I've spoken at universities. There are people there, usually not the university kids, who've decided ahead of time what they think I think, and I'm trying to explain to them that that's not what I think.

The nephilim are straight out of scripture. *Many Waters* came from lines of Genesis, which a lot of people skipped: there were nephilim on the earth in those days. They saw the daughters of men, that they were beautiful. They went into them and married them. My book came from those lines, so I didn't make up nephilim. They're scriptural.

Hearne: That reminds me of a radio show I was on where a caller objected to aspects of sex, violence, and obscenity in a children's book and quoted scripture. I had to point out that there was an awful lot of sex, violence, and obscenity in the Bible.

L'Engle: If you had to cut it all out, you'd be left with a very small book. I think there are powers of evil. You can't live in the middle of New York City and not know that. I think the best thing we can do is to give a child light to see them.

Hearne: Religion is a neglected subject in children's literature, partly because we have become a secular society and partly out of concern for offending or violating private sensibilities in a multicultural milieu. Yet many children have deep spiritual questions. Can you tell us about your own spiritual quest and how it relates to the worlds you've created in your books?

L'Engle: I am an Episcopalian. Which simply means to me that I have more elbow room, more freedom [than some other Christians] to ask questions. Yet I have a tradition, a literary structure that is beautiful. When things go wrong, a beautiful structure can be very helpful in holding you together.

I think kids are interested in religion. They ask questions about it. Not teaching religion in classrooms simply doesn't work because the children know what the teacher thinks. The teacher doesn't have to say a thing about it. The kids know who the person is. Most kids are concerned about the pattern of the universe and their place in it. Do I matter? Does anybody care? Is there a God? Am I loved?

Briefly, back to the science—to me, particle physics and quantum mechanics are extremely theological because they are dealing with the nature of being, so they are just as theological as a tome on morals. Before I wrote *Wrinkle*, I picked up a book in which Einstein was quoted as saying, "Anyone who is not lost in rapturous awe at the power and glory of the mind behind the universe is as good as a burnt-out candle." And I thought, "Oh, I have found my theologian." So I began reading in that area.

Hearne: You've woven biblical stories, figures, and passages into your fiction. Even though you solved the problem of Noah's daughter, in *Many Waters*, by having her gathered unto God directly by the seraphim, what do you think of a patriarchal tradition that allows only Noah's sons and their wives to board the ark? I use this as an example of cases in which women such as Eve, weighted down by sin, insure that future generations of institutionalized religions will continue to be patriarchal.

L'Engle: The story of Eve that I like is that God made Adam and looked at him and said, "Hmmm, I can do better."

Hearne: You made that up!

L'Engle: No, I didn't. I got it from a friend who grew up in a very fundamentalist church.

Hearne: So it's an ongoing dialogue?

L'Engle: Look, the Bible is a very chauvinistic book. Women are not important. Most of them are not named—Potiphar's wife, Jepthah's daughter, Pharaoh's daughter—and when you have a named woman, you have to sit up and take notice. But I've always seen the Bible as a wonderful storybook. One young woman told me she had been taught by her parents never to criticize any of the biblical characters because they were all good and moral people. And I said, "When did you last open your Bible?"

Hearne: In your juvenile fiction, good and evil are almost always clearly delineated. Have you considered developing the kind of situation where there really are no right or wrong choices? Or do you feel that doesn't belong in juvenile fiction?

L'Engle: Oh, I think it does. I think kids, particularly in today's society, are faced with choices, yet they don't have the background they need to think of creative answers.

Hearne: Let's talk about the fine line between wisdom and self-righteousness in projecting social and religious ideals through story.
L'Engle: Self-righteousness seldom leads to wisdom. It's an assumption that I know what is right, and if I am right therefore you must be wrong. Wisdom tends to see both right and wrong in almost everything. It's very seldom clearly delineated for us. Some of the people I have admired most of all have done terrible things, and yet that doesn't take away from the great things they did. Some of the people who I've thought were completely awful have awed me by doing something wonderful.

Hearne: Universal connectedness is a keynote throughout your fiction. Do you ever feel uneasy about generalizing from a white, middle-class, Christian perspective, as in identifying "Silent Night" as a song universally loved in *A House Like a Lotus*?
L'Engle: In the group I wrote about, it would be. I was writing from something I had experienced.

The idea of interrelatedness comes from particle physics because in particle physics nothing happens in isolation. Everything is interrelated, and everything affects everything else. Scientists have learned that you cannot study anything objectively because to look at something is to change it and be changed by it.

Hearne: That also supports your idea that religion and science reflect each other.
L'Engle: Yes, and certainly as we learn more in science we have to change what we think about God. Once we believed that planet Earth was the center of the universe and the focus of God's attention. Things changed when we discovered we are just an ordinary planet in a nice middle-aged solar system at the edge of an ordinary galaxy, one of many galaxies. So there can't be the same single-minded creator who cares only about Earth.

Hearne: What about when science changes its mind? I am thinking of the character Max in *A House Like a Lotus*. We've now seen studies indicating that sexual orientation is inherent in physiological aspects of brain structure and genetic coding. When you look back on a novel where Max's homosexuality is attributed to an abusive father . . .

L'Engle: But not Ursula's!

Hearne: What about Ursula's?

L'Engle: I think it is encoded in her DNA. I think that is generally the conclusion that most physicians have come to.

Hearne: So science, like the Bible, is in constant dialogue with what's going on around us?

L'Engle: Yes. Many years ago, I was autographing in a college town. At the end of the day a young man said, "I rather like what you've been saying to people, but I haven't read your books because I hear they're religious." All my little red flags of warning unfurled and flapped in the wind. I said, "What do you mean by religious? Jerry Falwell's religious. Khomeini's religious." Then I heard myself saying, "My religion is subject to change without notice." I thought, "Well, I've received my revelation for the year because if my religion is not subject to change, it's dead."

Hearne: It must be satisfying to find answers for yourself when you're answering other people's questions.

L'Engle: That's when the best answers come, when I don't have time to think.

Hearne: Based on your fan mail, do your readers express an overwhelming preference for one book or series over another?

L'Engle: I get a lot of mail on the *Crosswicks Journals* [four volumes of autobiography], largely but not entirely from women. I'm getting more and more mail from high school students on the "grown-up" novels. The mail on *Wrinkle*, etc., continues. I get about 100 letters a week, and I write what I call my general epistles about every six weeks. All I have to add is "Thanks for your letter," or I can write a short paragraph rather than have to tell everything in every letter. When people write letters I believe they deserve to have an answer.

Hearne: And at the same time you deserve time to write your books.

L'Engle: That's right. I'm at a period now where I've been very frustrated about getting to my books.

Hearne: There are too many people calling you for interviews! When fans write to you, do they identify something specific that has appealed to them?

L'Engle: They do that by telling me about their own lives. Quite often somebody will say, "You've said what I've needed to say and wasn't able to say myself," which is a wonderful response. I've had practically no criticism in letters, and the criticism that does come is, alas, always from Christians, usually from fundamentalists: "You are writing about a medium!" I'll say, "No, no. She was a happy medium." Meg was always accused of never having a happy medium, so I gave her one. It's a play on words. It's a joke. It's funny. Fundamentalists don't seem to have much of a sense of humor. If you take things lightly you can't get as angry about them.

Hearne: That's an interesting diagnosis, doctor. People do sometimes react more intensely to children's books than to those for adults. You've written for both audiences. Could you talk a little about the differences between writing for children and for adults?
L'Engle: The age of the protagonist. There isn't any other difference. I write the best I can possibly write. If I am writing about a ten-year-old, I stay within the framework of what I think a ten-year-old will be thinking. I'm writing about Meg's kids now. Rosie is the youngest and she's ten, one is in college, two in medical school up at the other end, and all those in the middle. I'm writing from seven different points of view.

Hearne: All the children you portray seem to go into professions, and yet the mother in the Austin family opts not to continue her music professionally.
L'Engle: I think that's a woman's right. When all this first started, women had to have professions. I thought, "No, if you're going to be free to choose you can go in either direction." And that's why I gave Meg all those children.

Hearne: Would you satisfy the voyeur in us and describe your writing process—both literally, as in when, where, and how, and conceptually, as in translating imagination into story?
L'Engle: Well, literally, I have moved from the pencil to the pen to the typewriter to the electric typewriter to the electronics of the computer. I like to start the day working before things get too heavy. I spend at least part of every day writing and if I don't, I get terribly frustrated. I revise a great deal.

Hearne: Can you write on the road when you're traveling?
L'Engle: Oh, it's wonderful—the phone doesn't ring, and I don't see the mail. Airplanes are great places because they really aren't anywhere in either time or space.

Hearne: What most interests you in your current writing?

L'Engle: Meg is talking with her daughter Peggy—and many years ago I saw about a ten-line squib in the newspaper from Niles, Michigan, which said that the way we fight cancer now is to try cut it out or kill it, whereas we should try to convert it. Meg says we are doing it in a masculine way, by killing and cutting; that the feminine way would be to try to convert these cancer cells back to normal cells. We've been doing things the male way for too long, and it has not proved successful.

Hearne: As you mention Meg and Peggy—both nicknames for Margaret— I'm thinking about the way names interweave in your books. Is that a way of talking about how women pass on their knowledge to their children and their children's children, through discussion and role modeling?

L'Engle: Yes, that's another reason grandparents are so important. Sometimes they have more time to talk about what has happened and why it was important or not important.

Hearne: Is there anything you'd like to say to your readers?

L'Engle: I would just like to say how grateful I am that—after ten years of nothing but rejection slips—when *A Wrinkle in Time* was published and did so well, I stopped getting the rejection slips. That is a wonderful thing. I would send something out and gear myself for the rejection slip, and I've still not entirely lost that stance. When you have it long enough, it prints itself pretty indelibly on your psyche.

Hearne: Now that you no longer take care of a family full-time, can you bring to your writing the full fruits of your experience and ideas?

L'Engle: Well, I have a large apartment—there are three bedrooms, each with a bath, and the maid's room with a bath. Still, there was one weekend in the autumn when there wasn't room for me! But I am free to say, "I am not going to be here this afternoon, or whenever."

Hearne: So I'm idealizing your state?

L'Engle: Yes. My granddaughter and her husband just moved out to their own apartment. My grandson finally found a place near college—he's downtown. People come through New York. Hotels are appallingly expensive, so they tend to stay with me. And I have a part-time roommate.

Hearne: Well, if stasis is death, changes must mean a full life. We all wish you many more years of writing!

Madeleine L'Engle

Leonard S. Marcus / 2006

For many years, one of Madeleine L'Engle's favorite places was a simple book-filled room above the garage at Crosswicks, her rural Connecticut home. It was in the quiet and privacy of that cozy hideaway, which she grandly named "the tower" for fun, that L'Engle wrote several of the books that the world has come to know her by, including *A Wrinkle in Time*. In the downstairs living room at Crosswicks is the piano, once her mother's, which she played whenever work at the typewriter keyboard was not going smoothly. A short hike from the house is a large flat rock where she and her family have their picnics and where, at night, L'Engle spent hours on end watching the "living fire" of the sky as it filled up with stars "leading out into the expanding universe."

When L'Engle wrote *A Wrinkle in Time*, historical fiction and realistic novels about family life were the fashion in literature for young people. As a result, when L'Engle's most famous book was originally published in 1962, it struck more than a few of its first adult readers as uncomfortably strange. Twenty-six publishers rejected *A Wrinkle in Time* before the author, who had begun to speak of it as the "book nobody likes," finally found an editor willing to take chance on it. Then, to the surprise of many, *A Wrinkle in Time* won the Newbery Medal. This unexpected outcome for a book that L'Engle says she "had to write" proved to be one of the milestone events on the way to reawakening readers worldwide to the power of fantasy.

In her Newbery Medal acceptance speech, L'Engle said that one of fantasy's great appeals for her is that it is written in "the only language in the world that cuts across all barriers of time, place, race, and culture." Then she spoke about her passion for stargazing, described her favorite stargazing rock, and, quoting British astronomer Fred Hoyle, concluded, "a book, too, can be a star, 'explosive material, capable of stirring up fresh life endlessly.'"

Leonard S. Marcus: What kind of child were you?
Madeleine L'Engle: I was an only child. Slightly lame. Couldn't run well. I was shy and gawky and didn't have many friends, so my imagination was very important to me. I was told that the first word I said was *clock*.

LSM: Later you became an actress. How did you find the courage for that?
ML: I just loved it. I began acting in high school. On stage, I wasn't Madeleine. I became someone else—Sir Toby Belch, for instance. I would love to have played the great dramatic roles, but I was always a comedian.

LSM: Did acting help prepare you to become a writer?
ML: Yes, because as an actor you hear words and see what they do, how words affect an audience.

LSM: Your characters are something like an acting company: so many of them return story after story.
ML: I like that idea. But I didn't plan it that way. It just seemed natural to bring certain characters back. You know: you meet somebody, and you like that person. You want to meet them again.

LSM: Several of your characters are stargazers. What do you think about when you look at the stars?
ML: Sometimes I think about time. That the star I am looking at is that star as it looked a hundred or four hundred years ago. That fascinates me.

LSM: What was it like to write *A Wrinkle in Time*?
ML: The story was unlike anything I had written before. Writing it felt wonderful.

LSM: Did you know from the start how the story would end?
ML: No. I've never done that! It is more fun to want to know. If you know exactly what's going to happen, it doesn't work. But if you start to write the story and listen to it, see where it wants to go . . . well, I think that's how God creates.

LSM: Did you know then that there was going to be a time quartet?
ML: I had no idea.

LSM: Did you try out the manuscript on your own children?

ML: Never. My children were seven, ten, and twelve at the time. But I didn't think to read it to them because I didn't think of it as being for children. That was my feeling at any rate. When people started calling me a "children's book author," I was very surprised. Baffled.

LSM: Why have you wanted to write a story about young characters?

ML: Because young people are still curious. They're still thinking and willing to change.

LSM: What is your earliest memory?

ML: It's New York. I'm wearing a dark brown leggings suit and being taken for a walk to Central Park, where my nanny Mrs. O. bought some of that forbidden chewy stuff—caramel toffee. She thought I didn't have enough nice things to eat, and she had no hesitation about breaking the rules if she thought it was a good idea.

LSM: That's something you may have learned from her.

ML: I learned a lot from her. Her name was Mary O'Connell. When I first knew her and I was a baby, I called her "O." And then "Mrs. O," and it stayed "Mrs. O." Her life was not easy but she had a wonderful sense of humor.

Her daughter Harriet would read to me. I had a little case of English children's books, which my grandfather would send me, and the 1911 edition of the *Encyclopaedia Britannica*. She got awfully tired of the book, and I'd say, "You skipped a page!" because she would have and would then have to go back and read the page she skipped. Once I learned to read, I read anything I could get my hands on.

LSM: You grew up with music all around.

ML: My mother's mother had a beautiful singing voice. My mother played the piano. I think she did a little performing when she was younger, but she hated to perform. She had stage fright. A different kind of shyness, I think, from mine.

When I was very young, my father took me to see *Madame Butterfly*. I thought it was just marvelous—but I wasn't prepared for an unhappy ending. So I said, "Is that all, Father?" And he said, "Yes. Well, did you like it?" I said, "Oh, yes, Father, thank you." And we went home, and he thought it was such a success that he took me to the next opera, which was *Pagliacci*. We sat in our seats, and I said, "Father, does it have an unhappy ending?" He said, "Yes." And I started to cry right there before the curtain ever went up, so he had to take me out. I didn't go back to the opera for quite a long time.

LSM: When did you first keep a journal?
ML: I began when I was eight. What I wrote then was very dull. "Today I went to school, and I hated it!"

LSM: At least, you knew your own mind.
ML: Later, I read other people's journals and began to model mine on theirs.

LSM: Were you a good student?
ML: I was a very poor student. I had found that I wasn't being taught much about life in school, so I didn't pay much attention. I was in high school when I finally met a teacher who offered me encouragement as a writer.

LSM: Was there a moment when you realized you were no longer a child?
ML: One day when I was twelve, I looked in on my mother and saw that she was looking very sad. My mother up until then had just been my mother. Suddenly, I saw her revealed as a person. It was scary because she was unhappy. I hadn't realized that grown-ups could be unhappy.

LSM: A fantasy version of that experience happens to Meg, in *A Wrinkle in Time.*
ML: Yes. Meg gets a glimpse of her mother that she's never had before, and it comes from an unlikely source: the Happy Medium. It's fantasy, and yet it's the real reality. Something has to be true to be real, but it doesn't have to be real to be true.

LSM: Do you like to read your manuscripts out loud as you work on them?
ML: If I can, I read them to my grown-up granddaughter, Charlotte. That's very helpful. You can't ask too many people for their opinions, or you get confused. You pick one or two and listen to them but nobody else. My husband was my best editor. He was a great cutter. He would say, "You don't need that word." I'd say, "You're right." Then he would say, "You don't need that sentence." And I would say, "All right. You want to cut the whole thing. Just cut it. Cut it all!"

LSM: *A Wrinkle in Time* was rejected by twenty-six publishers. What was it like to have your work turned down repeatedly?

ML: It was awful! I cried. I yelled. I stamped. I begged. It makes you think, Am I really a failure? Is what I think is so wonderful not wonderful after all? One editor said, "I may be turning down an *Alice in Wonderland*, but I'm afraid of it."

LSM: When you finally did find a publisher, was your book completely finished? Or did your editor ask you to make changes?
ML: I dropped one fairly short chapter because they said the book was too long. And then I added another, much longer chapter! But it worked.

LSM: Do you like to revise your work?
ML: I don't like to, but I do it. I do and do and do and do and do. I'm as lazy as anyone else. When I finish a book, I say, "That's it. I've done it!" And then I realize I have to do a lot more work. I scrawl my first draft, and then I revise and revise and revise. I write in notebooks and type later.

LSM: Your books have such vivid titles. Do they come easily to you?
ML: Titles are iffy. Sometimes I'm wonderful at it. Sometimes I'm terrible.
My mother came up with the title of *A Wrinkle in Time*. I went to take her her early morning coffee one day, and she said, "I think I have a title for you right out of your text." I said, "Oh, Mother, you've got it."

LSM: How did you come up with a name for the planet Camazotz?
ML: Camazotz is a nasty South American god. I have a little book of names of gods of all religions. It's very useful.

LSM: Has religion always been important to you?
ML: My religion has. World religion has not. I have always believed that if God made everything, He had to have liked it. I didn't want a God who hated me, who thought that babies were born in sin. I like some saints because they're funny. St. Teresa of Avila, for instance, who was out in her carriage and got stuck in the mud. God said, "This is how I treat my friends, Teresa." To which she replied, "No wonder you have so few." I think we don't all have to think of God the same way.

LSM: What is your workday like?
ML: I get up and I write—sometimes a short time, sometimes all day. I never like not to be writing. It is living, eating, everything for me. I write with music playing—whatever happens to be on the classical music station WQXR.

What happens is you've got to let your conscious and subconscious mind marry each other. My ideas come in the morning before I get up and at night before I slide into sleep. An idea for a story may sit around me for years before I actually use it.

LSM: What else, besides writing, do you enjoy?

ML: I love to swim. Swimming has a definite rhythm, and writing should have, too. If you are using the rhythm in one aspect of your life, it makes it easier to feel it in other aspects of your life. If I hadn't swum, I probably wouldn't have written some of the things I've written.

LSM: Do you sometimes get stuck while writing?

ML: Every other page, probably.

LSM: What do you do to get unstuck?

ML: Play the piano. If I can't swim, I play the piano. If I can't play the piano, I listen to music. It breaks the barrier I've built up.

LSM: What about research? Is that sometimes part of your work?

ML: I enjoy research, although library research isn't that appealing to me because I like to write in the margins of the books I read, and you can't write in library books. I'll write, "No, I don't agree with you there!" Or, "Wow, that's just right. I think you're wonderful!"

I've been lucky and have traveled a lot. My husband and I went across the Mohave Desert, which was beautiful and far greener than I had expected. Later I was able to draw on that experience when I wrote *Many Waters*.

LSM: Why, in *Many Waters*, did you want to retell the story of Noah and the flood?

ML: I was living in the world at the time when we were very precarious. The idea that something could happen that would wipe out nearly everybody was perfectly possible and very frightening. In *A Swiftly Tilting Planet*, I had already written about the possibility of nuclear war. The two books are complementary in that sense. I'm dealing with the same thing in two different ways.

LSM: Tell me about the impact of war on your life.

ML: I have always been under the shadow of war. I've always been aware of it and afraid of it. I was born just after World War I. My father died because of that war. He had been gassed in the trenches and lived for seventeen more years, slowly coughing his lungs out. So I knew war was terrible. I would say to my father, "We're never going to have another war, are we, Father?" Well, he wouldn't lie to me.

To me the great villain was war. When World War II began I was in my late teens. It was terribly conflicting. I didn't want to think that we should be involved, and yet I knew I couldn't sit back and let my Jewish friends be killed. So we had to be involved.

LSM: Do your feelings about war have something to do with why you have so often written fantasy?
ML: Oh, yes. Fantasy was to me the way to write about it. There's the story of the princess who, whenever she was good and opened her mouth, beautiful things would come out, and whenever she was bad, nasty things came out: toads and snails. That's a story. The images may seem strange, but they make the meaning clear.

LSM: Why do you write so often about unicorns?
ML: I believe in unicorns. I always have. Unicorns keep coming into my work. I didn't study them. I learned about them inadvertently. There are a lot of ugly beasts. I needed something to put up against the ugly beast that was good, and that's the unicorn.

LSM: Why do you write about multiple characters—the Murry twins, the Camazotz world of look-alikes in *A Wrinkle in Time*, the three Mr. Jenkinses in *A Wind in the Door*?
ML: My mother had twin brothers. My father had twin sisters and was a twin. So I'm surrounded by twins. And I expected to have twins, but I didn't.

Camazotz is the world they would like to push us into, where we all have to think the same thoughts, like the same music, eat the same foods. When a child or grown-up comes along who insists on doing it differently, that person is going to have a hard time.

LSM: You were like that yourself as a child, weren't you?
ML: Yes, without realizing it.

LSM: And so is your character, Meg.
ML: Of course. I'm Meg. I made her good at math, and I was good English, but other than that . . .

LSM: What do you tell children who say they want to write?
ML: I say, "Write. That's the only way you'll find out. Just do it."

LSM: Do you hear from any children about your books?
ML: An eleven-year-old boy said to me once, "I read *A Wrinkle in Time*. I didn't understand it, but I knew what it was about." I loved that.

I had what started out as a very typical letter from a little boy, which ended, "P.S. I read your book (*A Wrinkle in Time*) while I was in bed. I have cancer." We corresponded until he died. It was hard and wonderful both. My books are not bad books to die with. What I mean by that is that when I read a book, if it makes me feel more alive, that it's a good book to die with. That's why certain books last.

LSM: Are you a *Star Wars* fan?
ML: Oh, yes!

LSM: Have you taken your grandchildren to see those movies?
ML: I go alone or with a friend. I like to be free to scream, and I can't do that if I'm with the kids.

LSM: Is fantasy writing more accepted now than it was when you were starting out as a writer?
ML: Heavens, yes. I think that's because it's a scarier world. Fantasy gives you options. It's an attempt to touch on reality, in a way that can't be done better otherwise.

LSM: What is the best part about being a writer?
ML: Writing helps you to keep open and not close down. It helps you to keep on growing.

Index

Abigail, 158

Adam, 75, 176

Adam Eddington (*The Arm of the Starfish* and *A Ring of Endless Light*), 109, 115–16, 118, 122–27

Adams, Richard, 161

"adult novels." *See* pornography

Aguecheek, Andrew, 129

Al-Anon, 85

Alexander, Lloyd, 161

Alice's Adventures in Wonderland, 10, 77, 91, 92, 185

All My Children, 44, 83

American Library Association, ix, xii

Androcles and the Lion, 94

Anglicans, 10, 34, 71, 92, 143

Anne of Green Gables, 19, 46

anthropomorphic animals, 94, 97

Apollo, 61

"Appassionata" sonata, 71

Arkenstone, 91, 96, 97

astrophysics, 88, 113, 135, 161

atheism, 71, 95, 144

Austen, Jane, 171

Austin family (*Meet the Austins*), 7, 8, 16, 33, 43, 57, 73, 164, 170–73, 179

Baal, 71

Bach, J. S., 74, 109, 110, 112, 128

Basil (*A Ring of Endless Light*), 109, 110, 116, 120

Beethoven, Ludwig van, 71, 125, 128, 168

Berkeley, George (Bishop of Cloyne), 165

Bible, 34, 77, 83, 99, 101, 134, 138, 151, 154, 175, 176, 178; women in, 176. *See also individual names*

biology, 44, 88, 109, 124, 166

"Birth of Language, The," 154

Bleak House, 104

Bohr, Niels, 119

Book of the Dun Cow, 139

Books of Trial Liturgies, 38

Bradbury, Ray, 161

Branch, Craig, xii

Branzillo, 169

breastfeeding, 30, 56, 62

Brigham Young University, 136, 146

Broadway, 13, 30, 79, 92

Bronowski, Jay, 112, 119

Brontë, Emily, 46, 49, 171

Brothers Karamazov, 155

Browning, Robert, 147

Buddhism, 81, 89, 95

Bulldog Drummond, 142

Bulwer-Lytton, Edward, 163

Calvin O'Keefe (Time triology and *The Arm of the Starfish*), 20, 21, 167

Camazotz, 185, 187

Camilla, 4, 58, 146, 160, 171

Camp, Charles Wadsworth (father), xii, 3–4, 17, 26, 27, 28, 44, 58, 69, 70, 101, 104, 136, 145, 174, 183, 186–87

Camp, Madeleine Hall Barnett (mother), xii, 3, 4, 6, 9, 17, 18, 19, 26, 27, 28, 39–40, 43–44, 58–59, 69, 80,

82, 85, 104, 112, 120, 131, 133, 136, 145, 146, 174, 179, 181, 183, 184, 185, 187
cancer, 33, 41, 148, 180, 188
Canon Tallis (character), 26, 42, 43, 173
Canterville Ghost, The, 104
Carroll, Lewis, 10, 77
Cathedral of St. John the Divine, 24–25, 26, 27, 40, 56, 69, 85, 173
Catholic University, 11
Catholicism, 37, 40, 70, 80, 96, 97, 101, 140, 148
Celebration of Discipline, 139
censorship, xii, 101, 140, 143, 148, 153
Charles Tyler (character), 44, 83
Charles Wallace (Time trilogy), 20, 57, 100, 161, 162, 167, 169
Charleston, South Carolina, 28, 52
Charlotte Napier (*The Love Letters*), 12
Charlotte's Web, 49
Chase, Mary Ellen, 28–29
Chekhov, Anton, 16, 30, 92
Cherry Orchard, The, 30, 92, 132
children: adults' memories of being, 50; changing world of, 20; dolphins like, 122; faith of, 139; imagination of, 135; protecting parents, 131; as readers, 9–10, 21, 24, 42, 103–6, 113–14; regeneration of severed fingers or toes, 167; restricting vocabulary of, 24; spiritual questions of, 175; teaching religious ideology to, 144; within adult writers, 153
children's literature, xvi, xvii, xxi, xxiii, 9, 19, 73, 75, 175, 179, 183
Children's Literature Association, xxiii
Chocolate War, The, 21
Christ, 71, 96; -figure, 98, 99. *See also* Jesus
Christianity, 22, 26, 33, 34, 40, 41, 69, 70, 71, 73, 74, 76, 79, 84, 87, 88, 92, 93, 95–100, 135, 130, 134–36, 139, 141, 150, 152, 154, 156, 159, 175, 177, 179
Christmas, 8, 9, 11, 70, 133, 144

Chuck (*A Swiftly Tilting Planet*), 169
Clapp, Margaret, 146
Clarke, Arthur C., 117
Columbia University, 26, 27, 49, 75, 166, 170
Commonweal, 95
Congregational Church, 10, 33, 34, 37, 40, 84, 91, 100
Copernicus, Nicholaus, 118
Cormier, Robert, 21
Cornell University, 144
cosmopolitanism, 52
Crosswicks, 49, 53, 91, 133, 178, 181
Crowell, 160
cryonics, 115–16

Damascus Road experience, 69
Daniel, 44, 62, 131
Dante, 10, 163
David, King, 158
David Copperfield, 104, 158
Davies, Robertson, 141
Deller, Alfred, 104
Delphi, 61
demons, 140, 141
Deptford Trilogy, 141
Dick and Jane, 103
Dinosaur Book, 37
DNA, 125, 178
dolphins, 80, 81, 83, 107, 109–11, 115, 116, 117, 120, 122–26
Dostoyevsky, Fyodor, 46, 141, 155, 163
Dragon Lake, 65
Dragons in the Waters, 43, 65
dreams, 19, 41, 66, 77, 83, 88, 107, 142, 143, 146
Dumitriu, Petru, 141
Dunn, Esther Cloudman, 29
Durr, Clifford, 128

Eastern Orthodox Church, 99
Eddington, Arthur, 35, 74
Egypt, 88, 98, 151

Einstein, Albert, 35, 45, 74, 76, 100, 106, 112, 119, 128, 176
Elijah, 89, 138
Eliot, George, 163
Emerson, Ralph Waldo, 24, 80, 141, 144
Emily of New Moon, 19, 46, 49, 171
Encyclopaedia Britannica, 183
England, 4, 13, 61, 125, 141, 143, 150, 155, 163
Episcopalianism, xvi, xviii, 26, 37, 40, 69, 77, 79, 80, 141, 156, 175
Esther, 29
evangelicalism, 79–81, 95, 87, 96, 97, 101, 137, 140, 151, 152, 156
Eve, 176
evil, 8, 47, 50, 130, 175, 176
Ezekiel, 83

faith, 33, 41, 71, 74, 76, 79, 81, 89, 132, 134, 137, 139, 140, 147, 148, 167, 168
Falwell, Jerry, 147, 178
fantasy, 10, 18, 26, 69, 83, 133, 134, 136, 144, 161, 170, 175, 181, 184, 187, 188
Farrar, John, 9
Farrar, Straus and Giroux, 9, 12, 98, 105
fear, xx, 7–8, 38, 50, 74, 128, 140, 152, 153, 167
feminism, 43, 142. *See also* women's liberation
Fifth Business, 142
forgiveness, 37, 81–82, 83, 94, 97, 137
Foster, Richard, 139
Francis, Dick, 89
Franklin, Hugh (husband), xi, xii, xv, xvi, xvii, xviii, 3, 5–8, 11, 12, 15, 26, 30, 31, 32, 35, 38, 39, 42, 44, 55, 57, 60, 63–65, 69–73, 75, 82–85, 92, 94, 111, 112, 131–33, 147, 148, 168, 170, 171, 184, 186
freedom, 53, 74, 86, 144, 175
Freud, Sigmund, 50
friendship, 132, 150, 151, 156
Frodo Baggins (character), 19
Fu Manchu, 142

Galileo, 76, 78, 118
Gaudior, 83, 169
Gauguin, Paul, 7, 31
Geltzer, Charlotte Weaver, 172
gender, xviii, xix–xx, 6, 7, 8, 14, 31, 43, 49–50, 53–54, 61–62, 66, 67, 72, 92, 142, 171, 179, 180
Genesis, 94, 137, 151, 175
Gideon, 138
Giroux, Bob, 47
God, 35–37, 41, 71, 76, 81, 82, 87, 97, 134, 135, 136, 137, 139, 148, 161, 166, 167, 177
God in the Dark, 157
Good Samaritan, 99
Goshen, Connecticut, 6, 16, 49
Gospels, 81, 87, 98, 139
Greece, 146
Green Book, 37
Greenwich Village, 63, 93
Gribbin, John, 88, 113
Griffin, Emilie, 135

Hamlet, 9
Hand, Cathy, 86
Happy Medium, The (*A Wrinkle in Time*), 179, 184
Happy Prince, The, 14
Hawthorne, Nathaniel, 141
Herald-Evening Sun, 3
heroes and heroines, 19, 27 43, 46, 48, 49, 50, 59, 104, 144, 173
Hitler, Adolf, 87, 143
Hobbit, The, 96
Holy Cross Monastery, 40
Holy Spirit, 84, 101, 153
homosexuality, 21, 61, 62, 177–78
House Like a Lotus, A, 177
Hoyle, Fred, 182

I Heard the Owl Call My Name, 141
imagination, 10, 148, 156
incarnation, 37, 38, 48, 76, 93, 100, 138, 139

Incognito, 141
Indiana University Press, 5
Indians, 43, 52, 65, 66
Inferno, 10, 164
intellect, 46, 47, 49–50, 61, 71–73, 84, 113, 134, 143
intuition, xviii, 49–50, 62, 69, 71, 84, 113, 143, 165
Isaac, Reid, 47

"Jabberwocky," 162
Jackson, Andrew, 52
Jacob, 134, 157
Jane Eyre, 29
Jeans, James, 35
Jeb Nutteley (*A Ring of Endless Light*), 122–25
Jefferson, Thomas, 53
Jepthah's wife, 176
Jesus, 38, 41, 70, 75, 76, 78, 81, 87–89, 96, 98–102, 134–39, 153, 167
Jews, 87, 95, 187
Jonah, 77, 93–95, 137
Jones, Alan, 45
Joseph, 88
Joshua (*The Arm of the Starfish*), 98
Joyous Season, The, 92, 132
Jung, Carl, 23

Katherine Forrester (*The Small Rain* and *A Severed Wasp*), 171
Keats, John, 118, 128
Kennedy, John Fitzgerald, 86
Kerr, Jean and Walter, 39, 57
Khomeini, Sayyid Ruholla Musavi, 87, 178
Kindlings, The, xiii
King Lear, 141
kything, 45, 162, 169

Lamaze, 56
Lao Tzu, 81
Larchmont, New York, 39, 57

Le Gallienne, Eva, 92
Lear, Norman, 86, 141
L'Engle, Madeleine: acting career of, 16, 29–30, 92, 182; adult vs. child understanding of books by, 42, 75, 113, 135, 153; advice to writers, 188; agnosticism of, xii, xviii, 33, 84, 100; ancestors of, 51, 52, 53; atheism of, 70; Bion (son), 14, 31, 32, 40, 45, 65, 67, 133, 170; Bion, as model for Rob Austin, 43; childhood, x, 3–5, 17–19, 27–28, 46, 50, 58–59, 69, 95, 110, 133, 136, 142–43, 145–46, 167, 182, 183, 184, 187; Charlotte (granddaughter), xxii, 61, 131, 104, 131, 180, 184; children of, 14, 39, 95, 164, 170; on chronos and kairos, 76, 77; cousins of, 52, 131; as a daughter, 66, 82; early adulthood of, xvi, 29–30; education of, 4, 5, 16, 27–29, 34, 58–59, 84, 95; films of books, 11, 12, 86–89; first novel, 4; in Goshen, xii, xvi, xviii, xxii, 5, 26, 33, 34, 49, 70, 73, 77, 132, 133, 181; grandchildren of, xiv, 19, 40, 57, 60, 129, 133, 138, 188; grandfather of, 45, 53, 80, 107, 109, 110, 115, 116, 119–21, 148, 183; grandmother of, 26, 31, 38, 39, 66, 82, 104, 130, 173; grandson of, 138, 180; Greatie (great-great-grandmother), 51–52; on guilt, 64, 82, 127, 128, 153; hospitalizations, 8, 11, 30, 31, 41, 56, 99, 120, 123; intended audience, ix, x, xi, xvi, xix, xxi, 11, 13, 75, 113, 135, 139, 160, 161, 163, 179; Josephine (daughter), 14, 56, 61, 64, 67, 133, 173; journal-writing of, 16, 36, 40, 46, 51–53, 146, 157, 158, 166, 167, 170, 178, 184; Laurie (daughter-in-law), 65, 67, 126; Maria (daughter), 60, 61, 133; marriage of, xvi, xx, 26, 30, 57, 63–64, 72, 130–32, 147; as a mother,

xvi, xviii, xxii, 6–8, 14, 19, 26, 31, 32, 42, 54–57, 59–60, 66, 82, 95, 104, 106, 130–31, 164; in New York City, x, 3, 4, 8, 16, 18, 22, 24, 27–28, 39, 44, 57, 64, 65, 69, 83, 109, 132, 145, 175, 180, 183; parenting philosophy of, xvii, 3, 8, 19–20, 27, 30, 31, 39, 54–56, 59, 60, 62, 64, 72–73, 132, 138, 171; public persona of, x, xi, xxi, xxiii; as public speaker, xviii, 69, 81, 815, 115, 150; school visits of, 144; as servant of the story, xxi, 26, 44–45, 75, 98; shyness of, 16, 29, 183; as teacher of writing, 22–23, 98; wedding anniversary of, 47

—**Works:** *And Was It Good?*, 151; *The Arm of the Starfish*, 15, 20, 97, 125, 161, 167; *Camilla*, 4, 58, 146, 160, 171; *Certain Women*, 158; *A Circle of Quiet*, 31, 34, 49, 150; *Crosswicks Journals*, x, xiv–xv, 178; *Dance in the Desert*, 88, 98; *Dragons in the Waters*, 43, 65; *18 Washington Square South*, 93, 94; *A House Like a Lotus*, 177; *How Now Brown Cow*, 93, 94; *Ilsa*, xvi; *The Irrational Season*, 67, 95, 101, 131; *Journey with Jonah*, 93–94; *Lines Scribbled on an Envelope*, 150; *A Live Coal in the Sea*, 171; *The Love Letters*, 11–12, 14; *Many Waters*, 161–62, 164–67, 172, 175, 176, 186; *Meet the Austins*, 7, 8, 33, 57, 73, 171, 174; *The Other Side of the Sun*, 53, 132; *Penguins and Golden Calves*, xiv; *A Ring of Endless Light*, xix, 75, 79, 80, 83, 87, 103, 106, 115–29; *A Severed Wasp*, xi, xiv, xv, 171, 172; *The Small Rain*, 5, 9, 171, 172; *Sold into Egypt*, 151; *A Stone for a Pillow*, 151; *Summer of the Great-Grandmother*, 41, 42, 48, 49, 65, 69, 80, 82, 120, 133; *A*

Swiftly Tilting Planet, 69, 75, 77, 79, 83, 162, 153, 167–69, 172, 186; *Troubling a Star*, 173; *Walking on Water*, xii, 79, 89, 98, 102, 151, 163, 167; *The Weather of the Heart*, 150; *The Wind in the Door*, 20, 42, 44, 51, 57, 69, 77, 79, 83, 162, 164, 165, 166, 168, 172, 187; *A Wrinkle in Time*, 8, 19–21, 23, 24, 26, 33, 36, 42–44, 47, 48, 50, 57, 69, 73, 74, 77, 79, 83–86, 95, 99–103, 105, 110, 114, 134, 140, 154, 161, 163–66, 170–72, 174–76, 178, 180–82, 184, 185, 187, 188; *The Young Unicorns*, 20, 22. *See also individual characters and places*

Leo (*A Ring of Endless Light*), 109

Life Paths, 158

Limitations of Science, The, 35, 74

Listening for Madeleine, xvi, xxii

"Little Gidding," 163

Lolita, 143

Lord of the Rings, The, 19

Lord Peter Wimsey (character), 46

love, 4, 5, 7, 9, 11–12, 14, 20, 24, 25, 31, 34, 37, 39, 40, 44, 50, 63, 72, 74, 76, 82, 83, 84, 87, 96, 100, 121, 131, 132, 134, 137, 138, 139, 147, 148, 164, 166, 175

Lucas, George, 88

Luke, 99, 158

Macbeth, 29

MacDonald, George, 10, 19

Madame Butterfly, 183

Maddog (*A Swiftly Tilting Planet*), 169

Maddox (*A Swiftly Tilting Planet*), 168, 169

Madison Avenue, 67

Manhattan, 35, 57, 109, 170

Manticore, The, 141

Maracaibo, Venezuela, 65

Marcus, Leonard, xvi, xxii

Margaret A. Edwards Award, xxi, 170

marriage, xvi, xx, 26, 30, 31, 44, 55, 57, 62–64, 72, 92, 94, 99, 130–32; faithfulness in, 12, 63, 147, 148

Maryana Alcoforado (*The Love Letters*), 11, 12

mathematics, 10, 34, 36, 61, 74, 112, 113, 118, 135, 187

matriarchs, 8, 173

Matthews, Joe, 121

Max (*A House Like a Lotus*), 91, 92, 177, 178

meditation, 26, 93, 48

Meg Murry (Time trilogy), 20, 43, 44, 57, 100, 141, 161, 162, 164, 166, 169, 172–74, 179, 180, 184, 187

Melrose, Andrea, 86

memory, 36, 47, 50, 51, 66, 130, 183

Mencken, H. L. xii, 33

Mitchell, Ed, 44

mitochondria, 166, 167

Molson, Francis J., 99

money, 5, 38, 39, 46, 55, 70, 86, 127, 132, 173

Montgomery, L. M., 19, 46

morality, xxi, 53, 99, 134, 142–43, 146–47, 176

Mother Teresa, 99

mothers and motherhood, xvi, 26, 31, 33, 43, 54–57, 59–60, 67, 74, 88, 107, 121, 125, 136, 179, 184

Mr. Jenkins (Time trilogy), 165

Mr. Rochester (character), 29

Multnomah Press, 158

Mundelein College, 80, 97, 130

Murry family (Time quartet) 172, 173; twins, 161, 162, 164, 165, 187

music, 3, 10, 34, 57, 62, 99, 110, 112, 115, 129, 143, 168, 174, 179, 183, 185–87

mysticism, 33, 40, 76, 84, 88, 175

myths, 18, 62, 83, 136, 160

National Council of Teachers of English, xxi, 85

nephilim, 175

New England, 35, 40, 70, 84, 121

New England Journal of Medicine, 166

New York Public Library, xvii

New York Times, 13, 162

New Yorker, xi, xiv, xv, xxii

Newbery Medal, 26, 69, 48, 74, 79, 85, 99, 103, 128, 170, 181

Newbigin, Leslie, 155

Newton, Isaac, 76, 106, 119

Nineveh, 94, 137

Noah, 186; and daughter, 176

nursing. *See* breastfeeding

O'Connell, Mary (nurse), 70, 183

opera, 11, 44, 65, 183, 184

opium, 142

Origen, 37

Pagliacci, 183

paradoxes, 9, 10, 21, 137, 138

parents and parenthood, 10, 20, 21, 25, 38, 39, 56, 69, 101, 131, 145, 160, 167, 173, 176

Parks, Cara, xiii, xxii

Paul, Saint, 50, 71, 74, 134, 138

Penguins and Golden Calves: Idols and Icons in Antarctica and Other Unexpected Places, xiv

Perry, Bernard, 5

Peter, Saint, 45, 46, 61, 138

Petya Trofimov (character), 30

philosophy, 14, 18, 26, 51

physics, 14, 44, 74, 76, 77, 88, 100, 106, 162, 165, 176, 177

Picasso, Pablo, 112

Planck's quantum theory, xviii, 35, 106

poetry, 4, 5, 10, 13, 54, 59, 62, 118, 150–54, 156, 159, 168, 174

Pollock, Jackson, 77

pornography, 99, 105, 143

porpoises, 123, 124

Potiphar's wife, 176

prayer, 41, 46, 53, 71, 74, 75, 76, 84, 93, 152, 156, 157, 158, 169
pregnancy, 54, 59–60
Prodigal Son, 99
Progo, 83
Psalms, 94, 128, 135
pseudoscience, 106
psychiatry, 12, 36, 40, 47, 50, 51
psychoanalysis, 47
psychology, 7, 61
punishment, 81, 82, 136, 137

Quiztano Indians, 65, 66

Raines, Theron, 9, 12, 15
Regent College, 157
religion, 33, 40, 43, 8, 115, 147, 174, 175, 176, 177, 178, 185
repression, 47, 50, 56, 148
resurrection, 41, 88, 96, 116
Rhys, Jean, 163
Rob Austin (Austin Family Chronicles), 43, 117, 119
Romania, 141

Sacraments, 100
Satan, 36, 37, 134, 153
Schildkraut, Joseph, 92
Scientific American, 89
scripture, 93, 134–38, 145, 154, 158, 175
Seabury Press, 47, 48
Sendak, Maurice, 166
seraphim, 161, 176
Serkin, Rudolf, 71, 168
Sermon on the Mount, 9
sex, 30, 49, 55, 57, 61, 62, 66, 92, 101, 131, 132, 143, 147, 175, 177; education, 14–15, 56
sexism 26, 43, 44
Shaffer, George, 11
Shakespeare, William, 10, 29, 46, 104, 106, 110, 112, 128, 129, 141, 143, 163
Shaw, Harold, 79, 98

Shaw, Luci, 98, 150–59
Shimin, Symeon, 88
Silvey, Anita, ix
sin, 11, 79, 89, 101, 137, 138, 153, 176, 185
Sir Toby Belch (character), 182
Smith, Lillian, 106–7
Smith College, 5, 8, 26, 28–29, 34, 92, 147
Spirit and Forms of Love, The, 62–63
spirituality, 40, 93, 142, 156, 158, 175
Star Wars, 188
starfish, 125, 167
stars, 35, 70, 77, 113, 118, 128, 130, 135, 161–62, 165, 181–82
Staub, Dick, xiii
subconsciousness, 7, 10, 13, 35, 46, 47, 50, 73, 113, 164, 172, 186
submarines, 122, 124, 125
Sullivan, J. W. N., 14, 35
Swerdferger, Steven and Martha, xiii

technocracy, 56, 125, 161, 167
technology, 56, 88, 125, 126, 155, 156, 161, 174
television, 20, 23, 44, 83, 147, 173
Tempest, The, 10, 29
temptation, 101, 102, 153, 154, 173
Tennyson, Alfred Lord, 124
Teresa of Avila, Saint, 185
tesseract, 24, 45
Theophon the Recluse, 46, 84
Thomas, Dylan, 113
Thomas, Lewis, 66
Thoreau, Henry David, 141
Three Musketeers, The, 104
To Kill a Mockingbird, 141
TODAY show, 44
tolerance, 15, 41, 128, 137
Tolkien, J. R. R., 96
transfiguration, 71, 138, 155
truth, x, xi, xii, xvii, 3, 8, 10, 26, 58, 70, 83, 118, 130, 133, 146, 153, 154, 167, 160, 163, 165, 169, 184

Twain, Mark, 24
Twelfth Night, 29, 104

Uncle Harry, 92, 94
unicorns, 20, 22, 83, 91, 166, 187
Union Theological Seminary, 131
universalism, 76, 81
Ursula (*A House Like a Lotus*), 178

Vaughan, Henry, 103, 104, 114
Venezuela, 20, 43, 65
Vicky Austin (Austin Family
    Chronicles), 80, 87, 104, 106–10,
    113, 114, 116–18, 120, 122, 123, 124,
    126–28, 129, 164
Virgin Mary, 78

Walking on Water, xii, 79, 89, 98, 102,
    151, 163, 167
Wangerin, Walter, Jr., 139
War of the Worlds, 14
Watchman Expositor, xii
Watergate, 66
West, Edward Nason, 26, 40, 42, 43, 45,
    86, 88, 89
Wheaton College, 69, 80, 97, 98, 130,
    150–52, 154
White Holes, 88–89, 113
Williams, Daniel Day, 44, 62, 89, 131,
    148
Winter's Tale, The, 141
women's liberation, xviii, 49, 55, 179
World of Wonders, 141
World War I, 3, 20, 28

Yale University, 40, 41

Zachary (Austin Family Chronicles),
    106–8, 115, 116, 120, 127, 128, 173
Zarin, Cynthia, x, xi, xiv, xv, xvi, xvii,
    xxii
zombies, 121, 122